Greek
Phrase Book
&
Dictionary

Berlitz Publishing
New York   Munich   Singapore

Contacting the Editors
Every effort has been made to provide accurate information in this publication, but changes are inevitable. The publisher cannot be responsible for any resulting loss, inconvenience or injury. We would appreciate it if readers would call our attention to any errors or outdated information. We also welcome your suggestions; if you come across a relevant expression not in our phrase book, please contact us: Berlitz Publishing, 193 Morris Avenue, Springfield, NJ 07081, USA. Email: comments@berlitzbooks.com.

First Printing: May 2008
Printed in Singapore

Publishing Director: Sheryl Olinsky Borg
Project Manager: Farida Aslanova
Greek Editorial: Renata Liapis, Nektaria Notaridou
Cover Design: Claudia Petrilli
Interior Design: Derrick Lim, Juergen Bartz
Production Manager: Elizabeth Gaynor
Cover Photo: © Philip Coblentz/Brand X Pictures/age fotostock
Interior Photos: p. 12 © Studio Fourteen/Brand X Pictures/age fotostock; p. 17 © European Central Bank; p. 20 © Pixtal/age fotostock; p. 34-35 © Roman Korchuk, 2006/Shutterstock, Inc.; p. 39 © Corbis/fotosearch.com; p. 49 © Purestock/Alamy; p. 55 © FoodCollection/Stockfood; p. 59 © Stockbyte Photography/2002-07 Veer Incorporated; p. 68 © Rena Schild/2003-2007 Shutterstock, Inc.; p. 79 © Javier Larrea/Pixtal/age fotostock; p. 82 © Netfalls/2003-2007 Shutterstock, Inc.; p. 90 © Natalia Sinjushina & Evgeniy Meyke/2003-2007 Shutterstock, Inc.; p. 95 © Imageshop.com; p. 99 © image100/Corbis; p. 101 © Ljupco Smokovski/2003-2007 Shutterstock, Inc.; p. 104, 107 © 2007 Jupiterimages Corporation; p. 115 © Olga Shelego/2003-2007 Shutterstock, Inc.; p. 123 © 2007 Jupiterimages Corporation; p. 131 © Jupiterimages/Brand X/Corbis; p. 133 © Stockbyte/Fotosearch.com; p. 137 © Corbis/2006 Jupiterimages Corporation; p. 139 © David McKee/2003-2007 Shutterstock, Inc.; p. 140, 149, 161 © 2007 Jupiterimages Corporation; inside back cover © H.W.A.C.

Contents

Survival

Food

People

Fun

Special Needs

Resources

Dictionary

Pronunciation

This section is designed to make you familiar with the sounds of Greek using our simplified phonetic transcription. You'll find the pronunciation of the Greek letters explained below, together with their "imitated" equivalents. This system is used throughout the phrase book; simply read the pronunciation as if it were English, noting any special rules below.

Stress is important in Greek, as often the meaning of the word changes depending upon which syllable is stressed. In written Greek, stress is indicated by a small mark (') on the syllable to be stressed. In the Greek phonetic transcription, stress is indicated with an underline.

Over the last 25 years, the Greek language has been greatly simplified, with the number of stress and breathing marks reduced; however, one may still encounter words written with the more elaborate stress marks, mainly in older Greek texts.

In the Greek language, the question mark is indicated by the semi-colon (;).

Consonants

Letter	Approximate Pronunciation	Symbol	Example	Pronunciation
β	like v in voice	v	βάζο	<u>vah</u>·zoh
δ	voiced th, like th in then	TH	δεν	THehn
ζ	like z in zoo	z	ζω	zoh
θ	unvoiced th, like th in thing	th	θέλω	<u>theh</u>·loh
κ	like k in key	k	κότα	<u>koh</u>·tah
λ	like l in lemon	l	λεμόνι	leh·<u>moh</u>·nee
μ	like m in man	m	μαμά	mah·<u>mah</u>
ν	like n in net	n	νέο	<u>neh</u>·oh
ξ	like x in fox	ks	ξένος	<u>kseh</u>·nohs
π	like p in pen	p	πένα	<u>peh</u>·nah
ρ	trilled like a Scottish r	r	ώρα	<u>oh</u>·rah

Letter	Approximate Pronunciation	Symbol	Example	Pronunciation
σ	like s in sit	s	σε	seh
ς*	like s in slim	s	ήλιος	<u>ee</u>·liohs
τ	like t in tea	t	τι	tee
φ	like f in fun	f	φως	fohs
x	like ch in Scottish loch	kh	χαρά	khah·<u>rah</u>
ψ	like ps in tops	ps	ψάρι	<u>psah</u>·ree
γ	like g + h	gh	γάλα	<u>ghah</u>·lah
γγ, γκ	like g in go, but in some cases a more nasal ng as in sing	g	γκαρσόν	gahr·<u>sohn</u>
μπ	like b in bath, but in some cases more like mp as in lamp	b	μπαρ	bahr
ντ	like d in do, but in some cases more like nd as in end	d	ντομάτα	doh·<u>mah</u>·tah
τζ	like j in jazz	j	τζατζίκι	jah·<u>jee</u>·kee
τσ	like ts in lets	ts	τσάντα	<u>tsahn</u>·dah

* This character is used instead of **σ**, when the latter falls at the end of a word.

Vowels

Letter	Approximate Pronunciation	Symbol	Example	Pronunciation
α	like a in father	ah	μα	mah
ε	like e in ten	eh	θέλω	<u>theh</u>·loh
η, ι, υ	like ee in keen	ee	πίνω	<u>pee</u>·noh
o, ω	like o in top	oh	πότε	<u>poh</u>·teh
αι	like e in ten	eh	μπαίνω	<u>beh</u>·noh
οι, ει, υι	like ee in keen	ee	πλοίο	<u>plee</u>·oh

Vowel Combinations

Letters	Approximate Pronunciation	Symbol	Example	Pronunciation
αυ	1) when followed by θ, κ, ξ, π, σ, τ, φ, χ, ψ, like af in after	ahf	αυτός	ahf·<u>tohs</u>
	2) in all other cases, like av in avocado	ahv	αύρα	<u>ahv</u>·rah
ευ	1) when followed by θ, κ, ξ, π, σ, τ, φ, χ, ψ, like ef in effect	ehf	λευκός	lehf·<u>kohs</u>
	2) in all other cases, like ev in ever	ehv	νεύρο	<u>nehv</u>·roh
ου	like oo in zoo	oo	ούζο	<u>oo</u>·zoh
για, γεια	like yah in yard	yah	για	yah
γε, γιε	like ye in yet	yeh	γερό	yeh·<u>roh</u>
ειο, γιο	like yo in yogurt	yoh	γιος	yohs
γι, γυ, γη	like yea in yeast	yee	γύρω	<u>yee</u>·roh
ια, οια	like ia in piano	iah	ποια	piah

i Greek is a language with a long history. The language itself has developed over the centuries into modern Greek spoken today by approximately 11 million people in Greece and Cyprus, as well as Greek-speaking communities within other countries. It is a phonetic language; the sound of each letter does not usually change with its position. The characters may appear confusing at first; don't be put off by this. With a bit of practice most people can read Greek in just a few hours.

How to Use This Book

These essential phrases can also be heard on the audio CD.

Sometimes you see two alternatives in italics, separated by a slash. Choose the one that's right for your situation.

Essential

I'm here on *vacation [holiday]*/business.	Είμαι εδώ για *διακοπές/δουλειά.* ee·meh eh·THoh yah *THiah·koh·pehs/THoo·liah*
I'm going to...	**Θα...** thah...
I'm staying at the...Hotel.	**Μένω στο...ξενοδοχείο.** meh·noh stoh... kseh·noh·THoh·khee·oh

You May See...

ΝΑΥΑΓΟΣΩΣΤΙΚΗ ΛΕΜΒΟΣ nah·vah·ghoh·sohs·tee·kee lehm·vohs	life boats
ΣΩΣΙΒΙΑ soh·see·vee·ah	life jackets

Train

Where *is/are*...?	**Πού είναι...;** poo ee·neh...
– the ticket office	– **το γραφείο εισιτηρίων** toh ghrah·fee·oh ee·see·tee·ree·ohn
– the information desk	– **το γραφείο πληροφοριών** toh ghrah·fee·oh plee·roh·foh·ree·ohn
– the luggage lockers	– **οι θυρίδες** ee thee·ree·THehs

Words you may see are shown in *You May See* boxes.

Any of the words or phrases preceded by dashes can be plugged into the sentence above.

Greek phrases appear in red.

Read the simplified pronunciation as if it were English. For more on pronunciation, see page 7.

Phone

Hello. This is... **Εμπρός. Είμαι o♂/η♀...** ehm·<u>brohs</u> <u>ee</u>·meh oh♂/ee♀...

I'd like to speak to... **Θα ήθελα να μιλήσω με τον♂/την♀...** thah <u>ee</u>·theh·lah nah mee·<u>lee</u>·soh meh tohn♂/teen♀...

Extension... **Εσωτερική γραμμή.** ghrah·<u>mee</u>...

Speak *louder/more slowly*. **Μιλείστε *πιο δυνατ***... pioh THee·nah·<u>tah</u>/ahr·<u>ghah</u>

When different gender forms apply, the masculine form is followed by ♂; feminine by ♀.

▶ For numbers, see page 158.

The arrow indicates a cross reference where you'll find related phrases.

Information boxes contain relevant country, culture and language tips.

i Athens is the only Greek city currently served by a **μετρό** (meh·<u>troh</u>), subway. Subway tickets can be purchased at ticket desks or machines located at each station. Validate your ticket by stamping it in a validation machine, found by the platform, before you get on the subway.

You May Hear...

Τα εισιτήριά σας, παρακαλώ. tah ee·see·<u>tee</u>·ree·<u>ah</u> sahs pah·rah·kah·<u>loh</u>

Tickets, please.

Expressions you may hear are shown in *You May Hear* boxes.

Color-coded side bars identify each section of the book.

11

Thívai
Akharnái
Athínai
(Athens)
Káristos
Mégara
Piraiévs
Kéa
Aíyna
Návplion

▼ Survival

Arrival and Departure

Essential

I'm here on *vacation* [*holiday*]/*business*.	**Είμαι εδώ για *διακοπές/δουλειά*.** <u>ee</u>·meh eh·<u>THoh</u> yah *THiah·koh·<u>pehs</u>/THoo·<u>liah</u>*
I'm going to...	**Θα...** thah...
I'm staying at the...Hotel.	**Μένω στο...ξενοδοχείο.** <u>meh</u>·noh stoh... kseh·noh·THoh·<u>khee</u>·oh

You May Hear...

Το *εισιτήριο/διαβατήριό* σας, παρακαλώ. toh ee·see·<u>tee</u>·ree·<u>oh</u>/THee·ah·vah·<u>tee</u>·ree·<u>oh</u> sahs pah·rah·kah·<u>loh</u>	Your *ticket/ passport*, please.
Ποιος είναι ο σκοπός του ταξιδιού σας; piohs <u>ee</u>·neh oh skoh·<u>pohs</u> too tah·ksee·THee·<u>oo</u> sahs	What's the purpose of your visit?
Πού μένετε; poo <u>meh</u>·neh·teh	Where are you staying?
Πόσο καιρό θα μείνετε; <u>poh</u>·soh keh·<u>roh</u> thah <u>mee</u>·neh·teh	How long are you staying?
Με ποιον είστε εδώ; meh piohn <u>ee</u>·steh eh·<u>THoh</u>	Who are you with?

Passport Control and Customs

I'm just passing through.	**Απλώς περνώ από εδώ.** ahp·<u>lohs</u> pehr·<u>noh</u> ah·<u>poh</u> eh·<u>THoh</u>
I would like to declare...	**Θα ήθελα να δηλώσω...** thah <u>ee</u>·theh·lah nah THee·<u>loh</u>·soh...
I have nothing to declare.	**Δεν έχω να δηλώσω τίποτα.** THehn <u>eh</u>·khoh nah THee·<u>loh</u>·soh <u>tee</u>·poh·tah

Έχετε τίποτα να δηλώσετε; eh·kheh·teh tee·poh·tah nah THee·loh·seh·teh — Do you have anything to declare?

Πρέπει να πληρώσετε φόρο για αυτό. preh·pee nah plee·roh·seh·teh foh·roh yah ahf·toh — You must pay duty on this.

Παρακαλώ ανοίξτε αυτή την τσάντα. pah·rah·kah·loh ah·nee·ksteh ahf·tee teen tsah·ndah — Please open this bag.

ΤΕΛΩΝΕΙΟ teh·loh·nee·oh — customs

ΑΦΟΡΟΛΟΓΗΤΑ ΕΙΔΗ ah·foh·roh·loh·yee·tah ee·THee — duty-free goods

ΕΙΔΗ ΓΙΑ ΔΗΛΩΣΗ ee·THee yah THee·loh·see — goods to declare

ΤΙΠΟΤΑ ΓΙΑ ΔΗΛΩΣΗ tee·poh·tah yah THee·loh·see — nothing to declare

ΕΛΕΓΧΟΣ ΔΙΑΒΑΤΗΡΙΩΝ eh·leh·ghohs THee·ah·vah·tee·ree·ohn — passport control

ΑΣΤΥΝΟΜΙΑ ah·stee·noh·mee·ah — police

Money and Banking

Essential

Where is...?	Πού είναι...; poo ee·neh...
- the ATM	- το αυτόματο μηχάνημα ανάληψης toh ahf·toh·mah·toh mee·khah·nee·mah ah·nah·lee·psees
- the bank	- η τράπεζα ee trah·peh·zah

- the currency exchange office	**- γραφείο ανταλλαγής συναλλάγματος** ghrah·<u>fee</u>·oh ahn·dah·lah·<u>ghees</u> see·nah·<u>lahgh</u>·mah·tohs
What time does the bank *open/close*?	**Τι ώρα *ανοίγει/κλείνει* η τράπεζα;** tee <u>oh</u>·rah ah·<u>nee</u>·ghee/<u>klee</u>·nee ee <u>trah</u>·peh·zah
I'd like to change *dollars/pounds* into euros.	**Θα ήθελα να αλλάξω *μερικά δολάρια/λίρες* σε ευρώ.** thah <u>ee</u>·theh·lah nah ah·<u>lah</u>·ksoh meh·ree·<u>kah</u> THoh·<u>lah</u>·ree·ah/meh·ree·<u>kehs</u> <u>lee</u>·rehs seh ehv·roh
I want to cash some traveler's checks [cheques].	**Θα ήθελα να εξαργυρώσω μερικές ταξιδιωτικές επιταγές.** thah <u>ee</u>·theh·lah nah eh·ksahr·yee·<u>roh</u>·soh meh·ree·<u>kehs</u> tah·ksee· THee·oh·tee·<u>kehs</u> eh·pee·tah·<u>yehs</u>

ATM, Bank and Currency Exchange

Can I exchange foreign currency here?	**Μπορώ να αλλάξω συνάλλαγμα εδώ;** boh·<u>roh</u> nah ah·<u>lah</u>·ksoh see·<u>nah</u>·lahgh·mah eh·THoh
What's the exchange rate?	**Ποια είναι η τιμή συναλλάγματος;** piah <u>ee</u>·neh ee tee·<u>mee</u> see·nah·<u>lahgh</u>·mah·tohs
How much is the fee?	**Πόση προμήθεια χρεώνετε;** <u>poh</u>·see proh·<u>mee</u>·thee·ah khreh·<u>oh</u>·neh·teh
I've lost my traveler's checks [cheques].	**Έχασα τις ταξιδιωτικές επιταγές μου.** <u>eh</u>·khah·sah tees tah·ksee·THee·oh·tee·<u>kehs</u> eh·pee·tah·<u>yehs</u> moo
My card was lost.	**Χάθηκε η κάρτα μου.** <u>khah</u>·thee·keh ee <u>kahr</u>·tah moo
My credit cards have been stolen.	**Μου έκλεψαν τις πιστωτικές μου κάρτες.** moo <u>ehk</u>·leh·psahn tees pees·toh·tee·<u>kehs</u> moo <u>kahr</u>·tehs
My card doesn't work.	**Η κάρτα μου δεν λειτουργεί.** ee <u>kahr</u>·tah moo THehn lee·toor·<u>ghee</u>

▶ For numbers, see page 158.

You May See...

ΕΙΣΑΓΕΤΕ ΤΗΝ ΚΑΡΤΑ ee·<u>sah</u>·yeh·teh teen <u>kahr</u>·tah	insert card
ΑΚΥΡΩΣΗ ah·<u>kee</u>·roh·see	cancel
ΔΙΑΓΡΑΦΗ THee·ahgh·rah·<u>fee</u>	clear
ΕΙΣΑΓΕΤΕ ee·<u>sah</u>·yeh·teh	enter
PIN peen	PIN
ΑΝΑΛΗΨΗ ah·<u>nah</u>·lee·psee	withdraw
ΑΠΟ ΛΟΓΑΡΙΑΣΜΟ ΟΨΕΩΣ ah·<u>poh</u> loh·ghahr·yahz·<u>moh</u> oh·pseh·ohs	from checking [current] account
ΑΠΟ ΛΟΓΑΡΙΑΣΜΟ ΤΑΜΙΕΥΤΗΡΙΟΥ ah·<u>poh</u> loh·ghahr·yahz·<u>moh</u> tah·mee·ehf·tee·<u>ree</u>·oo	from savings account
ΑΠΟΔΕΙΞΗ ah·<u>poh</u>·THee·ksee	receipt

i All major foreign currencies, traveler's checks and Eurocheques are widely accepted at banks and currency cxchange offices throughout Greece. In addition, ATMs can be found outside most main banks; these accept VISA, MasterCard, American Express, Eurocard and a variety of other international bank and credit cards.
Banks are generally open Monday through Friday from 7:30 a.m. or 8:00 a.m. to 2:30 p.m. (1:30 p.m. on Friday). Centrally located banks are also open on Saturday. Currency exchange offices stay open until late evening.

16

You May See...

In 2002, the Greek drachma was replaced with the European Union currency, euro (**ευρώ**/ehv·<u>roh</u>), divided into 100 cents (**λεπτό**/ lehp·<u>toh</u>).
Coins: 1, 2, 5, 10, 20, 50 cents; 1, 2 euro
Notes: 5, 10, 20, 50, 100, 200, 500 euro

Transportation

Essential

How do I get to town?	**Πώς μπορώ να πάω στην πόλη;** pohs boh·<u>roh</u> nah <u>pah</u>·oh steen <u>poh</u>·lee
Where's...?	**Πού είναι...;** poo <u>ee</u>·neh...
– the airport	**– το αεροδρόμιο** toh ah·eh·roh·<u>THroh</u>·mee·oh
– the train [railway] station	**– ο σταθμός των τρένων** oh stahth·<u>mohs</u> ton <u>treh</u>·nohn
– the bus station	**– ο σταθμός των λεωφορείων** oh stahth·<u>mohs</u> tohn leh·oh·foh·<u>ree</u>·ohn
– the subway [underground] station	**– ο σταθμός του μετρό** oh stahth·<u>mohs</u> too meh·<u>troh</u>
How far is it?	**Πόσο απέχει;** <u>poh</u>·soh ah·<u>peh</u>·khee
Where can I buy tickets?	**Από πού μπορώ να αγοράσω εισιτήρια;** ah·<u>poh</u> poo boh·<u>roh</u> nah ah·ghoh·<u>rah</u>·soh ee·see·<u>tee</u>·ree·ah
A *one-way [single]/ round-trip [return]* ticket.	**Ένα απλό εισιτήριο/εισιτήριο με επιστροφή.** <u>eh</u>·nah *ahp·<u>loh</u>* ee·see·<u>tee</u>·ree·oh/ ee·see·<u>tee</u>·ree·oh meh eh·pees·troh·<u>fee</u>
How much?	**Πόσο;** <u>poh</u>·soh
Is there a discount?	**Υπάρχει μειωμένο εισιτήριο;** ee·<u>pahr</u>·khee mee·oh·<u>meh</u>·noh ee·see·<u>tee</u>·ree·oh
Which...?	**Ποια...;** piah...
– gate	**– είσοδος** <u>ee</u>·soh·THohs
– line	**– γραμμή** ghrah·<u>mee</u>
– platform	**– πλατφόρμα** plaht·<u>fohr</u>·mah

Where can I get a taxi?	**Πού μπορώ να βρω ταξί;** poo boh·<u>roh</u> nah vroh tah·<u>ksee</u>
Please take me to this address.	**Παρακαλώ πηγαίνετέ με σε αυτή τη διεύθυνση.** pah·rah·kah·<u>loh</u> pee·<u>yeh</u>·neh·<u>teh</u> meh seh ahf·<u>tee</u> tee THee·<u>ehf</u>·theen·see
Where can I rent a car?	**Πού μπορώ να νοικιάσω ένα αυτοκίνητο;** poo boh·<u>roh</u> nah nee·kee·<u>ah</u>·soh <u>eh</u>·nah ahf·toh·<u>kee</u>·nee·toh
Can I have a map?	**Μπορώ να έχω ένα χάρτη;** boh·<u>roh</u> nah <u>eh</u>·khoh <u>eh</u>·nah <u>khahr</u>·tee

Ticketing

When's...to Athens?	**Πότε αναχωρεί...για Αθήνα;** <u>poh</u>·teh ah·nah·khoh·<u>ree</u>...yah ah·<u>thee</u>·nah
– the (first) bus	**– το (πρώτο) λεωφορείο** toh (<u>proh</u>·toh) leh·oh·foh·<u>ree</u>·oh
– the (next) flight	**– η (επόμενη) πτήση** ee (eh·<u>poh</u>·meh·nee) <u>ptee</u>·see
– the (last) train	**– το (τελευταίο) τρένο** toh (teh·lehf·<u>teh</u>·oh) <u>treh</u>·noh
Where can I buy tickets?	**Από πού μπορώ να αγοράσω εισιτήρια;** ah·<u>poh</u> poo boh·<u>roh</u> nah ah·ghoh·<u>rah</u>·soh ee·see·<u>tee</u>·ree·ah
One ticket./Two tickets.	**Ένα εισιτήριο./Δύο εισιτήρια.** <u>eh</u>·nah ee·see·<u>tee</u>·ree·oh/<u>THee</u>·oh ee·see·<u>tee</u>·ree·ah
For *today/tomorrow*.	**Για *σήμερα/αύριο*.** yah <u>see</u>·meh·rah/<u>ahv</u>·ree·oh

▶ For days, see page 160.

▶ For time, see page 160.

A *first/economy* class ticket.	**Ένα *πρώτης/ οικονομικής θέσης* εισιτήριο.** <u>eh</u>·nah <u>proh</u>·tees/ee·koh·noh·mee·<u>kees</u> <u>theh</u>·sees ee·see·<u>tee</u>·ree·oh
How much?	**Πόσο;** <u>poh</u>·soh

Is there a discount for...?	**Υπάρχει μειωμένο εισιτήριο για...;** ee·<u>pahr</u>·khee mee·oh·<u>meh</u>·noh ee·see·<u>tee</u>·ree·oh yah...
– children	**– παιδιά** peh·<u>THyah</u>
– students	**– φοιτητές** fee·tee·<u>tehs</u>
– senior citizens	**– ηλικιωμένοι** ee·lee·kee·oh·<u>meh</u>·nee
I have an e-ticket.	**Έχω e-ticket.** <u>eh</u>·khoh ee tee·keht
Can I buy a ticket on the *bus/train*?	**Μπορώ να αγοράσω εισιτήριο στο** *λεωφορείο/τρένο*; boh·<u>roh</u> nah ah·ghoh·<u>rah</u>·soh ee·see·<u>tee</u>·ree·oh stoh *leh·oh·foh·<u>ree</u>·oh/<u>treh</u>·noh*
I'd like to...my reservation.	**Θα ήθελα να...την κράτησή μου.** thah <u>ee</u>·theh·lah nah...teen krah·tee·<u>see</u> moo
– cancel	**– ακυρώσω** ah·kee·<u>roh</u>·soh
– change	**– αλλάξω** ah·<u>lah</u>·ksoh
– confirm	**– επιβεβαιώσω** eh·pee·veh·veh·<u>oh</u>·soh

Plane

Getting to the Airport

How much is a taxi to the airport?	**Πόσο κοστίζει το ταξί ως το αεροδρόμιο;** poh·soh kohs·tee·zee toh tah·ksee ohs toh ah·eh·roh·THroh·mee·oh
To...Airport, please.	**Στο...αεροδρόμιο, παρακαλώ.** stoh... ah·eh·roh·THroh·mee·oh pah·rah·kah·loh
My airline is...	**Πετάω με την εταιρία...** peh·tah·oh meh teen eh·teh·ree·ah...
My flight leaves at...	**Η πτήση μου φεύγει στις...** ee ptee·see moo fehv·ghee stees...

▶ For time, see page 160.

I'm in a rush.	**Βιάζομαι.** vee·ah·zoh·meh
Can you take an alternate route?	**Μπορείτε να πάτε από άλλο δρόμο;** boh·ree·teh nah pah·teh ah·poh ah·loh THroh·moh
Can you drive *faster/slower*?	**Μπορείτε να πάτε *πιο γρήγορα/αργά*;** boh·ree·teh nah pah·teh *pioh ghree·ghoh·rah/ ahr·ghah*

You May Hear...

Με ποια εταιρία πετάτε; meh piah eh·teh·ree·ah peh·tah·teh	What airline are you flying?
Τοπική ή Διεθνή; toh·pee·kee ee THee·ehth·nee	Domestic or International?
Σε ποιον τερματικό σταθμό; seh piohn tehr·mah·tee·koh stahth·moh	What terminal?

You May See...

ΑΦΙΞΕΙΣ ah·<u>fee</u>·ksees	arrivals
ΑΝΑΧΩΡΗΣΕΙΣ ah·nah·khoh·<u>ree</u>·sees	departures
ΠΑΡΑΛΑΒΗ ΑΠΟΣΚΕΥΩΝ pah·rah·lah·<u>vee</u> ah·pohs·keh·<u>vohn</u>	baggage claim
ΠΤΗΣΕΙΣ ΕΣΩΤΕΡΙΚΟΥ <u>ptee</u>·sees eh·soh·teh·ree·<u>koo</u>	domestic flights
ΠΤΗΣΕΙΣ ΕΞΩΤΕΡΙΚΟΥ <u>ptee</u>·sees eh·ksoh·teh·ree·<u>koo</u>	international flights
ΕΛΕΓΧΟΣ ΑΠΟΣΚΕΥΩΝ <u>eh</u>·legh·khos ah·pos·keh·<u>vohn</u>	check-in
E-TICKET CHECK-IN ee·<u>tee</u>·keht tsehk·een	e-ticket check-in
ΠΥΛΕΣ ΕΠΙΒΙΒΑΣΗΣ <u>pee</u>·lehs eh·pee·<u>vee</u>·vah·sees	boarding gates

Check-in and Boarding

Where is the check-in desk for flight...?	**Πού είναι το γραφείο παράδοσης αποσκευών για την πτήση...;** poo <u>ee</u>·neh toh ghrah·<u>fee</u>·oh pah·<u>rah</u>·THoh·sees ah·poh·skeh·<u>vohn</u> yah teen <u>ptee</u>·see...
My name is...	**Λέγομαι...** <u>leh</u>·ghoh·meh...
I'm going to...	**Πηγαίνω...** pee·<u>gheh</u>·noh...
How much luggage is allowed?	**Πόσο είναι το επιτρεπόμενο βάρος;** <u>poh</u>·soh <u>ee</u>·neh toh eh·pee·treh·<u>poh</u>·meh·noh <u>vah</u>·rohs
Which gate does flight...leave from?	**Από ποια έξοδο φεύγει η πτήση...;** ah·<u>poh</u> piah <u>eh</u>·ksoh·THoh <u>fehv</u>·yee ee <u>ptee</u>·see...
I'd like *a window/ an aisle* seat.	**Θα ήθελα μια θέση στο *παράθυρο/ διάδρομο.*** thah <u>ee</u>·theh·lah mee·<u>ah theh</u>·see stoh pah·<u>rah</u>·thee·roh/THee·<u>ah</u>·THroh·moh
When do we *leave/ arrive*?	**Πότε *φεύγουμε/φθάνουμε;*** <u>poh</u>·teh <u>fehv</u>·ghoo·meh/<u>fthah</u>·noo·meh

Is flight...delayed?	**Υπάρχει καθυστέρηση στην πτήση...;**
	ee·<u>pahr</u>·khee kah·thee·<u>steh</u>·ree·see steen <u>ptee</u>·see...
How late will it be?	**Πόσο θα αργήσει;** <u>poh</u>·soh thah ahr·<u>ghee</u>·see

▶ For numbers, see page 158.

You May Hear...

Ο επόμενος! oh eh·<u>poh</u>·meh·nohs	Next!
Το *εισιτήριο/διαβατήριο* σας, παρακαλώ. toh ee·see·<u>tee</u>·ree·oh/THee·ah·vah·<u>tee</u>·ree·oh sahs pah·rah·kah·<u>loh</u>	Your *ticket/ passport*, please.
Πόσες αποσκευές έχετε; <u>poh</u>·sehs ah·poh·skeh·<u>vehs</u> <u>eh</u>·kheh·teh	How much luggage do you have?
Έχετε υπέρβαρο. <u>eh</u>·kheh·teh ee·<u>pehr</u>·vah·roh	You have excess baggage.
Αυτό είναι πολύ *βαρύ/μεγάλο* για αποσκευή χειρός. ahf·<u>toh</u> ee·neh poh·<u>lee</u> *vah·<u>ree</u>/ meh·<u>gha</u>·loh* yah ah·pohs·keh·<u>vee</u> khee·<u>rohs</u>	That's too *heavy/ large* for a carry-on [to carry on board].
Φτιάξατε τις βαλίτσες σας *μόνος σας♂/μόνη σας♀*; ftee·<u>ah</u>·ksah·teh tees vah·<u>lee</u>·tses sahs <u>moh</u>·nohs sahs♂/<u>moh</u>·nee sahs♀	Did you pack these bags yourself?
Σας έδωσε κανείς να μεταφέρετε κάτι; sahs <u>eh</u>·THoh·seh kah·<u>nees</u> nah meh·tah·<u>feh</u>·reh·teh <u>kah</u>·tee	Did anyone give you anything to carry?
Αδειάστε τις τσέπες σας. ah·<u>THiah</u>·steh tees <u>tseh</u>·pehs sahs	Empty your pockets.
Βγάλτε τα παπούτσια σας. <u>vghahl</u>·teh tah pah·<u>poo</u>·tsiah sahs	Take off your shoes.
Τώρα αρχίζει η επιβίβαση για την πτήση... <u>toh</u>·rah ahr·<u>khee</u>·zee ee eh·pee·<u>vee</u>·vah·see yah teen <u>ptee</u>·see...	Now boarding flight...

Luggage

Where *is/are*...?	**Πού είναι...;** poo <u>ee</u>·neh...
– the luggage carts [trolleys]	– **τα καροτσάκια αποσκευών** tah kah·roh·<u>tsah</u>·kee·ah ah·pohs·keh·<u>vohn</u>
– the luggage lockers	– **οι θυρίδες** ee thee·<u>ree</u>·THehs
– the luggage claim	– **η φύλαξη αποσκευών** ee <u>fee</u>·lah·ksee ah·poh·skeh·<u>vohn</u>
I've lost my luggage.	**Έχασα τις αποσκευές μου.** <u>eh</u>·khah·sah tees ah·pohs·keh·<u>vehs</u> moo
My luggage has been stolen.	**Μου έκλεψαν τις αποσκευές.** moo <u>ehk</u>·leh·psahn tees ah·pohs·keh·<u>vehs</u>
My suitcase was damaged.	**Η βαλίτσα μου χάλασε στη μεταφορά.** ee vah·<u>lee</u>·tsah moo <u>khah</u>·lah·seh stee meh·tah·foh·<u>rah</u>

Finding Your Way

Where *is/are*...?	**Πού είναι...;** poo <u>ee</u>·neh...
– the currency exchange office	– **το γραφείο ανταλλαγής συναλλάγματος** toh ghrah·<u>fee</u>·oh ahn·dah·lah·<u>ghees</u> see·nah·<u>lahgh</u>·mah·tohs
– the car rental [hire]	– **το γραφείο ενοικιάσεως αυτοκινήτων** toh ghrah·<u>fee</u>·oh eh·nee·kee·<u>ah</u>·seh·ohs ahf·toh·kee·<u>nee</u>·tohn
– the exit	– **η έξοδος** ee <u>eh</u>·ksoh·THohs
– the taxis	– **τα ταξί** tah tah·<u>ksee</u>
Is there...into town?	**Υπάρχει...για την πόλη;** ee·<u>pahr</u>·khee...yah teen <u>poh</u>·lee
– a bus	– **λεωφορείο** leh·oh·foh·<u>ree</u>·oh
– a train	– **τρένο** <u>treh</u>·noh
– a subway [underground]	– **μετρό** meh·<u>troh</u>

▶ For directions, see page 33.

Train

How do I get to the (main) train station?	**Πώς πάνε στον (κεντρικό) σιδηροδρομικό σταθμό;** pohs pah·neh stohn (kehn·dree·koh) see·THee·roh·THroh·mee·koh stahth·moh
How far is it?	**Πόσο απέχει;** poh·soh ah·peh·khee
Where *is/are*...?	**Πού είναι...;** poo ee·neh...
- the ticket office	**- το γραφείο εισιτηρίων** toh ghrah·fee·oh ee·see·tee·ree·ohn
- the luggage lockers	**- οι θυρίδες** ee thee·ree·THehs
- the platform	**- η αποβάθρα** ee ah·poh·vahth·rah

▶ For directions, see page 33.

▶ For ticketing, see page 19.

You May See...

ΠΡΟΣ ΑΠΟΒΑΘΡΕΣ prohs ah·poh·vahth·rehs	to the platforms
ΠΛΗΡΟΦΟΡΙΕΣ plee·roh·foh·ree·ehs	information
ΚΡΑΤΗΣΕΙΣ krah·tee·sees	reservations
ΑΦΙΞΕΙΣ ah·fee·ksees	arrivals
ΑΝΑΧΩΡΗΣΕΙΣ ah·nah·khoh·ree·sees	departures

Questions

Could I have a schedule [timetable]?	**Μπορώ να έχω ένα πρόγραμμα δρομολογίων;** boh·roh nah eh·khoh eh·nah proh·ghrah·mah THroh·moh·loh·yee·ohn
How long is the trip?	**Πόση ώρα διαρκεί το ταξίδι;** poh·see oh·rah THee·ahr·kee toh tah·ksee·THee
Do I have to change trains?	**Χρειάζεται να αλλάξω τρένο;** khree·ah·zeh·teh nah ah·lah·ksoh treh·noh

25

Departures

When is the train to...?	**Πότε φεύγει το τρένο για...;** poh·teh fehv·ghee toh treh·noh yah...
Is this the right platform for...?	**Είναι αυτή η σωστή αποβάθρα για το τρένο για...;** ee·neh ahf·tee ee sohs·tee ah·poh·vahth·rah yah toh treh·noh yah...
Where is platform...?	**Πού είναι η αποβάθρα...;** poo ee·neh ee ah·poh·vahth·rah...
Where do I change for...?	**Πού αλλάζω για...;** poo ah·lah·zoh yah...

Boarding

Can I sit here?	**Μπορώ να καθίσω εδώ;** boh·roh nah kah·thee·soh eh·THoh
That's my seat.	**Νομίζω αυτή είναι η θέση μου.** noh·mee·zoh ahf·tee ee·neh ee theh·see moo

You May Hear...

Επιβιβαστείτε! eh·pee·vee·vahs·tee·teh	All aboard!
Τα εισιτήριά σας, παρακαλώ. tah ee·see·tee·ree·ah sahs pah·rah·kah·loh	Tickets, please.

Πρέπει να αλλάξετε σε... <u>preh</u>·pee nah ah·<u>lah</u>·kseh·teh seh...	You have to change at...
Επόμενη στάση... eh·<u>poh</u>·meh·nee <u>stah</u>·see...	Next stop...

Bus

Where's the bus station?	**Πού είναι ο σταθμός λεωφορείων;** poo <u>ee</u>·neh oh stahth·<u>mohs</u> leh·oh·foh·<u>ree</u>·ohn
How far is it?	**Πόσο απέχει;** <u>poh</u>·soh ah·<u>peh</u>·khee
How do I get to...?	**Πώς πάνε σε...;** pohs <u>pah</u>·neh seh...
Is this the bus to...?	**Είναι αυτό το λεωφορείο για...;** <u>ee</u>·neh ahf·<u>toh</u> toh leh·oh·foh·<u>ree</u>·oh yah...
Could you tell me when to get off?	**Μπορείτε να μου πείτε πού να κατέβω;** boh·<u>ree</u>·teh nah moo <u>pee</u>·teh poo nah kah·<u>teh</u>·voh
Do I have to change buses?	**Χρειάζεται να αλλάξω λεωφορείο;** khree·<u>ah</u>·zeh·teh nah ah·<u>lah</u>·ksoh leh·oh·foh·<u>ree</u>·oh
Stop here, please!	**Σταματείστε εδώ, παρακαλώ!** stah·mah·<u>tees</u>·teh eh·<u>THoh</u> pah·rah·kah·<u>loh</u>

▶ For ticketing, see page 19.

Before boarding public transportation you need to buy a ticket at the special kiosks or automatic ticketing machines marked **ΕΙΣΙΤΗΡΙΑ** (ee·see·<u>tee</u>·ree·ah). In Athens, tickets are valid for 90 minutes after they have been validated and can be used for buses, the subway, trolleybuses, trams and part of the suburban railway. Daily, weekly or monthly tickets and reduced fares are available.

▶ For useful websites, see page 165.

Subway [Underground]

Where's the nearest subway [underground] station?	**Πού είναι ο κοντινότερος σταθμός του μετρό;** poo <u>ee</u>·neh oh koh·ndee·<u>noh</u>·teh·rohs stahth·<u>mohs</u> too meh·<u>troh</u>
Could I have a map of the subway [underground]?	**Μπορώ να έχω ένα χάρτη του μετρό;** boh·<u>roh</u> nah <u>eh</u>·khoh <u>eh</u>·nah <u>khahr</u>·tee too meh·<u>troh</u>
Which line should I take for...?	**Ποια γραμμή πρέπει να πάρω για...;** piah ghrah·<u>mee</u> <u>preh</u>·pee nah <u>pah</u>·roh yah...
Where do I change for...?	**Πού αλλάζω για...;** poo ah·<u>lah</u>·zoh yah...
Is this the right train for...?	**Είναι αυτό το σωστό τρένο για...;** <u>ee</u>·neh ahf·<u>toh</u> toh sohs·<u>toh</u> treh·noh yah...
Where are we?	**Πού είμαστε;** poo <u>ee</u>·mahs·teh

► For ticketing, see page 19.

 Athens is the only Greek city currently served by a **μετρό** (meh·<u>troh</u>), subway. Subway tickets can be purchased at ticket desks or machines located at each station. Validate your ticket by stamping it in a validation machine, found by the platform, before you get on the subway.

Boat and Ferry

When is the ferry to...?	**Πότε φεύγει το φέρρυ-μπωτ για...;** <u>poh</u>·teh <u>fehv</u>·ghee toh <u>feh</u>·ree boht yah...
Can I take my car onboard?	**Μπορώ να επιβιβάσω το αυτοκίνητό μου;** boh·<u>roh</u> nah eh·pee·vee·<u>vah</u>·soh toh ahf·toh·<u>kee</u>·nee·<u>toh</u> moo
Where are the life jackets?	**Πού είναι τα σωσίβια;** poo <u>ee</u>·neh tah soh·<u>see</u>·vee·ah

▶ For ticketing, see page 19.

You May See...

| **ΝΑΥΑΓΟΣΩΣΤΙΚΗ ΛΕΜΒΟΣ** nah·vah·ghoh·sohs·tee·<u>kee</u> <u>lehm</u>·vohs | life boats |
| **ΣΩΣΙΒΙΑ** soh·<u>see</u>·vee·ah | life jackets |

i It is likely that after your arrival in Athens, you will be heading straight for the port of Piraeus to catch a ferry. The harbor front is lined with ticket agents; ferry prices are fixed. Each agent tends to sell tickets for one company serving a particular route. A window display (usually in Greek and English) will tell you exactly what islands that ferry goes to. Sleeping on the deck is allowed, but make sure to take a sleeping bag and wear warm clothes, even in July!
Once on an island, you may decide to go on an island tour. Several converted fishing boats run daily trips. Note that throwing anything into the sea off a boat deck is an offense in Greece, and you will be fined if caught.

Bicycle and Motorcycle

I'd like to rent [hire]...	**Θα ήθελα να νοικιάσω...** thah <u>ee</u>·theh·lah nah nee·<u>kiah</u>·soh...
- a bicycle	**– ένα ποδήλατο** <u>eh</u>·nah poh·<u>THee</u>·lah·toh
- a moped	**– ένα μοτοποδήλατο** <u>eh</u>·nah moh·toh·poh·<u>THee</u>·lah·toh
- a motorbike	**– μία μοτοσικλέτα** <u>mee</u>·ah moh·toh·see·<u>kleh</u>·tah
How much per *day/week*?	**Πόσο κοστίζει *την ημέρα/την εβδομάδα*;** <u>poh</u>·soh koh·<u>stee</u>·zee teen ee·<u>meh</u>·rah/teen ehv·THoh·<u>mah</u>·THah
Can I have a *helmet/lock*?	**Μπορώ να έχω *ένα κράνος/μία κλειδαριά*;** boh·<u>roh</u> nah <u>eh</u>·khoh <u>eh</u>·nah <u>krah</u>·nohs/<u>mee</u>·ah klee·<u>THah</u>·riah

Taxi

Where can I get a taxi?	**Πού μπορώ να βρω ταξί;** poo boh·<u>roh</u> nah vroh tah·<u>ksee</u>
I'd like a taxi *now/ for tomorrow* at...	**Θα ήθελα ένα ταξί *τώρα/για αύριο* στις...** thah <u>ee</u>·theh·lah <u>eh</u>·nah tah·<u>ksee</u> <u>toh</u>·rah/yah <u>ahv</u>·ree·oh stees...
Pick me up at *(place/time)*...	**Ελάτε να με πάρετε *από/ στις*...** eh·<u>lah</u>·teh nah meh <u>pah</u>·reh·teh ah·<u>poh</u>/stees...
I'm going to...	**Πηγαίνω...** pee·<u>gheh</u>·noh...
- this address	**– σε αυτή τη διεύθυνση** seh ahf·<u>tee</u> tee THee·<u>ehf</u>·theen·see
- the airport	**– στο αεροδρόμιο** stoh ah·eh·roh·<u>THroh</u>·mee·oh
- the train [railway] station	**– στον σιδηροδρομικό σταθμό** stohn see·THee·roh·THroh·mee·<u>koh</u> stahth·<u>moh</u>
I'm late.	**Έχω αργήσει.** <u>eh</u>·hoh ahr·<u>ghee</u>·see

Can you drive *faster/slower*?	**Μπορείτε να πάτε πιο *γρήγορα/αργά*;** boh·_ree_·teh nah _pah_·teh pioh _gree_·ghoh·rah/ ahr·_ghah_
Stop/Wait here.	***Σταματήστε/Περιμένετε εδώ.*** stah·mah·_tee_·steh/peh·ree·_meh_·neh·teh eh·_THoh_
How much?	**Πόσο;** poh·soh
You said it would cost...euros.	**Είπατε ότι θα κόστιζε...ευρώ.** _ee_·pah·teh _oh_·tee thah _kohs_·tee·zeh...ehv·_roh_
Keep the change.	**Κρατείστε τα ρέστα.** krah·_tees_·teh tah _rehs_·tah
A receipt, please.	**Μια απόδειξη, παρακαλώ.** miah ah·_poh_·THee·ksee pah·rah·kah·_loh_

You May Hear...

Πού μπορώ να; poo boh·_roh_ nah	Where to?
Πού είναι η διεύθυνση; poo _ee_·neh ee THee·_ehf_·theen·see	What's the address?

i In Athens, licensed taxis are yellow with a blue stripe. In all major cities, fares are fixed. For longer distances you should agree to a fare before the trip. Tipping is not compulsory, but it is common to round up the amount due.

Car

Car Rental [Hire]

Where can I rent [hire] a car?	**Πού μπορώ να νοικιάσω ένα αυτοκίνητο;** poo boh·_roh_ nah nee·_kiah_·soh eh·nah ahf·toh·_kee_·nee·toh
I'd like to rent [hire]...	**Θα ήθελα να νοικιάσω ένα...** thah _ee_·theh·lah nah nee·_kiah_·soh eh·nah...
– a 2-/4-door car	– ***δίπορτο/τετράπορτο* αυτοκίνητο** _ee_·poh·rtoh/ teh·_trah_·poh·rtoh ahf·toh·_kee_·nee·toh

I'd like to rent [hire]...	**Θα ήθελα να νοικιάσω ένα...** thah ee·theh·lah nah nee·kiah·soh eh·nah...
- an automatic car	**- αυτόματο αυτοκίνητο** ahf·toh·mah·toh ahf·toh·kee·nee·toh
- a car with air conditioning	**- αυτοκίνητο με κλιματισμό** ahf·toh·kee·nee·toh meh klee·mah·tee·smoh
- a car seat	**- παιδικό κάθισμα αυτοκινήτου** peh·THee·koh kah·thee·smah ahf·toh·kee·nee·too
How much...?	**Πόσο κάνει...;** poh·soh kah·nee...
- per day/week	**- την ημέρα/ενδομάδα** teen ee·meh·rah/ ehv·THoh·mah·THah
- per kilometer	**- το χιλιόμετρο** toh khee·lee·oh·meht·roh
- for unlimited mileage	**- για απεριόριστη απόσταση** yah ah·peh·ree·oh·rees·tee ah·poh·stah·see
- with insurance	**- με ασφάλεια** meh ah·sfah·lee·ah
Are there any discounts?	**Υπάρχει έκπτωση;** ee·pahr·khee ehk·ptoh·see

You May Hear...

Έχετε διεθνή άδεια οδήγησης; eh·kheh·teh THee·ehth·nee ah·THee·ah oh·THee·ghee·sees — Do you have an international driver's license?

Μπορώ να δω το διαβατήριό σας, παρακαλώ; boh·roh nah THoh toh THee·ah·vah·tee·ree·oh sahs pah·rah·kah·loh — May I see your passport, please?

Θέλετε ασφάλεια; theh·leh·teh ah·sfah·lee·ah — Do you want insurance?

Υπάρχει μία προκαταβολή των... ee·pahr·khee miah proh·kah·tah·voh·lee tohn... — There is a deposit of...

Παρακαλώ υπογράψτε εδώ. pah·rah·kah·loh ee·poh·ghrah·psteh eh·THoh — Please sign here.

Gas [Petrol] Station

Where's the next gas [petrol] station, please?	**Πού είναι το επόμενο βενζινάδικο, παρακαλώ;** poo ee·neh toh eh·<u>poh</u>·meh·noh vehn·zee·<u>nah</u>·THee·koh pah·rah·kah·<u>loh</u>
Fill it up, please.	**Γεμίστε το, παρακαλώ.** yeh·<u>mee</u>·steh toh pah·rah·kah·<u>loh</u>
...liters, please.	**...λίτρα βενζίνη, παρακαλώ.** ...<u>lee</u>·trah vehn·<u>zee</u>·nee pah·rah·kah·<u>loh</u>
I'll pay in cash/by credit card.	**Θα πληρώσω τοις μετρητοίς/με πιστωτική κάρτα.** thah plee·<u>roh</u>·soh tees meh·tree·<u>tees</u>/ meh pee·stoh·tee·<u>kee</u> <u>kah</u>·rtah

You May See...

ΑΠΛΗ ah·<u>plee</u>	regular
ΣΟΥΠΕΡ <u>soo</u>·pehr	premium [super]
ΝΤΗΖΕΛ <u>dee</u>·zehl	diesel

Asking Directions

Is this the right road to...?	**Είναι αυτός ο σωστός δρόμος για...;** <u>ee</u>·neh ahf·<u>tohs</u> oh sohs·<u>tohs</u> <u>THroh</u>·mohs yah...
How far is it to...?	**Πόσο μακριά είναι για...;** <u>poh</u>·soh mahk·ree·<u>ah</u> <u>ee</u>·neh yah...
Where's...?	**Πού είναι...;** poo <u>ee</u>·neh...
– ...Street	**– η οδός...** ee oh·<u>THohs</u>...
– this address	**– αυτή η διεύθυνση** ahf·<u>tee</u> ee THee·<u>ehf</u>·theen·see
– the highway [motorway]	**– η εθνική οδός** ee ehth·nee·<u>kee</u> oh·<u>THohs</u>
Can you show me on the map?	**Μπορείτε να μου δείξετε στο χάρτη;** boh·<u>ree</u>·teh nah moo <u>THee</u>·kseh·teh stoh <u>khahr</u>·tee
I'm lost.	**Έχω χαθεί.** <u>eh</u>·hoh khah·<u>thee</u>

You May Hear...

ευθεία/ίσια ehf·<u>thee</u>·ah/<u>ee</u>·see·ah	straight ahead
στα αριστερά stah ah·rees·teh·<u>rah</u>	on the left
στα δεξιά stah THeh·ksee·<u>ah</u>	on the right
στη/μετά τη γωνία stee/meh·<u>tah</u> tee ghoh·<u>nee</u>·ah	*on/around* the corner
απέναντι ah·<u>peh</u>·nahn·dee	opposite
πίσω <u>pee</u>·soh	behind
δίπλα <u>THee</u>·plah	next to
μετά meh·<u>tah</u>	after
βόρεια/νότεια <u>voh</u>·ree·ah/<u>noh</u>·tee·ah	north/south
ανατολικά/δυτικά ah·nah·toh·lee·<u>kah</u>/THee·tee·<u>kah</u>	east/west
στο φανάρι stoh fah·<u>nah</u>·ree	at the traffic light
στη διασταύρωση stee THee·ah·<u>stahv</u>·roh·see	at the intersection

You May See...

ΑΠΑΓΟΡΕΥΕΤΑΙ Η ΕΠΙ ΤΟΠΟΥ ΣΤΡΟΦΗ
ah·pah·ghoh·<u>reh</u>·veh·teh ee eh·<u>pee</u> <u>toh</u>·poo stroh·<u>fee</u>

no u-turn

ΥΠΟΧΡΕΩΤΙΚΗ ΠΑΡΑΧΩΡΗΣΗ ΠΡΟΤΕΡΑΙΟΤΗΤΑΣ
ee·pohkh·reh·oh·tee·<u>kee</u> pah·rah·<u>khoh</u>·ree·see proh·teh·reh·<u>oh</u>·tee·tahs

yield

	ΥΠΟΧΡΕΩΤΙΚΗ ΔΙΑΚΟΠΗ ΠΟΡΕΙΑΣ ee·pohkh·reh·oh·tee·<u>kee</u> THee·ah·koh·<u>pee</u> poh·<u>ree</u>·ahs	stop
	ΠΕΡΙΟΧΗ ΑΠΑΓΟΡΕΥΣΗΣ ΣΤΑΘΜΕΥΣΗΣ peh·ree·oh·<u>khee</u> ah·pah·<u>ghoh</u>·rehf·sees <u>stahth</u>·mehf·sees	no parking
	ΑΠΑΓΟΡΕΥΕΤΑΙ Η ΣΤΑΣΗ ΚΑΙ Η ΣΤΑΘΜΕΥΣΗ ah·pah·ghoh·<u>reh</u>·veh·teh ee <u>stah</u>·see keh ee <u>stahth</u>·mehf·see	no stopping
	ΜΟΝΟΔΡΟΜΟΣ moh·<u>noh</u>·THroh·mohs	one way

Parking

Can I park here?	**Μπορώ να παρκάρω εδώ;** boh·<u>roh</u> nah pahr·<u>kah</u>·roh eh·<u>THoh</u>
Is there a parking lot [car park] nearby?	**Υπάρχει χώρος στάθμευσης εδώ κοντά;** ee·<u>pahr</u>·khee <u>khoh</u>·rohs <u>stath</u>·mehf·sees eh·<u>THoh</u> kohn·<u>dah</u>
How much...?	**Πόσο κοστίζει...;** <u>poh</u>·soh koh·<u>stee</u>·zee...
– per hour	**– την ώρα** teen <u>oh</u>·rah
– per day	**– την ημέρα** teen ee·<u>meh</u>·rah
– overnight	**– τη νύχτα** tee <u>neeh</u>·khtah

 Parking in large cities, particularly Athens, can be a problem as spaces are limited. It is likely that you will need to park in an indoor or outdoor parking lot. Prices vary greatly, depending on your location.

Breakdown and Repairs

My car *broke down/won't start.*	**Το αυτοκίνητό μου *χάλασε/δεν παίρνει μπρος.*** toh ahf·toh·<u>kee</u>·nee·<u>toh</u> moo *khah·lah·seh/THehn <u>pehr</u>·nee brohs*
Can you fix it today?	**Μπορείτε να το επισκευάσετε σήμερα;** boh·<u>ree</u>·teh nah toh eh·pees·keh·<u>vah</u>·seh·teh <u>see</u>·meh·rah
When will it be ready?	**Πότε θα είναι έτοιμο;** <u>poh</u>·teh thah <u>ee</u>·neh <u>eh</u>·tee·moh
How much?	**Πόσο;** <u>poh</u>·soh

Accidents

There's been an accident.	**Έγινε ένα ατύχημα.** <u>eh</u>·yee·neh <u>eh</u>·nah ah·<u>tee</u>·khee·mah
Call *an ambulance/ the police.*	**Καλέστε *ένα ασθενοφόρο/την αστυνομία.*** kah·<u>lehs</u>·teh <u>eh</u>·nah ahs·theh·noh·<u>foh</u>·roh/teen ahs·tee·noh·<u>mee</u>·ah

Accommodations

Essential

Can you recommend a hotel?	**Μπορείτε να μου συστήσετε ένα ξενοδοχείο;** boh·<u>ree</u>·teh nah moo sees·<u>tee</u>·seh·teh <u>eh</u>·nah kseh·noh·THoh·<u>khee</u>·oh
I have a reservation.	**Έχω κλείσει δωμάτιο.** <u>eh</u>·khoh <u>klee</u>·see THoh·<u>mah</u>·tee·oh
My name is...	**Λέγομαι...** <u>leh</u>·ghoh·meh...
Do you have a room...?	**Έχετε ελεύθερο δωμάτιο...;** <u>eh</u>·kheh·teh eh·<u>lehf</u>·theh·roh THoh·<u>mah</u>·tee·oh...

– for *one/two*	– **μονόκλινο/δίκλινο** moh·<u>noh</u>·klee·noh/ <u>THee</u>·klee·noh
– with a bathroom	– **με μπάνιο** meh <u>bah</u>·nioh
– with air conditioning	– **με κλιματισμό** meh klee·mah·teez·<u>moh</u>
For tonight.	**Γι' απόψε.** yah·<u>poh</u>·pseh
For two nights.	**Για δύο βράδια.** yah <u>THee</u>·oh vrah·THee·ah
For one week.	**Για μια εβδομάδα.** yah <u>mee</u>·ah ev·THoh·<u>mah</u>·THah
How much?	**Πόσο;** <u>poh</u>·soh
Do you have anything cheaper?	**Έχετε τίποτα φθηνότερο;** <u>eh</u>·kheh·teh <u>tee</u>·poh·tah fthee·<u>noh</u>·teh·roh
When's check-out?	**Τι ώρα πρέπει να αδειάσουμε το δωμάτιο;** tee <u>oh</u>·rah <u>preh</u>·pee nah ah·THee·<u>ah</u>·soo·meh toh THoh·<u>mah</u>·tee·oh
Can I leave this in the safe?	**Μπορώ να αφήσω αυτό στη θυρίδα;** boh·<u>roh</u> nah ah·<u>fee</u>·soh ahf·<u>toh</u> stee thee·<u>ree</u>·THah
Could we leave our baggage here until...?	**Μπορούμε να αφήσουμε τα πράγματά μας εδώ ως τις...;** boh·<u>roo</u>·meh nah ah·<u>fee</u>·soo·meh tah <u>prahgh</u>·mah·<u>tah</u> mahs eh·<u>THoh</u> ohs tees...
Could I have *the bill/a receipt*?	**Μπορώ να έχω *τον λογαριασμό/μια απόδειξη*;** boh·<u>roh</u> nah <u>eh</u>·hoh *tohn loh·ghahr·yahs·<u>moh</u>/miah ah·<u>poh</u>·THee·ksee*
I'll pay *in cash/by credit card*.	**Θα πληρώσω *τοις μετρητοίς/με πιστωτική κάρτα*.** thah plee·<u>roh</u>·soh *tees meht·ree·<u>tees</u>/ meh pees·toh·tee·<u>kee</u> <u>kahr</u>·tah*

If you didn't reserve your accommodations before your trip, visit the local tourist information office for a list of places to stay. Booking ahead is recommended in the high season, from mid-July to the end of August.

Finding Lodging

Can you recommend a hotel?	**Μπορείτε να μου συστήσετε ένα ξενοδοχείο...;** boh·<u>ree</u>·teh nah moo sees·<u>tee</u>·seh·teh <u>eh</u>·nah kseh·noh·THoh·<u>khee</u>·oh...
What is it near?	**Πού κοντά είναι;** poo kohn·<u>dah</u> ee·neh
How do I get there?	**Πώς πάω εκεί;** pohs <u>pah</u>·oh eh·<u>kee</u>

---

i Greece offers a large variety of accommodation options: **Ξενοδοχεία** (ksehn·oh·THoh·<u>khee</u>·ah), hotels; **Διαμερίσματα** (THee·ah·meh·<u>reez</u>·mah·tah), furnished apartments; **Δωμάτια** (THoh·<u>mah</u>·tee·ah) furnished rooms, with or without a private bath; **Παραδοσιακά δωμάτια** (pah·rah·THoh·see·ah·<u>kah</u> THoh·<u>mah</u>·tee·ah), apartments in traditional but renovated homes; **Ξενώνας νεότητας** (kseh·<u>noh</u>·nahs neh·<u>oh</u>·tee·tahs), youth hostels; **Κάμπιγκ** (<u>kahm</u>·peeng) campsites and more.

At the Hotel

I have a reservation.	**Έχω κλείσει δωμάτιο.** <u>eh</u>·hoh <u>klee</u>·see THoh·<u>mah</u>·tee·oh
My name is...	**Λέγομαι...** <u>leh</u>·ghoh·meh...
Do you have a room...?	**Έχετε δωμάτιο...;** <u>eh</u>·kheh·teh THoh·mah·tee·oh...
– with a *bathroom [toilet]/shower*	– **με μπάνιο/ντους** meh <u>bah</u>·nioh/doos
– with air conditioning	– **με κλιματισμό** meh klee·mah·teez·<u>moh</u>
– that's *smoking/ non-smoking*	– **για καπνιστές/μη καπνιστές** yah kahp·nees·<u>tehs</u>/mee kahp·nees·<u>tehs</u>
For tonight.	**Γι' απόψε.** yah·<u>poh</u>·pseh
For two nights.	**Για δύο βράδια.** yah THee·oh vrah·THiah
For one week.	**Για μία εβδομάδα.** yah <u>mee</u>·ah ev·THoh·<u>mah</u>·THah

▶ For numbers, see page 158.

Does the hotel have...?	**Έχει το ξενοδοχείο...;** <u>eh</u>·khee toh kseh·noh·<u>THoh</u>·<u>khee</u>·oh...
– a computer	**– υπολογιστή** ee·poh·loh·ghees·<u>tee</u>
– an elevator [lift]	**– ασανσέρ** ah·sahn·<u>sehr</u>
– (wireless) internet service	**– υπηρεσία (ασύρματου) internet** ee·pee·reh·<u>see</u>·ah (ah·<u>seer</u>·mah·too) een·tehr·<u>neht</u>
– room service	**– υπηρεσία δωματίου** ee·pee·reh·<u>see</u>·ah THoh·mah·<u>tee</u>·oo
– a pool	**– πισίνα** pee·<u>see</u>·nah
– a gym	**– γυμναστήριο** gheem·nahs·<u>tee</u>·ree·oh
I need...	**χρειάζομαι...** khree·<u>ah</u>·zoh·meh...
– an extra bed	**– άλλο ένα κρεβάτι** <u>ah</u>·loh <u>eh</u>·nah kreh·<u>vah</u>·tee
– a cot	**– ένα ράντζο** <u>eh</u>·nah <u>rahn</u>·joh
– a crib [child's cot]	**– ένα παιδικό κρεβάτι** <u>eh</u>·nah peh·THee·<u>koh</u> kreh·<u>vah</u>·tee

Το διαβατήριό σας/ την πιστωτική σας κάρτα, **παρακαλώ.** toh ee·ah·vah·<u>tee</u>·ree·<u>oh</u> sahs/teen pees·toh·tee·<u>kee</u> sahs <u>kahr</u>·tah pah·rah·kah·<u>loh</u>

Your *passport/ credit card*, please.

Παρακαλώ συμπληρώστε αυτό το έντυπο. pah·rah·kah·<u>loh</u> seem·blee·<u>rohs</u>·teh ahf·<u>toh</u> toh <u>ehn</u>·dee·poh

Please fill out this form.

Υπογράψτε εδώ. ee·pohgh·<u>rahp</u>·steh eh·<u>THoh</u>

Sign here.

Price

How much per *night/week*?	**Πόσο κάνει** *τη βραδιά/την εβδομάδα;* <u>poh</u>·soh <u>kah</u>·nee tee vrah·<u>iah</u>/teen ehv·oh·<u>mah</u>·ah	
Does the price include *breakfast/ sales tax [VAT]*?	**Η τιμή συμπεριλαμβάνει** *πρωινό/ΦΠΑ;* ee tee·<u>mee</u> seem·beh·ree·lahm·<u>vah</u>·nee proh·ee·<u>noh</u>/fee·pee·<u>ah</u>	

Questions

Where's...?	**Πού είναι...;** poo <u>ee</u>·neh...
– the bar	**– το μπαρ** toh bahr
– the bathroom	**– το μπάνιο** toh <u>bah</u>·nioh
– the elevator [lift]	**– το ασανσέρ** toh ah·sahn·<u>sehr</u>
Can I have...?	**Μπορώ να έχω...;** boh·<u>roh</u> nah <u>eh</u>·khoh...
– a blanket	**– μια κουβέρτα** miah koo·<u>vehr</u>·tah
– an iron	**– ένα σίδερο** <u>eh</u>·nah <u>see</u>·THeh·roh
– a pillow	**– ένα μαξιλάρι** <u>eh</u>·nah mah·ksee·<u>lah</u>·ree
– soap	**– σαπούνι** sah·<u>poo</u>·nee
– toilet paper	**– χαρτί υγείας** khahr·<u>tee</u> ee·<u>ghee</u>·ahs
– a towel	**– μια πετσέτα μπάνιου** miah peh·<u>tseh</u>·tah <u>bah</u>·nee·oo

Can I use this adapter here?	**Μπορώ να χρησιμοποιήσω αυτόν τον προσαρμοστή εδώ;** boh·<u>roh</u> nah khree·see·moh·pee·<u>ee</u>·soh ahf·<u>tohn</u> tohn proh·sahr·mohs·<u>tee</u> eh·<u>THoh</u>
How do I turn on the lights?	**Πώς ανάβουν τα φώτα;** pohs ah·<u>nah</u>·voon tah <u>foh</u>·tah
Could you wake me at...?	**Μπορείτε να με ξυπνήσετε στις...;** boh·<u>ree</u>·teh nah meh kseep·<u>nee</u>·seh·teh stees...
Could I have my things from the safe?	**Μπορώ να έχω τα πράγματά μου από τη θυρίδα;** boh·<u>roh</u> nah <u>eh</u>·khoh tah <u>prahgh</u>·mah·<u>tah</u> moo ah·<u>poh</u> tee thee·<u>ree</u>·THah
Is there *mail/ a message* for me?	**Υπάρχει αλληλογραφία/κάποιο μήνυμα για μένα;** ee·<u>pahr</u>·khee *ah·lee·lohgh·rah·<u>fee</u>·ah/ <u>kah</u>·pioh <u>mee</u>·nee·mah* yah <u>meh</u>·nah

You May See...

ΩΘΗΣΑΤΕ/ΕΛΞΑΤΕ oh·<u>thee</u>·sah·teh/ <u>ehl</u>·ksah·teh	push/pull
ΜΠΑΝΙΟ/ΤΟΥΑΛΕΤΑ <u>bah</u>·nioh/too·ah·<u>leh</u>·tah	bathroom/ restroom [toilet]
ΝΤΟΥΣ dooz	shower
ΑΣΑΝΣΕΡ ah·sahn·<u>sehr</u>	elevator [lift]
ΣΚΑΛΑ <u>skah</u>·lah	stairs
ΠΛΥΝΤΗΡΙΟ pleen·<u>dee</u>·ree·oh	laundry
ΜΗΝ ΕΝΟΧΛΕΙΤΕ meen eh·nohkh·<u>lee</u>·teh	do not disturb
ΠΥΡΟΣΤΕΓΗΣ ΘΥΡΑ pee·rohs·teh·<u>ghees</u> thee·rah	fire door
ΕΞΟΔΟΣ ΚΙΝΔΥΝΟΥ <u>eh</u>·ksoh·THohs keen·<u>THee</u>·noo	emergency exit
ΥΠΗΡΕΣΙΑ ΑΦΥΠΝΙΣΗΣ ee·pee·reh·<u>see</u>·ah ah·<u>feep</u>·nee·sees	wake-up call

Problems

There's a problem.	**Υπάρχει ένα πρόβλημα.** ee·<u>pahr</u>·hee <u>eh</u>·nah <u>prohv</u>·lee·mah
I've lost my *key/key card*.	**Έχασα *το κλειδί/την κάρτα* μου.** <u>eh</u>·hah·sah toh klee·<u>THee</u>/teen <u>kahr</u>·tah moo
I've locked myself out of my room.	**Κλειδώθηκα έξω από το δωμάτιό μου.** klee·<u>THoh</u>·thee·kah <u>eh</u>·ksoh ah·<u>poh</u> toh THoh·<u>mah</u>·tee·<u>oh</u> moo
There's no *hot water/toilet paper*.	**Δεν υπάρχει *ζεστό νερό/χαρτί υγείας*.** THen ee·<u>pahr</u>·khee zeh·<u>stoh</u> neh·<u>roh</u>/khahr·<u>tee</u> ee·<u>yee</u>·ahs
The room is dirty.	**Το δωμάτιο είναι βρώμικο.** toh THoh·<u>mah</u>·tee·oh <u>ee</u>·neh vroh·mee·koh
There are bugs in our room.	**Υπάρχουν έντομα στο δωμάτιό μας.** ee·<u>pahr</u>·hoon <u>ehn</u>·doh·mah stoh THoh·<u>mah</u>·tee·<u>oh</u> mahs
...is broken.	**...είναι σπασμένος♂/σπασμένη♀/σπασμένο((Neuter)).** ...ee·neh spahs·<u>mehn</u>·ohs♂/spahs·<u>mehn</u>·ee♀/spahs·<u>mehn</u>·oh((Neuter))
Can you fix...?	**Μπορείτε να φτιάξετε...;** boh·<u>ree</u>·teh nah <u>ftiah</u>·kseh·teh...
– the air conditioning	**– τον κλιματισμό** tohn klee·mah·teez·<u>moh</u>
– the fan	**– τον ανεμιστήρα** tohn ah·neh·mee·<u>stee</u>·rah
– the heating	**– τη θέρμανση** tee <u>thehr</u>·mahn·see
– the light	**– το φως** toh fohs
– the TV	**– την τηλεόραση** teen tee·leh·<u>oh</u>·rah·see
– the toilet	**– την τουαλέτα** teen too·ah·<u>leh</u>·tah

| I'd like to move to another room. | **Θα ήθελα να μεταφερθώ σε άλλο δωμάτιο.** thah <u>ee</u>·theh·lah nah meh·tah·fehr·<u>thoh</u> seh <u>ah</u>·loh THoh·<u>mah</u>·tee·oh |

In Greece the electricity supply is 220 V, with standard continental 2-pin or 3-pin plugs. A multi-adapter is recommended.

Check-out

When's check-out?	**Τι ώρα πρέπει να αδειάσουμε το δωμάτιο;** tee <u>oh</u>·rah <u>preh</u>·pee nah ah·THee·<u>ah</u>·soo·meh toh THoh·<u>mah</u>·tee·oh
Could we leave our baggage here until...?	**Μπορούμε να αφήσουμε τα πράγματά μας εδώ ως τις...;** boh·<u>roo</u>·meh nah ah·<u>fee</u>·soo·meh tah <u>prahgh</u>·mah·tah mahs eh·<u>THoh</u> ohs tees...
Can I have *an itemized bill/ a receipt*?	**Μπορώ να έχω έναν αναλυτικό λογαριασμό/ μια απόδειξη;** boh·<u>roh</u> nah <u>eh</u>·khoh <u>eh</u>·nahn ah·nah·lee·tee·<u>koh</u> loh·ghahr·yahz·<u>moh</u>/miah ah·<u>poh</u>·ee·ksee
I think there's a mistake in this bill.	**Νομίζω ότι έγινε ένα λάθος στο λογαριασμό.** noh·<u>mee</u>·zoh <u>oh</u>·tee <u>eh</u>·yee·neh <u>eh</u>·nah <u>lah</u>·thohs stoh loh·ghahr·yahz·<u>moh</u>
I'll pay *in cash/by credit card*.	**Θα πληρώσω *τοις μετρητοίς/με πιστωτική κάρτα*.** thah plee·<u>roh</u>·soh tees meht·ree·<u>tees</u>/ meh pees·toh·tee·<u>kee</u> <u>kahr</u>·tah

Tipping depends largely on your class of hotel; the higher the class, the more generous the tip. As a guideline, a euro or two per service rendered is recommended in standard hotels.

Renting

I've reserved *an apartment/a room*.	**Έχω κλείσει ένα *διαμέρισμα/δωμάτιο.*** eh·hoh klee·see eh·nah ee·ah·meh·rees·mah/ oh·mah·tee·oh
My name is...	**Λέγομαι...** leh·ghoh·meh...
Can I have the key/key card?	**Μπορώ να έχω *το κλειδί/την κάρτα;*** boh·roh nah eh·hoh toh klee·THee/teen kahr·tah
Are there...?	**Υπάρχουν...;** ee·pahr·khoon...
– dishes	**– πιάτα** piah·tah
– pillows	**– μαξιλάρια** mah·ksee·lah·ree·ah
– sheets	**– σεντόνια** sehn·doh·niah
– towels	**– πετσέτες** peh·tseh·tehs
– utensils	**– οικιακά σκεύη** ee·kee·ah·kah skeh·vee
When do I put out the trash [rubbish]?	**Πότε να βγάλω έξω τα σκουπίδια;** poh·teh nah vghah·loh eh·ksoh tah skoo·pee·THiah
...has broken down.	**...χάλασε.** ...khah·lah·seh
How does...work?	**Πώς λειτουργεί...;** pohs lee·toor·ghee...
– the air conditioner	**– το κλιματιστικό** toh klee·mah·tees·tee·koh
– the dishwasher	**– το πλυντήριο πιάτων** toh plee·ndee·ree·oh piah·tohn
– the freezer	**– ο καταψύκτης** oh kah·tah·psee·ktees
– the heater	**– ο θερμοσίφωνας** oh thehr·moh·see·foh·nahs
– the microwave	**– ο φούρνος μικροκυμάτων** oh foor·nohs meek·roh·kee·mah·tohn
– the refrigerator	**– το ψυγείο** toh psee·ghee·oh
– the stove	**– η κουζίνα** ee koo·zee·nah
– the washing machine	**– το πλυντήριο** toh pleen·dee·ree·oh

Household Items

I need...	Χρειάζομαι... khree·ah·zoh·meh...
– an adapter	– **έναν προσαρμοστή** eh·nahn proh·sahr·mohs·tee
– aluminum [kitchen] foil	– **λίγο αλουμινόχαρτο** lee·ghoh ah·loo·mee·noh·khahr·toh
– a bottle opener	– **ένα τιρμπουσόν** eh·nah teer·boo·sohn
– a broom	– **μια σκούπα** miah skoo·pah
– a can opener	– **ένα ανοιχτήρι** eh·nah ah·neeh·tee·ree
– cleaning supplies	– **μερικά καθαριστικά** meh·ree·kah kah·thah·rees·tee·kah
– a corkscrew	– **ένα τιρμπουσόν** eh·nah teer·boo·sohn
– detergent	– **λίγο απορρυπαντικό** lee·ghoh ah·poh·ree·pahn·dee·koh
– dishwashing liquid	– **λίγο υγρό πιάτων** lee·ghoh ee·ghroh piah·tohn
– garbage [rubbish] bags	– **μερικές σακκούλες σκουπιδιών** meh·ree·kehs sah·koo·lehs skoo·pee·THee·ohn
– a light bulb	– **μια λάμπα** miah lah·mbah
– matches	– **μερικά σπίρτα** meh·ree·kah speer·tah
– a mop	– **μια σφουγγαρίστρα** miah sfoo·ghahr·ees·trah
– napkins	– **χαρτοπετσέτες** khah·rtoh·peh·tseh·tehs
– plastic wrap [cling film]	– **διαφανή μεμβράνη** THee·ah·fah·nee mehm·vrah·nee
– a plunger	– **μια βεντούζα** miah vehn·doo·zah
– scissors	– **ένα ψαλίδι** eh·nah psah·lee·THee
– a vacuum cleaner	– **μια ηλεκτρική σκούπα** miah ee·lehk·tree·kee skoo·pah

▶ For dishes, utensils and kitchen tools, see page 65.

Hostel

Do you have any places left for tonight?	**Έχετε θέση για απόψε;** <u>eh</u>·kheh·teh <u>theh</u>·see yah ah·<u>poh</u>·pseh
Can I have...?	**Μπορώ να έχω...;** boh·<u>roh</u> nah <u>eh</u>·khoh...
- a blanket	**- μια κουβέρτα** miah koo·<u>vehr</u>·tah
- a pillow	**- ένα μαξιλάρι** <u>eh</u>·nah mah·ksee·<u>lah</u>·ree
- sheets	**- σεντόνια** sehn·<u>doh</u>·niah
- a towel	**- μια πετσέτα μπάνιου** miah peh·<u>tseh</u>·tah <u>bah</u>·nioo
What time are the doors locked?	**Τί ώρα κλειδώνετε;** tee <u>oh</u>·rah klee·<u>THoh</u>·neh·teh

Camping

Can I camp here?	**Μπορώ να κάνω κάμπινγκ εδώ;** boh·<u>roh</u> nah <u>kah</u>·noh <u>kahm</u>·peeng·<u>THoh</u>
Is there a campsite near here?	**Υπάρχει χώρος κάμπινγκ εδώ κοντά;** ee·<u>pahr</u>·khee <u>khoh</u>·rohs <u>kahm</u>·peeng eh·<u>THoh</u> kohn·<u>dah</u>
What is the charge per *day/week*?	**Ποιό είναι το κόστος για *την ημέρα/την εβδομάδα;*** pioh <u>ee</u>·neh toh <u>kohs</u>·tohs yah teen ee·<u>meh</u>·rah/ehv·THoh·<u>mah</u>·THah
Are there...?	**Υπάρχουν...;** ee·<u>pahr</u>·hoon...
- cooking facilities	**- ηλεκτρική κουζίνα** ee·lehk·tree·<u>kee</u> koo·<u>zee</u>·nah
- electrical outlets	**- πρίζες** <u>pree</u>·zehs
- laundry facilities	**- πλυντήρια** pleen·<u>dee</u>·ree·ah
- showers	**- ντους** dooz
- tents for rent [hire]	**- σκηνές για ενοικίαση** skee·nehs yah eh·nee·<u>kee</u>·ah·see

| Where can I empty the chemical toilet? | **Πού μπορώ να αδειάσω τη χημική τουαλέτα;** poo boh·<u>roh</u> nah ah·THee·<u>ah</u>·soh tee khee·mee·<u>kee</u> too·ah·<u>leh</u>·tah |

You May See...

ΠΟΣΙΜΟ ΝΕΡΟ <u>poh</u>·see·moh neh·<u>roh</u>	drinking water
ΑΠΑΓΟΡΕΥΕΤΑΙ Η ΚΑΤΑΣΚΗΝΩΣΗ ah·pah·ghoh·<u>reh</u>·veh·teh ee kah·tahs·<u>kee</u>·noh·see	no camping
ΜΗΝ ΑΝΑΒΕΤΕ ΦΩΤΙΑ <u>meen</u> ah·<u>nah</u>·veh·teh foh·tee·<u>ah</u>	no fires/barbecues

▶ For household items, see page 45.

▶ For dishes, utensils and kitchen tools, see page 65.

Internet and Communications

Essential

Where's an internet cafe?	**Πού υπάρχει internet cafe;** poo ee·<u>pahr</u>·khee <u>een</u>·tehr·neht kah·<u>feh</u>
Can I access the internet/check e-mail here?	**Μπορώ να μπω στο internet/να ελέγξω τα e-mail μου εδώ;** boh·<u>roh</u> nah boh stoh een·tehr·<u>neht</u>/nah eh·<u>lehng</u>·ksoh tah ee·<u>meh</u>·eel moo eh·<u>THoh</u>
How much per hour/half hour?	**Πόσο χρεώνεται η ώρα/μισή ώρα;** <u>poh</u>·soh hreh·<u>oh</u>·neh·teh ee <u>oh</u>·rah/mee·<u>see</u> <u>oh</u>·rah
How do I connect?	**Πώς μπορώ να συνδεθώ;** pohs boh·<u>roh</u> nah seehn·THeh·<u>thoh</u>
I'd like a phone card.	**Θα ήθελα μια τηλεκάρτα.** thah <u>ee</u>·theh·lah miah tee·leh·<u>kahr</u>·tah

Can I have your phone number?	Μπορώ να έχω τον αριθμό τηλεφώνου σας; boh·<u>roh</u> nah eh·hoh tohn ah·reeth·<u>moh</u> tee·leh·<u>foh</u>·noo sahs
Here's my *number/ e-mail address*.	Ορίστε το *τηλέφωνό μου/e-mail μου*. oh·<u>rees</u>·teh toh tee·<u>leh</u>·foh·<u>noh</u> moo/ ee·<u>meh</u>·eel moo
Call me.	Πάρτε με τηλέφωνο. <u>pahr</u>·teh meh tee·<u>leh</u>·foh·noh
E-mail me.	Στείλτε μου e-mail. <u>steel</u>·teh moo ee·<u>meh</u>·eel
Hello. This is...	Εμπρός. Είμαι... ehm·<u>brohs</u> ee·meh...
I'd like to speak to...	Θα ήθελα να μιλήσω με... thah ee·theh·lah nah mee·<u>lee</u>·soh meh...
Repeat that, please.	Επαναλάβετέ το, παρακαλώ. eh·pah·nah·lah·veh·<u>teh</u> toh pah·rah·kah·<u>loh</u>
I'll be in touch.	Θα επικοινωνήσω μαζί σας. thah eh·pee·kee·noh·<u>nee</u>·soh mah·<u>zee</u> sahs
Bye.	Αντίο. ah·<u>dee</u>·oh
Where is the *nearest/main* post office?	Πού είναι το *κοντινότερο/κεντρικό* ταχυδρομείο; poo <u>ee</u>·neh toh koh·ndee·<u>noh</u>·teh·roh/kehn·dree·<u>koh</u> tah·khee·THroh·<u>mee</u>·oh
I'd like to send this to...	Θα ήθελα να στείλω αυτό σε... thah ee·theh·lah nah <u>stee</u>·loh ahf·<u>toh</u> seh...

Computer, Internet and E-mail

Where's an internet cafe?	Πού υπάρχει ένα internet cafe; poo ee·<u>pahr</u>·khee eh·nah een·tehr·<u>neht</u> kah·<u>feh</u>
Does it have wireless internet?	Έχει ασύρματο internet; <u>eh</u>·khee ah·<u>seer</u>·mah·toh een·tehr·<u>neht</u>
How do I turn the computer *on/off*?	Πώς *ανοίγει/κλείνει* ο υπολογιστής; pohs ah·<u>nee</u>·ghee/<u>klee</u>·nee oh ee·poh·loh·ghees·<u>tees</u>

Can I...?	**Μπορώ...;** boh·<u>roh</u>...
– access the internet here	**– να έχω πρόσβαση στο internet από εδώ** nah <u>eh</u>·hoh <u>prohs</u>·vah·see stoh een·tehr·<u>neht</u> ah·<u>poh</u> eh·<u>THoh</u>
– check e-mail	**– να ελέγξω τα e-mail μου** nah eh·<u>leng</u>·ksoh tah ee·<u>meh</u>·eel moo
– print	**– εκτυπώσω** ehk·tee·<u>poh</u>·soh
How much per *hour/half hour*?	**Πόσο χρεώνεται η *ώρα/μισή ώρα*;** <u>poh</u>·soh hreh·<u>oh</u>·neh·teh ee <u>oh</u>·rah/mee·<u>see</u> <u>oh</u>·rah
How do I...?	**Πώς μπορώ να...;** pohs boh·<u>roh</u> nah
– connect/ disconnect	**– συνδεθώ/αποσυνδεθώ** seen·theh·<u>THoh</u>/ ah·poh·seen·theh·<u>THoh</u>
– log *on/off*	**– συνδεθώ/αποσυνδεθώ** seen·theh·<u>THoh</u>/ ah·poh·seen·theh·<u>THoh</u>
– type this symbol	**– πληκτρολογήσω αυτό το σύμβολο** pleek·troh·loh·<u>ghee</u>·soh ahf·<u>toh</u> toh <u>seem</u>·voh·loh

| What's your e-mail? | **Ποιο είναι το e-mail σας;** pioh ee·neh toh ee·<u>meh</u>·eel sahs |
| My e-mail is... | **Το e-mail μου είναι...** toh ee·<u>meh</u>·eel moo ee·neh... |

You May See...

ΚΛΕΙΣΙΜΟ <u>klee</u>·see·moh	close
ΔΙΑΓΡΑΦΗ THee·ahgh·rah·<u>fee</u>	delete
EMAIL ee·<u>meh</u>·eel	e-mail
ΕΞΟΔΟΣ <u>eh</u>·ksoh·THohs	exit
ΒΟΗΘΕΙΑ voh·<u>ee</u>·thee·ah	help
ΕΦΑΡΜΟΓΗ ΑΜΕΣΟΥ ΜΗΝΥΜΑΤΟΣ eh·fahr·moh·<u>yee</u> <u>ah</u>·meh·soo mee·<u>nee</u>·mah·tohs	instant messenger
INTERNET een·tehr·<u>neht</u>	internet
ΣΥΝΔΕΣΗ <u>seen</u>·theh·see	login
ΝΕΟ (ΜΗΝΥΜΑ) <u>neh</u>·oh <u>mee</u>·nee·mah	new (message)
ON/OFF ohn/ohf	on/off
ΑΝΟΙΧΤΟ ah·neekh·<u>toh</u>	open
ΕΚΤΥΠΩΣΗ ehk·<u>tee</u>·poh·see	print
ΑΠΟΘΗΚΕΥΣΗ ah·poh·<u>thee</u>·kehf·see	save
ΑΠΟΣΤΟΛΗ ah·pohs·toh·<u>lee</u>	send
ΟΝΟΜΑ ΧΡΗΣΤΗ/ΚΩΔΙΚΟΣ ΠΡΟΣΒΑΣΗΣ <u>oh</u>·noh·mah <u>khrees</u>·tee/koh·THee·<u>kohs</u> prohs·vah·sees	username/ password
ΑΣΥΡΜΑΤΟ INTERNET ah·<u>seer</u>·mah·toh een·tehr·<u>neht</u>	wireless internet

Phone

A *phone card/ prepaid phone*, please.	**Μια τηλεκάρτα/χρονοκάρτα.** miah tee·leh·<u>kahr</u>·tah/khroh·noh·<u>kahr</u>·tah
How much?	**Πόσο;** <u>poh</u>·soh
My phone doesn't work here.	**Το τηλέφωνό μου δεν λειτουργεί εδώ.** toh tee·<u>leh</u>·foh·<u>noh</u> moo THehn lee·toor·<u>ghee</u> eh·<u>THoh</u>
What's the *area/ country* code for...?	**Ποιος είναι ο κωδικός *περιοχής/χώρας* για...;** piohs <u>ee</u>·neh oh koh·THee·<u>kohs</u> peh·ree·oh·<u>khees</u>/<u>khoh</u>·rahs yah...
What's the number for Information?	**Ποιος είναι ο αριθμός για Πληροφορίες;** piohs <u>ee</u>·neh oh ah·reeth·<u>mohs</u> yah plee·roh·foh·<u>ree</u>·ehs
I'd like the number for...	**Θα ήθελα έναν αριθμό για...** thah <u>ee</u>·theh·lah <u>eh</u>·nahn ah·reeth·<u>moh</u> yah...
Can I have your number?	**Μπορώ να έχω τον αριθμό τηλεφώνου σας;** boh·<u>roh</u> nah <u>eh</u>·khoh tohn ah·reeth·<u>moh</u> tee·leh·<u>foh</u>·noo sahs
Here's my number.	**Ορίστε ο αριθμός τηλεφώνου μου.** oh·<u>ree</u>·steh oh ah·reeth·<u>mohs</u> tee·leh·<u>foh</u>·noo moo

▶ For numbers, see page 158.

Please text me.	**Παρακαλώ, στείλτε μου μήνυμα.** pah·rah·kah·<u>loh</u> steel·teh moo <u>mee</u>·nee·mah
I'll call you.	**Θα σας πάρω τηλέφωνο.** thah sahs <u>pah</u>·roh tee·leh·<u>foh</u>·noh

On the Phone

Hello. This is...	**Εμπρός. Είμαι ο♂/η♀...** ehm·<u>brohs</u> <u>ee</u>·meh oh♂/ee♀...

I'd like to speak to...	**Θα ήθελα να μιλήσω με τον♂/την♀...** thah <u>ee</u>·theh·lah nah mee·<u>lee</u>·soh meh tohn♂/ teen♀...
Extension...	**Εσωτερική γραμμή...** eh·soh·teh·ree·<u>kee</u> ghrah·<u>mee</u>...
Speak *louder/more slowly*.	**Μιλείστε *πιο δυνατά/πιο αργά*.** mee·<u>lees</u>·teh pioh *THee·nah·<u>tah</u>/ahr·<u>ghah</u>*
Repeat that, please.	**Επαναλάβετέ το, παρακαλώ.** eh·pah·nah·<u>lah</u>·veh·teh toh pah·rah·kah·<u>loh</u>
I'll call back later.	**Θα έρθω σε επαφή μαζί σας αργότερα.** thah <u>ehr</u>·thoh seh eh·pah·<u>fee</u> mah·<u>zee</u> sahs ahr·<u>ghoh</u>·teh·rah
Bye.	**Αντίο.** ah·<u>dee</u>·oh

▶ For business travel, see page 132.

You May Hear...

Ποιος είστε; piohs <u>ee</u>·steh
Who's calling?

Περιμένετε, παρακαλώ. peh·ree·<u>meh</u>·neh·teh pah·rah·kah·<u>loh</u>
Hold on, please.

Θα σας συνδέσω. thah sahs seen·<u>THeh</u>·soh
I'll put you through.

Θέλετε να αφήσετε μήνυμα; <u>theh</u>·leh·teh nah ah·<u>fee</u>·seh·teh <u>mee</u>·nee·mah
Would you like to leave a message?

Ξανακαλέστε *αργότερα/σε δέκα λεπτά.* ksah·nah·kah·<u>lehs</u>·teh *ahr·<u>ghoh</u>·teh·rah/seh <u>eh</u>·kah lehp·<u>tah</u>*
Call back *later/in ten minutes.*

Να σας πάρει *εκείνος/εκείνη;* nah sahs <u>pah</u>·ree *eh·<u>kee</u>·nohs/eh·<u>kee</u>·nee*
Can *he/she* call you back?

Ποιος είναι ο αριθμός σας; piohs <u>ee</u>·neh oh ah·reeth·<u>mohs</u> sahs
What's your number?

Fax

Can I *send/receive* a fax here?
Μπορώ να *στείλω/λάβω* **φαξ από εδώ;** boh·<u>roh</u> nah *<u>stee</u>·loh/<u>lah</u>·voh* fahks ah·<u>poh</u> eh·<u>THoh</u>

What's the fax number?
Ποιος είναι ο αριθμός φαξ; piohs <u>ee</u>·neh oh ah·reeth·<u>mohs</u> fahks

Please fax this to...
Παρακαλώ στείλτε αυτό το φαξ σε... pah·rah·kah·<u>loh</u> <u>steel</u>·teh ahf·<u>toh</u> toh fahks seh...

Throughout Greece, even in remote areas, there are plenty of public phones; these are mainly card operated. Phone cards can be purchased from **περίπτερα** (peh·<u>ree</u>·pteh·rah), kiosks. You can also purchase a **κάρτα για κινητό** (<u>kah</u>·rtah yiah kee·nee·<u>toh</u>) prepaid card for your wireless phone from any of the conveniently located wireless phone stores.

Post Office

Where's the post office/mailbox [postbox]?	**Πού είναι το ταχυδρομείο/το γραμματοκιβώτιο;** poo <u>ee</u>·neh *toh tah·khee·roh·<u>mee</u>·oh/toh ghrah·mah·toh·kee·<u>voh</u>·tee·oh*
A stamp for this postcard/letter.	**Ένα γραμματόσημο γι' αυτή την κάρτα/αυτό το γράμμα.** <u>eh</u>·nah ghrah·mah·<u>toh</u>·see·moh yah ahf·<u>teen</u> teen <u>kahr</u>·tah/ahf·<u>toh</u> toh <u>ghrah</u>·mah
How much?	**Πόσο;** <u>poh</u>·soh
I want to send this package by airmail/express.	**Θέλω να στείλω αυτό το πακέτο αεροπορικώς/εξπρές.** <u>theh</u>·loh nah <u>stee</u>·loh ahf·<u>toh</u> toh pah·<u>keh</u>·toh ah·eh·roh·poh·ree·<u>kohs</u>/ehks·<u>prehs</u>
Can I have a receipt?	**Μπορώ να έχω μια απόδειξη;** boh·<u>roh</u> nah <u>eh</u>·khoh miah ah·<u>poh</u>·THee·ksee

You May Hear...

Παρακαλώ συμπληρώστε αυτήν την τελωνειακή δήλωση. pah·rah·kah·<u>loh</u> seem·blee·<u>rohs</u>·teh ahf·<u>teen</u> teen teh·loh·nee·ah·<u>kee</u> <u>THee</u>·loh·see	Please fill out the customs declaration form.
Ποια είναι η αξία; piah <u>ee</u>·neh ee ah·<u>ksee</u>·ah	What's the value?
Τι είναι μέσα; tee <u>ee</u>·neh <u>meh</u>·sah	What's inside?

i The post office is open from 8 a.m. to 8 p.m., except on Wednesday and Saturday when it closes at around 1 p.m. Main post offices are open Sunday morning. Mailboxes are yellow and bear the initials **ΕΛΤΑ** (ehl·<u>tah</u>).

▼ Food

Eating Out

Essential

Can you recommend a good *restaurant/bar*?
Μπορείτε να συστήσετε ένα καλό *εστιατόριο/μπαρ*; boh·<u>ree</u>·teh nah sees·<u>tee</u>·seh·teh <u>eh</u>·nah kah·<u>loh</u> ehs·tee·ah·<u>toh</u>·ree·oh/bahr

Is there a *traditional Greek/ an inexpensive* restaurant near here?
Υπάρχει κανένα *ελληνικό/φθηνό* εστιατόριο εδώ κοντά; ee·<u>pahr</u>·khee kah·<u>neh</u>·nah *eh·lee·nee·<u>koh</u>/fthee·<u>noh</u>* ehs·tee·ah·<u>toh</u>·ree·oh eh·<u>THoh</u> kohn·<u>dah</u>

A table for..., please.
Ένα τραπέζι για..., παρακαλώ. <u>eh</u>·nah trah·<u>peh</u>·zee yah...pah·rah·kah·<u>loh</u>

Could we sit...?
Μπορούμε να καθήσουμε...; boh·<u>roo</u>·meh nah kah·<u>thee</u>·soo·meh...

– here/there
– **εδώ/εκεί** eh·<u>THoh</u>/eh·<u>kee</u>

– outside
– **έξω** <u>eh</u>·ksoh

– in a non-smoking area
– **σε έναν χώρο για μη καπνίζοντες** seh <u>eh</u>·nahn <u>khoh</u>·roh yah mee kahp·<u>nee</u>·zohn·dehs

I'm waiting for someone.
Περιμένω κάποιον. peh·ree·<u>meh</u>·noh <u>kah</u>·piohn

Where is the restroom [toilet]?
Πού είναι η τουαλέτα; poo <u>ee</u>·neh ee too·ah·<u>leh</u>·tah

A menu, please.
Έναν κατάλογο, παρακαλώ. <u>eh</u>·nahn kah·<u>tah</u>·loh·ghoh pah·rah·kah·<u>loh</u>

What do you recommend?
Τι προτείνετε; tee proh·<u>tee</u>·neh·teh

I'd like...
Θα ήθελα... thah <u>ee</u>·theh·lah...

Some more..., please.
Λίγο ακόμη..., παρακαλώ. <u>lee</u>·ghoh ah·<u>koh</u>·mee...pah·rah·kah·<u>loh</u>

Enjoy your meal!	**Καλή όρεξη!** kah·lee oh·reh·ksee
The check [bill], please.	**Τον λογαριασμό, παρακαλώ.** tohn loh·ghah·riahs·moh pah·rah·kah·loh
Is service included?	**Συμπεριλαμβάνεται και το φιλοδώρημα;** seem·beh·ree·lahm·vah·neh·teh keh toh fee·loh·THoh·ree·mah
Can I pay by credit card?	**Μπορώ να πληρώσω με πιστωτική κάρτα;** boh·roh nah plee·roh·soh meh pee·stoh·tee·kee kahr·tah
Can I have a receipt?	**Μπορώ να έχω απόδειξη;** boh·roh nah eh·khoh ah·poh·THee·ksee
Thank you.	**Ευχαριστώ.** ehf·hah·ree·stoh

Restaurant Types

Can you recommend...?	**Μπορείτε να συστήσετε...;** boh·ree·teh nah sees·tee·seh·teh...
– a restaurant	**– ένα εστιατόριο** eh·nah ehs·tee·ah·toh·ree·oh
– a bar	**– ένα μπαρ** eh·nah bahr
– a cafe	**– μια καφετέρια** miah kah·feh·teh·ree·ah
– a fast-food place	**– ένα φάστ φουντ** eh·nah fahst food
– a *souvlaki/gyros* stand	**– ένα σουβλατζίδικο** eh·nah soov·la·jee·THee·koh

Reservations and Questions

I'd like to reserve a table...	**Θα ήθελα να κλείσω ένα τραπέζι...** thah ee·theh·lah nah klee·soh eh·nah trah·peh·zee...
– for two	**– για δύο** yah THee·oh
– for this evening	**– γι' απόψε** yah ah·poh·pseh
– for tomorrow at...	**– για αύριο στις...** yah ahv·ree·oh stees...

A table for two, please.	**Ένα τραπέζι για δύο, παρακαλώ.** eh·nah trah·<u>peh</u>·zee yah <u>THee</u>·oh pah·rah·kah·<u>loh</u>
We have a reservation.	**Έχουμε κλείσει τραπέζι.** eh·khoo·meh <u>klee</u>·see trah·<u>peh</u>·zee
My name is...	**Λέγομαι...** <u>leh</u>·ghoh·meh...
Where is the restroom [toilet]?	**Πού είναι η τουαλέτα;** poo <u>ee</u>·neh ee too·ah·<u>leh</u>·tah

You May Hear...

Έχετε κάνει κράτηση; <u>eh</u>·kheh·teh <u>kah</u>·nee <u>krah</u>·tee·see	Do you have a reservation?
Πόσα άτομα; <u>poh</u>·sah <u>ah</u>·toh·mah	How many?
Καπνίζοντες ή μη καπνίζοντες; kah·<u>pnee</u>·zohn·dehs ee mee kah·<u>pnee</u>·zohn·dehs	Smoking or non-smoking?
Είσαστε έτοιμοι να παραγγείλετε; <u>ee</u>·sahs·teh <u>eh</u>·tee·mee nah pah·rah·<u>gee</u>·leh·teh	Are you ready to order?
Τι θα πάρετε; tee thah <u>pah</u>·reh·teh	What would you like?
Σας συστήνω... sahs sees·<u>tee</u>·noh...	I recommend...
Καλή όρεξη. kah·<u>lee</u> <u>oh</u>·reh·ksee	Enjoy your meal.

Ordering

Waiter!/Waitress!	**Γκαρσόν!/Δεσποινίς!** gahr·<u>sohn</u>/ THehs·pee·<u>nees</u>
We're ready to order.	**Είμαστε έτοιμοι να παραγγείλουμε.** <u>ee</u>·mahs·teh <u>eh</u>·tee·mee nah pah·rah·<u>gee</u>·loo·meh
May I see the wine list?	**Μπορώ να δω τον κατάλογο κρασιών;** boh·<u>roh</u> nah THoh tohn kah·<u>tah</u>·loh·ghoh krah·<u>siohn</u>

I'd like...	**Θα ήθελα...** thah <u>ee</u>·theh·lah...
- a bottle of...	**- ένα μπουκάλι...** <u>eh</u>·nah boo·<u>kah</u>·lee...
- glass of...	**- ένα ποτήρι...** <u>eh</u>·nah poh·<u>tee</u>·ree...
- carafe of...	**- μια καράφα...** miah kah·<u>rah</u>·fah...

▶ For alcoholic and non-alcoholic drinks, see page 77.

The menu, please.	**Τον κατάλογο, παρακαλώ.** tohn kah·<u>tah</u>·loh·ghoh pah·rah·kah·<u>loh</u>
Do you have...?	**Έχετε...;** <u>eh</u>·kheh·teh...
- a menu in English	**- έναν κατάλογο στα Αγγλικά** <u>eh</u>·nahn kah·<u>tah</u>·loh·ghoh stah ahng·lee·<u>kah</u>
- a fixed-price menu	**- έναν κατάλογο με σταθερές τιμές** <u>eh</u>·nahn kah·<u>tah</u>·loh·ghoh meh stah·theh·<u>rehs</u> tee·<u>mehs</u>
- a children's menu	**- παιδικό μενού** peh·THee·<u>koh</u> meh·<u>noo</u>
What do you recommend?	**Τι προτείνετε;** tee proh·<u>tee</u>·neh·teh

What's this?	**Τι είναι αυτό;** tee <u>ee</u>·neh ahf·<u>toh</u>
What's in it?	**Τι περιέχει;** tee peh·ree·<u>eh</u>·khee
Is it spicy?	**Είναι πικάντικο;** <u>ee</u>·neh pee·<u>kahn</u>·dee·koh
It's to go [take away].	**Είναι για το σπίτι.** <u>ee</u>·neh yah toh <u>spee</u>·tee

You May See...

ΚΟΥΒΕΡ koo·<u>vehr</u>	cover charge
ΣΤΑΘΕΡΗ ΤΙΜΗ stah·theh·<u>ree</u> tee·<u>mee</u>	fixed-price
ΚΑΤΑΛΟΓΟΣ kah·<u>tah</u>·loh·ghohs	menu
ΜΕΝΟΥ ΤΗΣ ΗΜΕΡΑΣ meh·<u>noo</u> tees ee·<u>meh</u>·rahs	menu of the day
Η ΕΞΥΠΗΡΕΤΗΣΗ (ΔΕΝ) ΠΕΡΙΛΑΜΒΑΝΕΤΑΙ ee eh·ksee·pee·<u>reh</u>·tee·see (THehn) peh·ree·lahm·<u>vahn</u>·eh·teh	service (not) included
ΠΙΑΤΑ ΤΗΣ ΗΜΕΡΑΣ pee·<u>ah</u>·tah tees ee·<u>meh</u>·rahs	specials

Cooking Methods

baked	**του φούρνου** too <u>foor</u>·noo
barbecued, grilled	**της σχάρας** tees <u>skhah</u>·rahs
boiled	**βραστό** vrah·<u>stoh</u>
braised	**κατσαρόλας** kah·tsah·<u>roh</u>·lahs
breaded	**πανέ** pah·<u>neh</u>
cooked in olive oil	**λαδερό** lah·THeh·<u>roh</u>
creamed	**με κρέμα γάλακτος** meh <u>kreh</u>·mah <u>ghah</u>·lah·ktohs
diced	**σε κύβους** seh <u>kee</u>·voos
filleted	**φιλέτο** fee·<u>leh</u>·toh
fried	**τηγανητό** tee·ghah·nee·<u>toh</u>

marinated	**μαρινάτο** mah·ree·<u>nah</u>·toh
poached	**ποσέ** poh·<u>seh</u>
roasted	**ψητό** psee·<u>toh</u>
sautéed	**σωτέ** soh·<u>teh</u>
steamed	**στον ατμό** stohn aht·<u>moh</u>
stewed	**μαγειρευτό** mah·yee·rehf·<u>toh</u>
stewed in tomato sauce	**γιαχνί** yahkh·<u>nee</u>
stewed in wine	**κρασάτο** krah·<u>sah</u>·toh
stuffed	**γεμιστό** yeh·mees·<u>toh</u>

Special Requirements

I'm...	**Είμαι...** <u>ee</u>·meh...
– diabetic	**-διαβητικός♂/διαβητική♀** THee·ah·vee·teek·<u>ohs</u>♂/THee·ah·vee·tee·<u>kee</u>♀
– lactose intolerant	**– έχω ευαισθησία στα γαλακτοκομικά** <u>eh</u>·khoh eh·vehs·thee·<u>see</u>·ah stah ghah·lahk·toh·koh·mee·<u>kah</u>
– vegetarian	**– χορτοφάγος** khohr·toh·<u>fah</u>·ghohs
I'm allergic to...	**είμαι αλλεργικός♂/αλλεργική♀ σε...** <u>ee</u>·meh ah·lehr·yeek·<u>ohs</u>♂/ah·lehr·yeek·<u>ee</u>♀ seh...
I can't eat...	**Δεν πρέπει να φάω φαγητό που περιέχει...** THehn <u>preh</u>·pee nah <u>fah</u>·oh fah·yee·<u>toh</u> poo peh·ree·<u>eh</u>·khee...
– dairy	**– γαλακτοκομικά** ghah·lahk·toh·koh·mee·<u>kah</u>
– gluten	**– γλουτένη** ghloo·<u>teh</u>·nee
– nuts	**– ξηρούς καρπούς** ksee·<u>roos</u> kahr·<u>poos</u>
– pork	**– χοιρινό** khee·ree·<u>noh</u>
– shellfish	**– οστρακοειδή** ohs·trah·koh·ee·<u>THee</u>

I can't eat...	**Δεν πρέπει να φάω φαγητό που περιέχει...** THehn <u>preh</u>·pee na <u>fah</u>·oh fah·yee·<u>toh</u> poo peh·ree·<u>eh</u>·khee...
– spicy foods	**– πικάντικα τρόφιμα** pee·<u>kahn</u>·dee·kah <u>troh</u>·fee·mah
– wheat	**– σιτάρι** see·<u>tah</u>·ree

Dining with Kids

Do you have a children's menu?	**Έχετε παιδικό μενού;** <u>eh</u>·kheh·teh peh·THee·<u>koh</u> meh·<u>noo</u>
Can we have a child's seat?	**Μπορούμε να έχουμε ένα παιδικό κάθισμα;** boh·<u>roo</u>·meh nah <u>eh</u>·khoo·meh <u>eh</u>·nah peh·THee·<u>koh</u> kah·theez·mah
Where can I *feed/ change* the baby?	**Πού μπορώ να *ταΐσω/αλλάξω* το μωρό;** poo boh·<u>roh</u> nah *tah·ee·soh/ah·<u>lah</u>·ksoh* toh moh·<u>roh</u>
Can you warm this?	**Μπορείτε να το ζεστάνετε;** boh·<u>ree</u>·teh nah toh zehs·<u>tah</u>·neh·teh

▶ For travel with children, see page 134.

Complaints

How much longer will our food be?	**Πόση ώρα ακόμη θα κάνει το φαγητό;** <u>poh</u>·see <u>oh</u>·rah ah·<u>koh</u>·mee thah <u>kah</u>·nee toh fah·yee·<u>toh</u>
We can't wait any longer.	**Δεν μπορούμε να περιμένουμε άλλο.** THehn boh·<u>roo</u>·meh nah peh·ree·<u>meh</u>·noo·meh ah·loh
We're leaving.	**Φεύγουμε.** <u>fehv</u>·ghoo·meh
That's not what I ordered.	**Δεν παρήγγειλα αυτό.** THehn pah·<u>ree</u>·ngee·lah ahf·<u>toh</u>
I asked for...	**Ζήτησα...** <u>zee</u>·tee·sah...
I can't eat this.	**Δεν μπορώ να το φάω.** THehn boh·<u>roh</u> nah toh <u>fah</u>·oh

This is too...	**Αυτό είναι πολύ...** ahf·toh ee·neh poh·lee...
– cold/hot	**– κρύο/ζεστό** kree·oh/zehs·toh
– salty/spicy	**– αλμυρό/πικάντικο** ahl·mee·roh/ pee·kahn·dee·koh
– tough/bland	**– σκληρό/ανάλατο** sklee·roh/ahl·mee·roh
This isn't *clean/ fresh*.	**Αυτό δεν είναι *καθαρό/φρέσκο*.** ahf·toh THehn ee·neh kah·thah·roh/frehs·koh

Paying

The check [bill], please.	**Τον λογαριασμό, παρακαλώ.** tohn loh·ghahr·yahs·moh pah·rah·kah·loh
We'd like to pay separately.	**Θα πληρώσουμε ξεχωριστά.** thah plee·roh·soo·meh kseh·khoh·rees·tah
It's all together.	**Όλοι μαζί.** oh·lee mah·zee
Is service included?	**Συμπεριλαμβάνεται και το σέρβις;** seem·beh·ree·lahm·vah·neh·teh keh toh sehr·vees
What's this amount for?	**Τί είναι αυτό το ποσό;** tee ee·neh ahf·toh toh poh·soh
I didn't have that. I had...	**Δεν πήρα αυτό. Πήρα...** THehn pee·rah ahf·toh pee·rah...
Can I pay by credit card?	**Μπορώ να πληρώσω με αυτήν την πιστωτική κάρτα;** boh·roh nah plee·roh·soh meh ahf·teen teen pees·toh·tee·kee kahr·tah
Can I have an *itemized bill/ a receipt*?	**Μπορώ να έχω έναν *αναλυτικό λογαριασμό/ μια αναλυτική απόδειξη*;** boh·roh nah eh·khoh eh·nahn ah·nah·lee·tee·koh loh·ghahr·yahs·moh/miah ah·nah·lee·tee·kee ah·poh·ee·ksee
That was a delicious meal.	**Ήταν ένα πολύ νόστιμο γεύμα.** ee·tahn eh·nah poh·lee nohs·tee·moh yehv·mah

> **i** In Greek restaurants the service charge is included in the price. However, it is still customary to leave a little extra if you are satisfied with the service.

Market

Where are the *carts* [trolleys]/*baskets*?	**Πού είναι τα *καροτσάκια*/*καλάθια*;** poo ee·neh tah kah·roh·tsah·kiah/kah·lah·thiah
Where *is/are*...?	**Πού είναι...;** poo ee·neh...

▶ For food items, see page 81.

I'd like some of *that/those*.	**Θα ήθελα μερικά από *αυτά*/*εκείνα*.** thah ee·theh·lah meh·ree·kah ah·poh ahf·tah/ eh·kee·nah
Can I taste it?	**Μπορώ να το δοκιμάσω;** boh·roh nah toh THoh·kee·mah·soh
I'd like...	**Θα ήθελα...** thah ee·theh·lah...
– a *kilo/half-kilo* of...	**– *ένα*/*μισό* κιλό...** eh·nah/mee·soh kee·loh...
– a *liter/half-liter* of...	**– *ένα*/*μισό* λίτρο...** eh·nah/mee·soh leet·roh...
– a piece of...	**– ένα κομμάτι...** eh·nah koh·mah·tee...
– a slice of...	**– μια φέτα...** miah feh·tah...
More./Less.	**Περισσότερο./Λιγότερο.** peh·ree·soh·teh·roh/lee·ghoh·teh·roh
How much?	**Πόσο;** poh·soh
Where do I pay?	**Πού πληρώνω;** poo plee·roh·noh
A bag, please.	**Μια σακούλα, παρακαλώ.** miah sah·koo·lah pah·rah·kah·loh
I'm being helped.	**Εξυπηρετούμαι.** eh·ksee·pee·reh·too·meh

▶ For conversion tables, see page 164.

You May Hear...

Μπορώ να σας βοηθήσω; boh·<u>roh</u> nah sahs voh·ee·<u>thee</u>·soh — Can I help you?

Τι θα πάρετε; tee thah <u>pah</u>·reh·teh — What would you like?

Τίποτε άλλο; tee·poh·teh <u>ah</u>·loh — Anything else?

Αυτά είναι...ευρώ. ahf·<u>tah</u> ee·neh...ehv·<u>roh</u> — That's...euros.

---

i Large-scale supermarkets can be found on the outskirts of most towns; smaller supermarkets are located near city centers. There are several large chains, including: **AB Βασιλόπουλος** (<u>ahl</u>·fah <u>vee</u>·tah vah·see·<u>loh</u>·poo·lohs), **Dia** (<u>dee</u>·ah), **Champion** (<u>chahm</u>·pee·ohn), **ΣΚΛΑΒΕΝΙΤΗΣ** (sklah·veh·<u>nee</u>·tees) and **Spar** (spahr).

You May See...

ΑΝΑΛΩΣΗ ΚΑΤΑ ΠΡΟΤΙΜΗΣΗ ΠΡΙΝ ΑΠΟ... ah·<u>nah</u>·loh·see kah·<u>tah</u> proh·<u>tee</u>·mee·see preen ah·<u>poh</u> — best before...

ΘΕΡΜΙΔΕΣ thehr·<u>mee</u>·THehs — calories

ΧΩΡΙΣ ΛΙΠΑΡΑ khoh·<u>rees</u> lee·pah·<u>rah</u> — fat free

ΔΙΑΤΗΡΕΙΤΑΙ ΣΤΟ ΨΥΓΕΙΟ THee·ah·tee·<u>ree</u>·teh stoh psee·<u>yee</u>·oh — keep refrigerated

ΜΠΟΡΕΙ ΝΑ ΠΕΡΙΕΧΕΙ ΙΧΝΗ ΑΠΟ... boh·<u>ree</u> nah peh·ree·<u>eh</u>·khee eekh·nee ah·<u>poh</u>... — may contain traces of...

Dishes, Utensils and Kitchen Tools

bottle opener	**τιρμπουσόν** teer·mboo·<u>sohn</u>	
bowls	**τα μπωλ** tah bohl	

can opener	**ανοιχτήρι** ah·neekh·<u>tee</u>·ree
corkscrew	**τιρμπουσόν** teer·boo·<u>sohn</u>
cups	**τα φλυτζάνια** tah flee·<u>jah</u>·niah
forks	**τα πηρούνια** tah pee·<u>roo</u>·niah
frying pan	**τηγάνι** tee·<u>ghah</u>·nee
glasses	**τα ποτήρια** tah poh·<u>teer</u>·yah
knives	**τα μαχαίρια** tah mah·<u>khehr</u>·yah
measuring *cup/* *spoon*	**μεζούρα φλυτζάνι/κουτάλι** meh·<u>zoo</u>·rah flee·<u>jah</u>·nee/koo·<u>tah</u>·lee
napkin	**χαρτοπετσέτα** khahr·toh·peh·<u>tseh</u>·tah
plates	**τα πιάτα** tah <u>piah</u>·tah
pot	**κανάτα** kah·<u>nah</u>·tah
saucepan	**κατσαρόλα** kah·tsah·<u>roh</u>·lah
spatula	**σπάτουλα** <u>spah</u>·too·lah
spoons	**κουτάλια** koo·<u>tah</u>·liah

Meals

i Greeks rarely eat breakfast (**πρωινό**/proh·ee·<u>noh</u>). They usually have a strong coffee with sugar (**βαρύ γλυκό**/vah·<u>ree</u> ghlee·<u>koh</u>) in the morning, followed by another one between 10 and 11 a.m., maybe with a pastry.
Lunch (**μεσημεριανό**/meh·see·meh·riah·<u>noh</u>) is the main meal, although because of the summer heat some Greeks eat lighter at lunchtime and have their main meal in the evening. It is usually eaten from 2 to 3 p.m., but most restaurants will serve it until 4 p.m.

| I'd like... | **Θα ήθελα...** thah <u>ee</u>·theh·lah... |
| More..., please. | **Λίγο ακόμη..., παρακαλώ.** <u>lee</u>·ghoh ah·<u>koh</u>·mee... pah·rah·kah·<u>loh</u> |

Dinner (**βραδυνό**/vrah·THee·<u>noh</u>) is often eaten late—normally at 9 or 10 p.m. It is not unusual to find restaurants serving food until midnight or later. Snacks can be bought at souvlaki stalls (**σουβλατζήδικα**/soov·lah·<u>jee</u>·THee·kah) or snack bars (**σνακ μπαρ**/snahk bahr) until the early hours of the morning. You can also buy tasty snacks, such as cheese pie (**τυρόπιτα**/ tee·<u>rhoh</u>·pee·tah), at bakeries, which are open from very early in the morning until the afternoon.

Breakfast

bacon	**μπέικον** <u>beh</u>·ee·kohn	
bread	**ψωμί** psoh·<u>mee</u>	
butter	**βούτυρο** <u>voo</u>·tee·roh	
cereal (*cold/hot*)	**δημητριακά με (ζεστό/κρύο) γάλα**	
	THee·meet·ree·ah·<u>kah</u> meh (zehs·<u>toh</u>/<u>kree</u>·oh) <u>ghah</u>·lah	
cheese	**τυρί** tee·<u>ree</u>	
coffee/tea	**καφέ/τσάι** kah·<u>feh</u>/<u>tsah</u>·ee	
cold cuts [charcuterie]	**αλλαντικά** ah·lah·ndee·<u>kah</u>	
scrambled eggs	**ομελέτα** oh·meh·<u>leh</u>·tah	
juice	**χυμός** khee·<u>mohs</u>	
granola [muesli]	**μούσλι** <u>moo</u>·slee	
honey	**μέλι** <u>meh</u>·lee	
muffin	**μάφιν** <u>mah</u>·feen	
milk	**γάλα** <u>ghah</u>·lah	
oatmeal	**κουάκερ** koo·<u>ah</u>·kehr	

With/Without...	**Με/Χωρίς...** meh/khoh·<u>rees</u>...
I can't have...	**Δεν πρέπει να φάω φαγητό που περιέχει...** THehn <u>preh</u>·pee nah <u>fah</u>·oh fah·yee·<u>toh</u> poo peh·ree·<u>eh</u>·khee...

omelet	**ομελέτα** oh·meh·<u>leh</u>·tah
roll	**ψωμάκι** psoh·<u>mah</u>·kee
sausage	**λουκάνικο** loo·<u>kah</u>·nee·koh
toast	**ψωμί φρυγανιά** psoh·<u>mee</u> free·ghah·<u>niah</u>
yogurt (with honey)	**γιαούρτι (με μέλι)** yah·<u>oor</u>·tee (meh <u>meh</u>·lee)

Appetizers [Starters]

cold meat	**κρύο κρέας** <u>kree</u>·oh <u>kreh</u>·ahs
fish roe dip	**ταραμοσαλάτα** tah·rah·moh·sah·<u>lah</u>·tah
fried baby squid	**καλαμαράκια** kah·lah·mah·<u>rah</u>·kiah
fried meatballs	**κεφτεδάκια** kef·teh·<u>THah</u>·kiah
fried whitebait	**μαρίδα τηγανητή** mah·<u>ree</u>·THah tee·ghah·nee·<u>tee</u>

I'd like...	**Θα ήθελα...** thah <u>ee</u>·theh·lah...
More..., please.	**Λίγο ακόμη..., παρακαλώ.** <u>lee</u>·ghoh ah·<u>koh</u>·mee... pah·rah·kah·<u>loh</u>

herring (smoked)	ρέγγα (καπνιστή) rehn·gah (kahp·nees·<u>tee</u>)
olive (stuffed)	ελιά (γεμιστή) eh·<u>liah</u> (yeh·mees·<u>tee</u>)
pâté	πατέ pah·<u>teh</u>
spinach and feta in pastry dough	σπανακόπιττα spah·nah·<u>koh</u>·pee·tah
stuffed grape leaves	ντολμαδάκι dohl·mah·<u>THah</u>·kee
yogurt, garlic and cucumber dip	τζατζίκι jah·<u>jee</u>·kee

> **Μεζέδες** (meh·<u>zeh</u>·dehs), appetizers, can be a meal alone.
> Greeks will often go out for a glass of **ούζο** (<u>oo</u>·zoh), an anise-flavored liqueur, accompanied by appetizers.

Soup

bean soup with tomatoes and parsley	φασολάδα fah·soh·<u>lah</u>·THah
chicken soup	κοτόσουπα koh·<u>toh</u>·soo·pah
chickpea soup	ρεβύθια σούπα reh·<u>vee</u>·thiah <u>soo</u>·pah
cracked wheat soup	τραχανάς trah·khah·<u>nahs</u>
fish soup thickened with egg and lemon	ψαρόσουπα αυγολέμονο psah·<u>roh</u>·soo·pah ahv·ghoh·<u>leh</u>·moh·noh
fish stew with tomatoes	κακαβιά kah·kahv·<u>yah</u>
lentil soup	φακές σούπα fah·<u>kehs</u> <u>soo</u>·pah
meat soup	κρεατόσουπα kreh·ah·<u>toh</u>·soo·pah

| With/Without... | Με/Χωρίς... meh/khoh·<u>rees</u>... |
| I can't have... | Δεν πρέπει να φάω φαγητό που περιέχει... THehn <u>preh</u>·pee nah <u>fah</u>·oh fah·yee·<u>toh</u> poo peh·ree·<u>eh</u>·khee... |

soup with rice, eggs and lemon juice	**σούπα αυγολέμονο** <u>soo</u>·pah ahv·ghoh·<u>leh</u>·moh·noh
tripe soup	**πατσάς** pah·<u>tsahs</u>
tahini (sesame paste) soup	**ταχινόσουπα** tah·khee·<u>noh</u>·soo·pah
tomato soup	**τοματόσουπα** toh·mah·<u>toh</u>·soo·pah
vegetable soup	**χορτόσουπα** khohr·<u>toh</u>·soo·pah

Fish and Seafood

anchovy	**αντσούγια** ahn·<u>joo</u>·yahs
crab	**καβούρι** kah·<u>voo</u>·ree
cuttlefish	**σουπιά** soo·<u>piah</u>
eel	**χέλι** <u>kheh</u>·lee
fresh cod	**μπακαλιάρος** bah·kah·<u>liah</u>·rohs
grouper	**σφυρίδα** sfee·<u>ree</u>·THah
mullet	**κέφαλος** <u>keh</u>·fah·lohs
lobster	**αστακός** ahs·tah·<u>kohs</u>
marinated mullet, sole or mackerel	**ψάρι μαρινάτο** <u>psah</u>·ree mah·ree·<u>nah</u>·toh
mussel	**μύδι** <u>mee</u>·THee
octopus	**χταπόδι** khtah·<u>poh</u>·THee
oyster	**στρείδι** <u>stree</u>·THee
red mullet	**μπαρμπούνι** bahr·<u>boo</u>·nee
salted cod	**μπακαλιάρος παστός** bah·kah·<u>liah</u>·rohs pahs·<u>tohs</u>

| I'd like... | **Θα ήθελα...** thah <u>ee</u>·theh·lah... |
| More..., please. | **Λίγο ακόμη..., παρακαλώ.** <u>lee</u>·ghoh ah·<u>koh</u>·mee... pah·rah·kah·<u>loh</u> |

sardine	σαρδέλα	sahr·THeh·lah
shrimp [prawn]	γαρίδα	ghah·ree·THah
sole	γλώσσα	ghloh·sah
squid	καλαμάρι	kah·lah·mah·ree
swordfish	ξιφίας	ksee·fee·ahs
tuna	τόννος	toh·nohs

Meat and Poultry

beef	βοδινό	voh·THee·noh
beef or veal stewed with tomatoes and eggplant [aubergine]	μελιτζανάτο	meh·lee·jah·nah·toh
brains	μυαλό	miah·loh
Greek burger	μπιφτέκι	beef·teh·kee
chicken	κοτόπουλο	koh·toh·poo·loh
cutlet	κοτολέτα	koh·toh·leh·tah
duck	πάπια	pah·piah
fillet	φιλέτο	fee·leh·toh
goat	κατσικάκι	kah·tsee·kah·kee
goose	χήνα	khee·nah
ham	ζαμπόν	zahm·bohn
kidney	νεφρό	neh·froh
lamb	αρνί	ahr·nee
liver	συκώτι	see·koh·tee

With/Without...	Με/Χωρίς... meh/khoh·rees...
I can't have...	Δεν πρέπει να φάω φαγητό που περιέχει... THehn preh·pee nah fah·oh fah·yee·toh poo peh·ree·eh·khee...

layers of eggplant [aubergine], meat and white sauce	**μουσακάς** moo·sah·<u>kahs</u>
meat with orzo pasta baked with tomatoes	**γιουβέτσι** yoo·<u>veh</u>·tsee
pheasant	**φασιανός** fah·siah·<u>nohs</u>
pork	**χοιρινό** khee·ree·<u>noh</u>
rabbit	**κουνέλι** koo·<u>neh</u>·lee
sausage	**λουκάνικο** loo·<u>kah</u>·nee·koh
skewered pork or lamb, well seasoned and cooked over charcoal	**κοντοσούβλι** koh·ndoh·<u>soov</u>·lee dohs
spiced lamb and potatoes baked in parchment or in filo dough	**αρνάκι εξοχικό** ahr·<u>nah</u>·kee eh·ksoh·khee·<u>koh</u>
turkey	**γαλοπούλα** ghah·loh·<u>poo</u>·lah
veal	**μοσχάρι** mohs·<u>khah</u>·ree
veal/pork steak	**μπριζόλα** *μοσχαρίσια/χοιρινή* bree·<u>zoh</u>·lah *mohs·khah·<u>ree</u>·siah/khee·ree·<u>nee</u>*

rare	**με το αίμα του, σενιάν** meh toh <u>eh</u>·mah too seh·<u>nian</u>
medium	**μέτρια ψημένο** <u>meht</u>·ree·ah psee·<u>meh</u>·noh
well-done	**καλοψημένο** kah·loh·psee·<u>meh</u>·noh
I'd like...	**Θα ήθελα...** thah <u>ee</u>·theh·lah...
More..., please.	**Λίγο ακόμη..., παρακαλώ.** <u>lee</u>·ghoh ah·<u>koh</u>·mee... pah·rah·kah·<u>loh</u>

Egg Dishes

...eggs	**αυγά...** ahv·<u>ghah</u>...
- soft-boiled	**– μελάτα** meh·<u>lah</u>·tah
- hard-boiled	**– σφικτά** sfeekh·<u>tah</u>
- fried	**– τηγανητά μάτια** tee·ghah·nee·<u>tah</u> <u>mah</u>·tiah
- poached	**– ποσέ** poh·<u>seh</u>
cheese omelet	**ομελέττα με τυρί** oh·meh·<u>leh</u>·tah meh tee·<u>ree</u>
ham omelet	**ομελέττα με ζαμπόν** oh·meh·<u>leh</u>·tah meh zahm·<u>bohn</u>

A traditional and very tasty egg dish in Greece is **στραπατσάδα** (strah·pah·<u>tsah</u>·THah), scrambled eggs with fresh tomato, but sometimes with other ingredients depending on the region. Another traditional method of using egg is in **αυγολέμονο** (ahv·ghoh·<u>leh</u>·moh·noh): egg yolk and lemon are added to a sauce or soup. This sauce usually accompanies warm stuffed grape leaves and other vegetable dishes or stews.

Vegetables

artichokes	**αγκινάρες** ahn·gkee·<u>nah</u>·rehs
asparagus	**σπαράγγια** spah·<u>rahn</u>·giah
broad beans	**κουκί** koo·<u>kee</u>
butter bean	**φασόλι γίγαντας** fah·<u>soh</u>·lee <u>yee</u>·ghahn·dahs
cabbage	**λάχανο** <u>lah</u>·khah·noh
carrot	**καρότο** kah·<u>roh</u>·toh
cauliflower	**κουνουπίδι** koo·noo·<u>pee</u>·THee

| With/Without... | **Με/Χωρίς...** meh/khoh·<u>rees</u>... |
| I can't have... | **Δεν πρέπει να φάω φαγητό που περιέχει...** THehn <u>preh</u>·pee nah <u>fah</u>·oh fah·yee·<u>toh</u> poo peh·ree·<u>eh</u>·khee... |

celery	**σέλερι**	<u>seh</u>·leh·ree
cucumber	**αγγούρι**	ahn·<u>goo</u>·ree
eggplant [aubergine]	**μελιτζάνα**	meh·lee·<u>jah</u>·nah
green bean	**φασολάκι**	fah·soh·<u>lah</u>·kee
green peppers	**πιπεριές πράσινες**	pee·pehr·<u>yehs</u> prah·see·nehs
leek	**πράσο**	<u>prah</u>·soh
mushroom	**μανιτάρι**	mah·nee·<u>tah</u>·ree
okra	**μπάμια**	<u>bah</u>·miah
onion	**κρεμμύδι**	kreh·<u>mee</u>·Thee
peas	**αρακάς**	ah·rah·<u>kahs</u>
peppers	**πιπεριές**	pee·pehr·<u>yehs</u>
potato	**πατάτα**	pah·<u>tah</u>·tah
red cabbage	**κόκκινο λάχανο**	<u>koh</u>·kee·noh <u>lah</u>·khah·noh
spinach	**σπανάκι**	spah·<u>nah</u>·kee
tomato	**ντομάτα**	ndoh·<u>mah</u>·tah
zucchini [courgette]	**κολοκυθάκι**	koh·loh·kee·<u>thah</u>·kee

Spices and Staples

basil	**βασιλικός**	vah·see·lee·<u>kohs</u>
bay leaf	**δαφνόφυλλο**	THah·<u>fnoh</u>·fee·loh
bread	**ψωμί**	psoh·<u>mee</u>
cinnamon	**κανέλλα**	kah·<u>neh</u>·lah
dill	**άνηθος**	<u>ah</u>·nee·thohs
garlic	**σκόρδο**	<u>skohr</u>·THoh
mastic	**μαστίχα**	mahs·<u>tee</u>·khah
mint	**δυόσμος**	THee·<u>ohz</u>·mohs

I'd like...	**Θα ήθελα...**	thah <u>ee</u>·theh·lah...
More..., please.	**Λίγο ακόμη..., παρακαλώ.**	<u>lee</u>·ghoh ah·<u>koh</u>·mee... pah·rah·kah·<u>loh</u>

oregano	ρίγανη <u>ree</u>·ghah·nee
parsley	μαϊντανός mah·ee·dah·<u>nohs</u>
pasta	ζυμαρικά zee·mah·ree·<u>kah</u>
rosemary	δεντρολίβανο THehn·droh·<u>lee</u>·vah·noh
sage	φασκόμηλο fahs·<u>koh</u>·mee·loh
sugar	ζάχαρη <u>zah</u>·khah·ree
thyme	θυμάρι thee·<u>mah</u>·ree
toast	ψωμί φρυγανιά psoh·<u>mee</u> free·ghah·<u>niah</u>
unleavened bread	λαγάνα lah·<u>ghah</u>·nah

Fruit

apple	μήλο <u>mee</u>·loh
apricot	βερύκοκο veh·<u>ree</u>·koh·koh
banana	μπανάνα bah·<u>nah</u>·nah
cherry	κεράσι keh·<u>rah</u>·see
date	χουρμάς khoor·<u>mahs</u>
fig	σύκο <u>see</u>·koh
grape	σταφύλι stah·<u>fee</u>·lee
grapefruit	γκρέιπφρουτ <u>greh</u>·eep·froot
lemon	λεμόνι leh·<u>moh</u>·nee
melon	πεπόνι peh·<u>poh</u>·nee
orange	πορτοκάλι pohr·toh·<u>kah</u>·lee
peach	ροδάκινο roh·<u>THah</u>·kee·noh
pear	αχλάδι akh·<u>lah</u>·THee
plum	δαμάσκηνο THah·<u>mahs</u>·kee·noh
pineapple	ανανάς ah·nah·<u>nahs</u>

With/Without...	Με/Χωρίς... meh/khoh·<u>rees</u>...
I can't have...	Δεν πρέπει να φάω φαγητό που περιέχει... THehn <u>preh</u>·pee nah <u>fah</u>·oh fah·yee·<u>toh</u> poo peh·ree·<u>eh</u>·khee...

| tangerine | μανταρίνι mahn·dah·<u>ree</u>·nee |
| watermelon | καρπούζι kahr·<u>poo</u>·zee |

Cheese

feta cheese	φέτα <u>feh</u>·tah
Gruyere cheese	γραβιέρα ghrah·<u>vieh</u>·rah
Kaseri, yellow cheese	κασέρι kah·<u>seh</u>·ree
cottage cheese	τυρί κότατζ tee·<u>ree</u> <u>koh</u>·tahtz

Dessert

apple pie	μηλόπιτα mee·<u>loh</u>·pee·tah
baklava, flaky pastry with nut filling	μπακλαβάς bah·klah·<u>vahs</u>
candy [sweets]	καραμέλα kah·rah·<u>meh</u>·lah
caramel custard	κρέμα καραμελέ <u>kreh</u>·mah kah·rah·meh·<u>leh</u>
filo pastry filled with almonds, orange juice and cinnamon	κοπεγχάγη koh·pehn·<u>khah</u>·ghee
flaky pastry filled with custard and steeped in syrup	γαλακτομπούρεκο ghah·lah·ktoh·<u>boo</u>·reh·koh
fruit salad	φρουτοσαλάτα froo·toh·sah·<u>lah</u>·tah
halva, sweet sesame seed paste	χαλβάς khahl·<u>vahs</u>
ice cream	παγωτό pah·ghoh·<u>toh</u>

I'd like...	Θα ήθελα... thah <u>ee</u>·theh·lah...
More..., please.	Λίγο ακόμη..., παρακαλώ. <u>lee</u>·ghoh ah·<u>koh</u>·mee... pah·rah·kah·<u>loh</u>
With/Without...	Με/Χωρίς... meh/khoh·<u>rees</u>...
I can't have...	Δεν πρέπει να φάω φαγητό που περιέχει... THehn <u>preh</u>·pee nah <u>fah</u>·oh fah·yee·<u>toh</u> poo peh·ree·<u>eh</u>·khee...

rice pudding	**ρυζόγαλο** ree·<u>zoh</u>·ghah·loh
shredded pastry roll filled with nuts and steeped in syrup	**καταΐφι** kah·tah·<u>ee</u>·fee
Turkish delight	**λουκούμι** loo·<u>koo</u>·mee
walnut cake	**καρυδόπιτα** kah·ree·<u>THoh</u>·pee·tah

Drinks

Essential

May I see the *wine list/drink menu*?	**Μπορώ να δω τον κατάλογο με τα *κρασιά/ ποτά*;** boh·<u>roh</u> nah THoh tohn kah·<u>tah</u>·loh·ghoh meh tah *krah·<u>siah</u>/poh·<u>tah</u>*
What do you recommend?	**Τι συστήνετε;** tee see·<u>stee</u>·neh·teh
I'd like a *bottle/ glass* of *red/white* wine.	**Θα ήθελα ένα *μπουκάλι/ποτήρι κόκκινο/ λευκό κρασί*.** thah <u>ee</u>·theh·lah <u>eh</u>·nah *boo·<u>kah</u>·lee/poh·<u>tee</u>·ree koh·<u>kee</u>·noh/lehf·<u>koh</u>* krah·<u>see</u>
The house wine, please.	**Το κρασί του καταστήματος, παρακαλώ.** toh krah·<u>see</u> too kah·tah·<u>stee</u>·mah·tohs pah·rah·kah·<u>loh</u>
Another *bottle/ glass*, please.	**Άλλο ένα *μπουκάλι/ποτήρι*, παρακαλώ.** <u>ah</u>·loh <u>eh</u>·nah *boo·<u>kah</u>·lee/poh·<u>tee</u>·ree* pah·rah·kah·<u>loh</u>
I'd like a local beer.	**Θα ήθελα μια τοπική μπύρα.** thah <u>ee</u>·theh·lah miah toh·pee·<u>kee</u> <u>bee</u>·rah
Let me buy you a drink.	**Να σαςκεράσω ένα ποτό.** nah sahs keh·<u>rah</u>·soh <u>eh</u>·nah poh·<u>toh</u>
Cheers!	**Στην υγειά σας!** steen ee·<u>ghiah</u> sahs

A coffee/tea, please.	Έναν καφέ/Ένα τσάι, παρακαλώ. _eh_·nahn kah·_feh_/_eh_·nah _tsah_·ee pah·rah·kah·_loh_
Black.	Σκέτος. _skeh_·tohs
With...	Με... meh...
– milk	– γάλα _ghah_·lah
– sugar	– ζάχαρη _zah_·khah·ree
– artificial sweetener	– ζαχαρίνη zah·khah·_ree_·nee
..., please.	..., παρακαλώ. ...pah·rah·kah·_loh_
– A juice	– Ένα χυμό _eh_·nah khee·_moh_
– A soda	– Μία σόδα _mee_·ah soh·THah
– A sparkling water	– Ένα ανθρακούχο νερό _eh_·nah ahn·thrah·_koo_·khoh neh·_roh_
– A still water	– Ένα νερό χωρίς ανθρακικό _eh_·nah neh·_roh_ khoh·_rees_ ahn·thrah·kee·_koh_
Is the tap water safe to drink?	Είναι το νερό βρύσης πόσιμο; _ee_·neh toh neh·_roh_ _vree_·sees _poh_·see·moh

Non-alcoholic Drinks

...coffee	έναν καφέ... _eh_·nahn kah·_feh_...
– instant	– ένα Νεσκαφέ _eh_·nah nehs·kah·_feh_
– Greek	– ελληνικό eh·lee·nee·_koh_
– with cream/milk	– με κρέμα/γάλα meh _kreh_·mah/_ghah_·lah
...juice	χυμός... khee·_mohs_...
– apple	– μήλο _mee_·loh
– grapefruit	– γκρέιπφρουτ _greh_·eep·froot
– orange	– πορτοκάλι poh·rtoh·_kah_·lee
iced tea	παγωμένο τσάι pah·ghoh·_meh_·noh _tsah_·ee

tea with *milk/ lemon*	**τσάι με *γάλα/λεμόνι*** <u>tsah</u>·ee meh <u>ghah</u>·lah/ leh·<u>moh</u>·nee
mineral water	**μεταλλικό νερό** meh·tah·lee·<u>koh</u> neh·<u>roh</u>

> ℹ️ The most popular drinks in the summer are **φραπέ** (frah·<u>peh</u>), iced instant coffee shaken to produce a thick coffee froth, with or without milk and sugar, and **φρέντο** (<u>frehd</u>·doh), iced espresso with or without milk, found at most coffee shops and bars. Freshly squeezed juices are also widely consumed. Tap water is drinkable almost everywhere, but if you prefer you can get **εμφιαλωμένο νερό** (ehm·fee·ah·loh·<u>meh</u>·noh neh·<u>roh</u>), bottled water.

You May Hear...

Θέλετε κάτι να πιείτε; <u>theh</u>·leh·teh <u>kah</u>·tee nah pee·<u>ee</u>·teh	Can I get you a drink?
Με *γάλα/ζάχαρη*; meh <u>ghah</u>·lah/<u>zah</u>·khah·ree	With *milk/sugar*?
Νερό *ανθρακούχο/χωρίς ανθρακικό*; neh·<u>roh</u> ahn·thrah·<u>koo</u>·khoh/khoh·<u>rees</u> ahn·thrah·kee·<u>koh</u>	*Sparkling/Still* water?

Aperitifs, Cocktails and Liqueurs

Greek brandy	**Μεταξά** meh·tah·<u>ksah</u>
kumquat liqueur (Corfu)	**κουμ-κουάτ** koom·koo·<u>aht</u>
straight [neat]	**σκέτο** <u>skeh</u>·toh
on the rocks	**με πάγο** meh <u>pah</u>·ghoh
ouzo	**ούζο** <u>oo</u>·zoh

Beer

beer	**μπύρα** <u>bee</u>·rah
bottled	**εμφιαλωμένη** ehm·fee·ah·loh·<u>meh</u>·nee
draft	**βαρελίσια** vah·reh·<u>lee</u>·siah
light/dark	**ξανθή/μαύρη** ksahn·<u>thee</u>/<u>mahv</u>·ree

Wine

blush [rosé]	**ροζέ** roh·<u>zeh</u>
chilled	**παγωμένο** pah·ghoh·<u>meh</u>·noh
dry	**ξηρό** ksee·<u>roh</u>
red	**μπουκάλι κόκκινο** boo·<u>kah</u>·lee <u>koh</u>·kee·noh
sweet	**γλυκό** ghlee·<u>koh</u>
white	**λευκό** <u>lehf</u>·koh
wine	**κρασί** krah·<u>see</u>

i A typical Greek wine that takes some getting used to is **ρετσίνα** (reh·<u>tsee</u>·nah), a white wine containing pine resin.
Wine is usually produced and consumed locally; it is often the case that a restaurant owner will bring you a carafe of his or her very own wine, if you ask for **κρασί βαρελίσιο** (krah·<u>see</u> vah·reh·<u>lee</u>·sioh), the house wine.

anchovy	**αντσούγια**	ahn·<u>joo</u>·yah
apple	**μήλο**	<u>mee</u>·loh
apple pie	**μηλόπιτα**	mee·<u>loh</u>·pee·tah
apricot	**βερίκοκο**	veh·<u>ree</u>·koh·koh
artichoke	**αγκινάρα**	ahn·gkee·<u>nah</u>·rah
artificial sweetener	**ζαχαρίνη**	zah·khah·<u>ree</u>·nee
asparagus	**σπαράγγι**	spah·<u>rahn</u>·gee
bacon	**μπέικον**	<u>beh</u>·ee·kohn
baklava, flaky pastry with nut filling	**μπακλαβάς**	bah·klah·<u>vahs</u>
banana	**μπανάνα**	bah·<u>nah</u>·nah
basil	**βασιλικός**	vah·see·lee·<u>kohs</u>
bay leaf	**δαφνόφυλλο**	THah·<u>fnoh</u>·fee·loh
bean soup with tomatoes and parsley	**φασολάδα**	fah·soh·<u>lah</u>·THah
beef	**βοδινό**	voh·THee·<u>noh</u>
beef or veal stewed with tomatoes and eggplant [aubergine]	**μελιτζανάτο**	meh·lee·jah·<u>nah</u>·toh
beer	**μπίρα**	<u>bee</u>·rah
brains	**μυαλό**	miah·<u>loh</u>
bread	**ψωμί**	psoh·<u>mee</u>
bread roll	**ψωμάκι**	psoh·<u>mah</u>·kee
broad bean	**κουκί**	koo·<u>kee</u>
butter	**βούτυρο**	<u>voo</u>·tee·roh
butter bean	**φασόλι γίγαντας**	fah·<u>soh</u>·lee <u>yee</u>·ghahn·dahs
cabbage	**λάχανο**	<u>lah</u>·khah·noh

candy [sweets]	**καραμέλα** kah·rah·<u>meh</u>·lah
caramel custard	**κρέμα καραμελέ** <u>kreh</u>·mah kah·rah·meh·<u>leh</u>
carrot	**καρότο** kah·<u>roh</u>·toh
cauliflower	**κουνουπίδι** koo·noo·<u>pee</u>·THee
celery	**σέλερι** <u>seh</u>·leh·ree
cereal (*cold/hot*)	**δημητριακά με (ζεστό/κρύο) γάλα** THee·meet·ree·ah·<u>kah</u> meh (zehs·<u>toh</u>/<u>kree</u>·oh) <u>ghah</u>·lah
cheese	**τυρί** tee·<u>ree</u>
cheese omelet	**ομελέττα με τυρί** oh·meh·<u>leh</u>·tah meh tee·<u>ree</u>
cherry	**κεράσι** keh·<u>rah</u>·see
chicken	**κοτόπουλο** koh·<u>toh</u>·poo·loh

chicken soup	κοτόσουπα	koh·toh·soo·pah
chickpea soup	ρεβύθια σούπα	reh·vee·thiah soo·pah
chilled	παγωμένο	pah·ghoh·meh·noh
cinnamon	κανέλλα	kah·neh·lah
club soda	σόδα	soh·THah
coffee	καφέ	kah·fehs
cold cuts [charcuterie]	αλλαντικά	ah·lah·ndee·kah
cold meat	κρύο κρέας	kree·oh kreh·ahs
cottage cheese	τυρί κότατζ	tee·ree koh·tahtz
crab	καβούρι	kah·voo·ree
cracked wheat soup	τραχανάς	trah·khah·nahs
cream	κρέμα	kreh·mah
cucumber	αγγούρι	ahn·goo·ree
cutlet	κοτολέτα	koh·toh·leh·tah
cuttlefish	σουπιά	soo·piah
date	χουρμάς	khoor·mahs
dill	άνηθος	ah·nee·thohs
draft	βαρελίσια	vah·reh·lee·siah
duck	πάπια	pah·piah
eel	χέλι	kheh·lee
egg	αυγό	ahv·ghoh
eggplant [aubergine]	μελιτζάνα	meh·lee·jah·nah
fig	σύκο	see·koh
fillet	φιλέτο	fee·leh·toh
filo pastry filled with almonds, orange juice and cinnamon	κοπεγχάγη	koh·pehn·khah·ghee

filo pastry filled with custard and steeped in syrup	**γαλακτομπούρεκο** ghah·lah·ktoh·<u>boo</u>·reh·koh
fish	**ψάρι** <u>psah</u>·ree
fish soup thickened with egg and lemon	**ψαρόσουπα αυγολέμονο** psah·<u>roh</u>·soo·pah ahv·ghoh·<u>leh</u>·moh·noh
fish stew with tomatoes	**κακαβιά** kah·kahv·<u>yah</u>
fresh cod	**μπακαλιάρος** bah·kah·<u>liah</u>·rohs
fried baby squid	**καλαμαράκια** kah·lah·mah·<u>rah</u>·kiah
fried meatballs	**κεφτεδάκια** kef·teh·<u>THah</u>·kiah
fried whitebait	**μαρίδα τηγανητή** mah·<u>ree</u>·THah tee·ghah·nee·<u>tee</u>
fruit	**φρούτο** <u>froo</u>·toh
fruit juice	**χυμός φρούτων** khee·<u>mohs</u> <u>froo</u>·tohn
fruit salad	**φρουτοσαλάτα** froo·toh·sah·<u>lah</u>·tah
garlic	**σκόρδο** <u>skohr</u>·THoh
goat	**κατσικάκι** kah·tsce·<u>kah</u>·kee
goose	**χήνα** <u>khee</u>·nah
granola [muesli]	**μούσλι** <u>moos</u>·lee
grape	**σταφύλι** stah·<u>fee</u>·lee
grapefruit	**γκρέιπφρουτ** greh·eep·froot
Greek brandy	**Μεταξά** meh·tah·<u>ksah</u>
green bean	**φασολάκι** fah·soh·<u>lah</u>·kee
green peppers	**πιπεριές πράσινες** pee·pehr·<u>yehs</u> <u>prah</u>·see·nehs
grouper	**σφυρίδα** sfee·<u>ree</u>·THah
halva, sweet sesame seed paste	**χαλβάς** khahl·<u>vahs</u>
ham	**ζαμπόν** zahm·<u>bohn</u>

ham omelet	**ομελέττα με ζαμπόν** oh·meh·<u>leh</u>·tah meh zahm·<u>bohn</u>
herring (smoked)	**ρέγγα (καπνιστή)** <u>rehn</u>·gah (kahp·nees·<u>tee</u>)
honey	**μέλι** <u>meh</u>·lee
ice cream	**παγωτό** pah·ghoh·<u>toh</u>
iced tea	**παγωμένο τσάι** pah·ghoh·<u>meh</u>·noh <u>tsah</u>·ee
instant coffee	**Νεσκαφέ** nehs·kah·<u>feh</u>
juice	**χυμός** khee·<u>mohs</u>
kidney	**νεφρό** neh·<u>froh</u>
kumquat liqueur (Corfu)	**κουμ-κουάτ** koom·koo·<u>aht</u>
lamb	**αρνί** ahr·<u>nee</u>
layers of eggplant [aubergine], meat and white sauce	**μουσακάς** moo·sah·<u>kahs</u>
leek	**πράσο** <u>prah</u>·soh
lemon	**λεμόνι** leh·<u>moh</u>·nee
lentil soup	**φακές σούπα** fah·<u>kehs</u> <u>soo</u>·pah
liqueur	**λικέρ** lee·<u>kehr</u>
liver	**συκώτι** see·<u>koh</u>·tee
lobster	**αστακός** ahs·tah·<u>kohs</u>
mackerel	**σκουμπρί** skoo·<u>mbree</u>
marinated mullet, sole or mackerel	**ψάρι μαρινάτο** <u>psah</u>·ree mah·ree·<u>nah</u>·toh
mastic	**μαστίχα** mahs·<u>tee</u>·khah
mayonnaise	**μαγιονέζα** mah·yoh·<u>neh</u>·zah
meat	**κρέας** <u>kreh</u>·ahs
meat soup	**κρεατόσουπα** kreh·ah·<u>toh</u>·soo·pah

meat with orzo pasta baked with tomatoes	γιουβέτσι	yoo·<u>veh</u>·tsee
melon	πεπόνι	peh·<u>poh</u>·nee
milk	γάλα	<u>ghah</u>·lah
mint	δυόσμος	THee·<u>ohz</u>·mohs
muffin	μάφιν	<u>mah</u>·feen
mullet	κέφαλος	<u>keh</u>·fah·lohs
mushroom	μανιτάρι	mah·nee·<u>tah</u>·ree
mussel	μύδι	<u>mee</u>·THee
nuts	ξηροί καρποί	ksee·<u>ree</u> kah·<u>rpee</u>
oatmeal	κουάκερ	koo·<u>ah</u>·kehr
octopus	χταπόδι	khtah·<u>poh</u>·THee
okra	μπάμια	<u>bah</u>·miah
olive (stuffed)	ελιά (γεμιστή)	eh·<u>liah</u> (yeh·mees·<u>tee</u>)
olive oil	ελαιόλαδο	eh·leh·<u>oh</u>·lah·THoh
omelet	ομελέτα	oh·meh·<u>leh</u>·tah
on the rocks	με πάγο	meh <u>pah</u>·ghoh
onion	κρεμμύδι	kreh·<u>mee</u>·THee
orange	πορτοκάλι	poh·rtoh·<u>kah</u>·lee
oregano	ρίγανη	<u>ree</u>·ghah·nee
ouzo	ούζο	<u>oo</u>·zoh
oyster	στρείδι	<u>stree</u>·THee
parsley	μαϊντανός	mah·ee·dah·<u>nohs</u>
pasta	ζυμαρικά	zee·mah·ree·<u>kah</u>
paté	πατέ	pah·<u>teh</u>
peach	ροδάκινο	roh·<u>THah</u>·kee·noh
pear	αχλάδι	akh·<u>lah</u>·THee
peas	αρακάς	ah·rah·<u>kahs</u>

pheasant	φασιανός fah·siah·<u>nohs</u>
pineapple	ανανάς ah·nah·<u>nahs</u>
plum	δαμάσκηνο THah·<u>mahs</u>·kee·noh
poached	ποσέ poh·<u>seh</u>
pork	χοιρινό khee·ree·<u>noh</u>
porksteak	μπριζόλα χοιρινή bree·<u>zoh</u>·lah khee·ree·<u>nee</u>
potato	πατάτα pah·<u>tah</u>·tah
rabbit	κουνέλι koo·<u>neh</u>·lee
red cabbage	κόκκινο λάχανο <u>koh</u>·kee·noh <u>lah</u>·khah·noh
red mullet	μπαρμπούνι bahr·<u>boo</u>·nee
red wine	κόκκινο κρασί <u>koh</u>·kee·noh krah·see
rice	ρύζι <u>ree</u>·zee
rice pudding	ρυζόγαλο ree·<u>zoh</u>·ghah·loh
roast	ψητό psee·<u>toh</u>
roll	ψωμάκι psoh·<u>mah</u>·kee
rosemary	δεντρολίβανο THehn·droh·<u>lee</u>·vah·noh
sage	φασκόμηλο fahs·<u>koh</u>·mee·loh
salad	σαλάτα sah·<u>lah</u>·tah
salted cod	μπακαλιάρος παστός bah·kah·<u>liah</u>·rohs pahs·<u>tohs</u>
sardine	σαρδέλα sahr·<u>THeh</u>·lah
sauce	σάλτσα <u>sah</u>·ltsah
sausage	λουκάνικο loo·<u>kah</u>·nee·koh
scrambled eggs	ομελέτα oh·meh·<u>leh</u>·tah
shellfish	όστρακα <u>oh</u>·strah·kah
shredded pastry roll filled with nuts and steeped in syrup	καταΐφι kah·tah·<u>ee</u>·fee
shrimp [prawn]	γαρίδα <u>ghah</u>·ree·THah

skewered pork or lamb, well seasoned and cooked over charcoal	**κοντοσούβλι** koh·ndoh·<u>soov</u>·lee
snack	**σνακ** snahk
soda	**αναψυκτικό** ah·nah·psee·ktee·<u>koh</u>
soft-boiled eggs	**μελάτα αυγά** meh·<u>lah</u>·tah ahv·<u>gah</u>
sole (fish)	**γλώσσα** <u>ghloh</u>·sah
soup	**σούπα** <u>soo</u>·pah
soup with rice, eggs and lemon juice	**σούπα αυγολέμονο** <u>soo</u>·pah ahv·ghoh·<u>leh</u>·moh·noh
spiced lamb and potatoes baked in parchment or in filo pastry	**αρνάκι εξοχικό** ahr·<u>nah</u>·kee eh·ksoh·khee·<u>koh</u>
spices	**μπαχαρικά** bah·khah·ree·<u>kah</u>
spinach	**σπανάκι** spah·<u>nah</u>·kee
spinach and feta in pastry dough	**σπανακόπιττα** spah·nah·<u>koh</u>·pee·tah
stuffed grape leaves	**ντολμαδάκι** dohl·mah·<u>THah</u>·kee
squid	**καλαμάρι** kah·lah·<u>mah</u>·ree
steak	**μπριζόλα** bree·<u>zoh</u>·lah
sugar	**ζάχαρη** <u>zah</u>·khah·ree
swordfish	**ξιφίας** ksee·<u>fee</u>·ahs
syrup	**σιρόπι** see·<u>roh</u>·pee
tahini (sesame paste) soup	**ταχινόσουπα** tah·khee·<u>noh</u>·soo·pah
tangerine	**μανταρίνι** mahn·dah·<u>ree</u>·nee
taramosalata, fish roe dip	**ταραμοσαλάτα** tah·rah·moh·sah·<u>lah</u>·tah

tea	**τσάι** <u>tsah</u>·ee
thyme	**θυμάρι** thee·<u>mah</u>·ree
toast	**ψωμί φρυγανιά** psoh·<u>mee</u> free·ghah·<u>niah</u>
tomato	**ντομάτα** ndoh·<u>mah</u>·tah
tomato soup	**τοματόσουπα** toh·mah·<u>toh</u>·soo·pah
tongue (meat)	**γλώσσα** <u>ghloh</u>·sah
tonic water	**τόνικ** <u>toh</u>·neek
tripe soup	**πατσάς** pah·<u>tsahs</u>
tuna	**τόννος** <u>toh</u>·nohs
turkey	**γαλοπούλα** ghah·loh·<u>poo</u>·lah
Turkish delight	**λουκούμι** loo·<u>koo</u>·mee
unleavened bread	**λαγάνα** lah·<u>ghah</u>·nah
veal	**μοσχάρι** mohs·<u>khah</u>·ree
veal steak	**μπριζόλα μοσχαρίσια** bree·<u>zoh</u>·lah mohs·khah·<u>ree</u>·siah
vegetable	**λαχανικό** lah·khah·nee·<u>koh</u>
vegetable soup	**χορτόσουπα** khohr·<u>toh</u>·soo·pah
walnut cake	**καρυδόπιτα** kah·ree·<u>THoh</u>·pee·tah
water	**νερό** neh·<u>roh</u>
watermelon	**καρπούζι** kahr·<u>poo</u>·zee
wheat	**σιτάρι** see·<u>tah</u>·ree
wine	**κρασί** krah·<u>see</u>
yogurt (with honey)	**γιαούρτι (με μέλι)** yah·<u>oor</u>·tee (meh <u>meh</u>·lee)
yogurt, garlic and cucumber dip	**τζατζίκι** jah·<u>jee</u>·kee
zucchini [courgette]	**κολοκυθάκι** koh·loh·kee·<u>thah</u>·kee

▼ People

Talking

Essential

Hello.	**Χαίρετε.** <u>kheh</u>·reh·teh
How are you?	**Πώς είστε;** pohs <u>ee</u>·steh
Fine, thanks. And you?	**Καλά, ευχαριστώ. Εσείς;** kah·<u>lah</u> ehf·khah·ree·<u>stoh</u> eh·<u>sees</u>
Excuse me!	**Συγγνώμη!** seegh·<u>noh</u>·mee
Do you speak English?	**Μιλάτε Αγγλικά;** mee·<u>lah</u>·teh ahng·lee·<u>kah</u>
What's your name?	**Πώς λέγεστε;** pohs <u>leh</u>·yeh·steh
My name is...	**Λέγομαι...** <u>leh</u>·ghoh·meh...
Nice to meet you.	**Χαίρω πολύ.** <u>kheh</u>·roh poh·<u>lee</u>
Where are you from?	**Από πού είστε;** ah·<u>poh</u> poo <u>ee</u>·steh
I'm from the U.S./U.K.	**Είμαι από *τις Ηνωμένες Πολιτείες/ το Ηνωμένο Βασίλειο.*** <u>ee</u>·<u>meh</u> ah·<u>poh</u> *tees ee·noh·<u>meh</u>·nehs poh·lee·<u>tee</u>·ehs/toh ee·noh·<u>meh</u>·noh vah·<u>see</u>·lee·oh*
What do you do?	**Τι δουλειά κάνετε;** tee THoo·<u>liah</u> <u>kah</u>·neh·teh
I work for...	**Δουλεύω για...** THoo·<u>leh</u>·voh yah...
I'm a student.	**Είμαι φοιτητής♂/φοιτήτρια♀.** <u>ee</u>·meh fee·tee·<u>tees</u>♂/fee·<u>tee</u>·tree·ah♀
I'm retired.	**Είμαι συνταξιούχος.** <u>ee</u>·meh seen·dah·ksee·<u>oo</u>·khohs
Do you like...?	**Σου αρέσει...;** soo ah·<u>reh</u>·see...
Goodbye.	**Γεια σας.** yah sahs
See you later.	**Τα λέμε αργότερα.** tah <u>leh</u>·meh ahr·<u>ghoh</u>·teh·rah

Communication Difficulties

Do you speak English?	**Μιλάτε Αγγλικά;** mee·<u>lah</u>·teh ahng·lee·<u>kah</u>
Does anyone here speak English?	**Μιλάει κανείς εδώ Αγγλικά;** mee·<u>lah</u>·ee kah·<u>nees</u> eh·<u>THoh</u> ahng·lee·<u>kah</u>
I don't speak Greek.	**Δεν μιλώ Ελληνικά.** THehn mee·<u>loh</u> eh·lee·nee·<u>kah</u>
Could you speak more slowly?	**Μπορείτε να μιλάτε πιο αργά;** boh·<u>ree</u>·teh nah mee·<u>lah</u>·teh pioh ahr·<u>ghah</u>
Could you repeat that?	**Μπορείτε να το επαναλάβετε;** boh·<u>ree</u>·teh nah toh eh·pah·nah·<u>lah</u>·veh·teh
Excuse me!	**Συγγνώμη!** seegh·<u>noh</u>·mee
What was that?	**Τι είπατε;** tee <u>ee</u>·pah·teh
Can you write it down, please?	**Μου το γράφετε παρακαλώ;** moo toh <u>ghrah</u>·feh·teh pah·rah·kah·<u>loh</u>
Can you translate this for me?	**Μπορείτε να μου μεταφράσετε αυτό;** boh·<u>ree</u>·teh nah moo meh·tahf·<u>rah</u>·seh·teh ahf·<u>toh</u>
What does *this/ that* mean?	**Τι σημαίνει *αυτό/εκείνο*;** tee see·<u>meh</u>·nee *ahf·<u>toh</u>/eh·<u>kee</u>·noh*
I (don't) understand.	**(Δεν) Καταλαβαίνω.** (THehn) kah·tah·lah·<u>veh</u>·noh
Do you understand?	**Καταλαβαίνετε;** kah·tah·lah·<u>veh</u>·neh·teh

You May Hear...

Μιλώ (μόνο) λίγα Αγγλικά. mee·<u>loh</u> (<u>moh</u>·noh)
lee·ghah ahng·lee·<u>kah</u>

I speak (only)
a little English.

Δεν μιλώ Αγγλικά. THehn mee·<u>loh</u> ahng·lee·<u>kah</u>

I don't speak English.

Making Friends

Hello.	**Χαίρετε.** <u>kheh</u>·reh·teh
Good morning.	**Καλημέρα.** kah·lee·<u>meh</u>·rah
Good *afternoon/ evening*.	**Καλησπέρα.** kah·lee·<u>speh</u>·rah
Good night.	**Καληνύχτα.** kah·lee·<u>neekh</u>·tah
My name is...	**Λέγομαι...** <u>leh</u>·ghoh·meh...
What's your name?	**Πώς λέγεστε;** pohs <u>leh</u>·yehs·teh
I'd like to introduce you to...	**Θα ήθελα να σας συστήσω τον♂/την♀...** thah <u>ee</u>·theh·lah nah sahs sees·<u>tee</u>·soh tohn♂/ teen♀...
Pleased to meet you.	**Χαίρω πολύ.** <u>kheh</u>·roh poh·<u>lee</u>
How are you?	**Πώς είστε;** pohs <u>ees</u>·teh
Fine, thanks.	**Καλά, ευχαριστώ.** kah·<u>lah</u> ehf·khah·rees·<u>toh</u>
And you?	**Εσείς;** Eh·<u>sees</u>

i Greeks shake hands when they meet for the first time and on subsequent meetings. With close friends, it is customary to exchange kisses on both cheeks when meeting and parting. It is polite to address people you meet for the first time by their surname until prompted to use their first name.

Travel Talk

I'm here...	**Είμαι εδώ...** <u>ee</u>·meh eh·<u>THoh</u>...
- on business	- **για δουλειά** yah THoo·lee·<u>ah</u>
- vacation [holiday]	- **για διακοπές** yah THiah·koh·<u>pehs</u>
- studying	- **για σπουδές** yah spoo·<u>THehs</u>
I'm staying here for...	**Μένω εδώ για...** meh·noh eh·<u>THoh</u> yah...
I've been here...	**Είμαι εδώ...** <u>ee</u>·meh eh·<u>THoh</u>...
- a day	- **μια ημέρα** miah <u>meh</u>·rah
- a week	- **μια εβδομάδα** miah ehv·THoh·<u>mah</u>·THah
- a month	- **ένα μήνα** eh·nah <u>mee</u>·nah

▶ For numbers, see page 158.

| Where are you from? | **Από πού είστε;** ah·<u>poh</u> poo <u>ee</u>·steh |
| I'm from... | **Είμαι από...** <u>ee</u>·meh ah·<u>poh</u>... |

Relationships

Who are you with?	**Με ποιον/ποιαν είστε;** meh piohn/piahn <u>ee</u>·steh
I'm on my own.	**Είμαι μόνος♂/μόνη♀ μου.** <u>ee</u>·meh <u>moh</u>·nohs♂/<u>moh</u>·nee♀ moo
I'm with...	**Είμαι με...** <u>ee</u>·meh meh...
- my *husband/wife*	- **τον σύζυγο/την σύζυγό μου** tohn <u>see</u>·zee·ghoh/teen <u>see</u>·zee·<u>ghoh</u> moo
- my *boyfriend/ girlfriend*	- **τον φίλο/την κοπέλα μου** tohn fee·loh/teen koh·<u>peh</u>·lah moo
- a friend	- **ένα φίλο♂/μια φίλη♀** <u>eh</u>·nah <u>fee</u>·loh♂/ miah <u>fee</u>·lee♀
- a colleague	- **έναν συνάδελφο** <u>eh</u>·nahn see·<u>nah</u>·THehl·foh
When's your birthday?	**Πότε είναι τα γενέθλιά σου;** <u>poh</u>·teh ee·neh tah gheh·<u>nehth</u>·lee·<u>ah</u> soo

How old are you?	**Πόσο χρονών είσαι;** <u>poh</u>·soh khroh·<u>nohn</u> ee·seh
I'm...	**Είμαι...** <u>ee</u>·meh...

▶ For numbers, see page 158.

I'm...	**Είμαι...** <u>ee</u>·meh...
– single	**– ελεύθερος**♂**/ελεύθερη**♀ eh·<u>lehf</u>·theh·rohs♂/eh·<u>lehf</u>·theh·ree♀
– in a relationship	**– δεσμευμένος**♂**/δεσμευμένη**♀ THehs·mehv·<u>meh</u>·nohs♂/ THehs·mehv·<u>meh</u>·nee♀
– married	**– παντρεμένος**♂**/παντρεμένη**♀ pahn·dreh·<u>meh</u>·nohs♂/pahn·dreh·<u>meh</u>·nee♀
– divorced	**– διαζευγμένος**♂**/διαζευγμένη**♀ THee·ah·zehv·<u>ghmeh</u>·nohs♂/ THee·ah·zehv·<u>ghmeh</u>·ee♀
– separated	**– σε διάσταση** seh THee·<u>ah</u>·stah·see
I'm widowed.	**Είμαι χήρος**♂**/χήρα**♀. ee·meh <u>khee</u>·rohs♂/ <u>khee</u>·rah♀
Do you have *children/ grandchildren*?	**Έχετε *παιδιά/εγγόνια*;** <u>eh</u>·kheh·teh *peh·<u>THyah</u>/eh·<u>goh</u>·niah*

95

Work and School

What do you do?	**Τι δουλειά κάνετε;** tee THoo·liah kah·neh·teh
What are you studying?	**Τι σπουδάζετε;** tee spoo·THah·zeh·teh
I'm studying...	**Σπουδάζω...** spoo·THah·zoh...
Who do you work for...?	**Για ποιον δουλεύετε...;** yah piohn THoo·leh·veh·teh...
I work for...	**Δουλεύω για...** THoo·leh·voh yah...
Here's my business card.	**Ορίστε η κάρτα μου.** oh·ree·steh ee kahr·tah moo

▶ For business travel, see page 132.

Weather

What's the weather forecast for tomorrow?	**Τι λέει η πρόβλεψη του καιρού για αύριο;** tee leh·ee ee proh·vleh·psee too keh·roo yah ah·vree·oh
What *beautiful/ terrible* weather!	**Τι *ωραίος/απαίσιος* καιρός!** tee oh·reh·ohs/ ah·peh·see·ohs keh·rohs
It's *cool/warm*.	**Έχει *δροσιά/ζέστη*.** eh·khee roh·siah/ zeh·stee
It's *rainy/sunny*.	**Ο καιρός είναι *βροχερός/ηλιόλουστος*.** oh keh·rohs ee·neh vroh·kheh·rohs/ ee·lioh·loo·stohs
It's *snowy/icy*.	**Έχει παγωνιά.** eh·khee pah·ghoh·niah
Do I need *a jacket/ an umbrella*?	**Να πάρω *ζακέτα/ομπρέλα*;** nah pah·roh zah·keh·tah/ohm·breh·lah

▶ For temperature, see page 164.

Romance

Essential

Would you like to go out for a *drink/ dinner*?	**Θέλετε να βγούμε για *ποτό/φαγητό*;** theh·leh·teh nah vghoo·meh yah poh·toh/ fah·yee·toh
What are your plans for *tonight/ tomorrow*?	**Ποια είναι τα σχέδιά σας για *απόψε/αύριο*;** piah ee·neh tah skheh·THee·ah sahs yah ah·poh·pseh/ahv·ree·oh
Can I have your number?	**Μπορώ να έχω τον αριθμό τηλεφώνου σας;** boh·roh nah eh·khoh tohn ah·reeth·moh tee·leh·foh·noo sahs
May we join you?	**Να έρθουμε μαζί σας;** nah ehr·thoo·meh mah·zee sahs
Let me buy you a drink.	**Να σε κεράσω ένα ποτό.** nah seh keh·rah·soh eh·nah poh·toh
I like you.	**Μου αρέσεις.** moo ah·reh·sees
I love you.	**Σ' αγαπώ.** sah·ghah·poh

Making Plans

Would you like to go out for coffee?	**Θα θέλατε να βγούμε για καφέ;** thah theh·lah·teh nah vghoo·meh yah kah·feh
What are your plans for...?	**Ποια είναι τα σχέδιά σας για...;** piah ee·neh tah skheh·THee·ah sahs yah...
– tonight	– **απόψε** ah·poh·pseh
– tomorrow	– **αύριο** ahv·ree·oh
– this weekend	– **αυτό το Σαββατοκύριακο** ahf·toh toh sah·vah·toh·kee·riah·koh
Where would you like to go?	**Πού θα θέλατε να πάμε;** poo thah theh·lah·teh nah pah·meh

| I'd like to go to... | **Θα ήθελα να πάω...** thah ee·theh·lah nah pah·oh... |

| Do you like...? | **Σου αρέσει...;** soo ah·reh·see... |

| Can I have your *number/e-mail*? | **Μου δίνετε το *τηλέφωνο/e-mail* σας;** moo THee·neh·teh toh tee·leh·foh·noh/ee·meh·eel sahs |

▶ For e-mail and phone, see page 47.

Pick-up [Chat-up] Lines

| Can I join you? | **Να έρθω κι εγώ στην παρέα σας;** nah ehr·thoh kee eh·ghoh steen pah·reh·ah sahs |

| You look great! | **Είστε πολύ όμορφος♂/όμορφη♀!** ee·steh poh·lee oh·mohr·fohs♂/oh·mohr·fee♀ |

| Shall we go somewhere quieter? | **Πάμε κάπου πιο ήσυχα;** pah·meh kah·poo pioh ee·see·khah |

Accepting and Rejecting

| Thank you. I'd love to. | **Ευχαριστώ. Θα το ήθελα πολύ.** ehf·khah·rees·toh thah toh ee·theh·lah poh·lee |

| Where should we meet? | **Πού θα συναντηθούμε;** poo thah see·nahn·dee·thoo·meh |

| I'll meet you at *the bar/your hotel*. | **Θα σε συναντήσω *στο μπαρ/στο ξενοδοχείο σου.*** thah seh see·nahn·dee·soh stoh bahr/stoh kseh·noh·THoh·khee·oh soo |

| I'll come by at... | **Θα περάσω στις...** thah peh·rah·soh stees... |

| Thank you, but I'm busy. | **Σας ευχαριστώ, αλλά είμαι πολύ απασχολημένος♂/απασχολημένη♀.** sahs ehf·khah·rees·toh ah·lah ee·meh poh·lee ah·pahs·khoh·lee·meh·nohs♂/ ah·pahs·khoh·lee·meh·nee♀ |

I'm not interested.	**Δεν ενδιαφέρομαι.** THehn ehn·THee·ah·<u>feh</u>·roh·meh
Leave me alone, please!	**Σας παρακαλώ, αφήστε με ήσυχο♂/ ήσυχη♀!** sahs pah·rah·kah·<u>loh</u> ah·<u>fees</u>·teh meh <u>ee</u>·see·khoh♂/<u>ee</u>·see·khee♀
Stop bothering me!	**Σταματείστε να με ενοχλείτε!** stah·mah·<u>tee</u>·steh nah meh eh·noh·<u>khlee</u>·teh

Getting Physical

Can I *hug/kiss* you?	**Μπορώ να σε αγκαλιάσω/φιλήσω;** boh·<u>roh</u> nah seh ahn·gah·<u>liah</u>·soh/fee·<u>lee</u>·soh
Yes.	**Ναι.** neh
No.	**Όχι.** <u>oh</u>·khee
Stop!	**Σταμάτα!** stah·<u>mah</u>·tah

Sexual Preferences ——————————————

Are you gay?	**Είσαι γκέι;** <u>ee</u>·seh <u>geh</u>·ee
I'm...	**Είμαι...** <u>ee</u>·meh...
– heterosexual	– **ετεροφυλόφιλος**♂/**ετεροφυλόφιλη**♀ eh·teh·roh·fee·<u>loh</u>·fee·lohs♂/ eh·teh·roh·fee·<u>loh</u>·fee·lee♀
– homosexual	– **ομοφυλόφιλος**♂/**ομοφυλόφιλη**♀ oh·moh·fee·<u>loh</u>·fee·lohs♂/ oh·moh·fee·<u>loh</u>·fee·lee♀
– bisexual	– **αμφιφυλόφιλος**♂/**αμφιφυλόφιλη**♀ ahm·fee·fee·<u>loh</u>·fee·lohs♂/ ahm·fee·fee·<u>loh</u>·fee·lee♀

▶ For informal and formal usage, see page 92.

▼ Fun

Sightseeing

Essential

Where's the tourist information office?	**Πού είναι το γραφείο τουρισμού;** poo <u>ee</u>·neh toh ghrah·<u>fee</u>·oh too·reez·<u>moo</u>
What are the main points of interest?	**Ποια είναι τα κυριότερα αξιοθέατα;** piah <u>ee</u>·neh tah kee·ree·<u>oh</u>·teh·rah ah·ksee·oh·<u>theh</u>·ah·tah
Do you have tours in English?	**Γίνονται ξεναγήσεις στα αγγλικά;** <u>ghee</u>·nohn·deh kseh·nah·<u>ghee</u>·sees stah ahng·lee·<u>kah</u>
Could I have a *map/guide*?	**Μπορώ να έχω έναν *χάρτη/οδηγό*;** boh·<u>roh</u> nah <u>eh</u>·khoh <u>eh</u>·nahn *khahr·tee/oh·THee·ghoh*

Tourist Information Office

Do you have any information on...?	**Έχετε πληροφορίες για...;** <u>eh</u>·kheh·teh plee·roh·foh·<u>ree</u>·ehs yah...
Can you recommend...?	**Μπορείτε να συστήσετε έναν/μία/ένα...;** boh·<u>ree</u>·teh nah sees·<u>tee</u>·seh·teh <u>eh</u>·nahn/ <u>mee</u>·ah/<u>eh</u>·nah...
– a boat trip	**– μια εκδρομή με βάρκα** <u>mee</u>·ah ehk·THroh·<u>mee</u> meh <u>vahr</u>·kah
– an excursion	**– μια εκδρομή** <u>mee</u>·ah ehk·THroh·<u>mee</u>
– a sightseeing tour	**– μια ξενάγηση στα αξιοθέατα** <u>mee</u>·ah kseh·<u>nah</u>·yee·see stah ah·ksee·oh·<u>theh</u>·ah·tah

---

i The official, government-run tourist information offices are known as **EOT** (eh·<u>oht</u>), **Ελληνικός Οργανισμός Τουρισμού** (eh·lee·nee·<u>kohs</u> ohr·ghah·nees·<u>mohs</u> too·rees·<u>moo</u>), in Greece and **KOT** (koht), **Κυπριακός Οργανισμός Τουρισμού** (keep·ree·ah·<u>kohs</u> ohr·ghah·nees·<u>mohs</u> too·rees·<u>moo</u>) in Cyprus. They can be found in most tourist resorts and major towns.

Tours

I'd like to go on the tour to...	**Θα ήθελα να πάω στην ξενάγηση στο...** thah <u>ee</u>·theh·lah nah <u>pah</u>·oh steen kseh·<u>nah</u>·yee·see stoh...
Are there tours in English?	**Γίνονται ξεναγήσεις στα αγγλικά;** <u>ghee</u>·nohn·deh kseh·nah·<u>yee</u>·sees stah ahng·lee·<u>kah</u>
What time do we *leave/return*?	**Τι ώρα *αναχωρούμε/επιστρέφουμε*;** tee <u>oh</u>·rah ah·nah·khoh·<u>roo</u>·meh/eh·pees·<u>treh</u>·foo·meh
We'd like to have a look at the...	**Θα θέλαμε να ρίξουμε μια ματιά...** thah <u>theh</u>·lah·meh nah <u>ree</u>·ksoo·meh miah mah·<u>tiah</u>...
Can we stop here...?	**Μπορούμε να σταματήσουμε εδώ...;** boh·<u>roo</u>·meh nah stah·mah·<u>tee</u>·soo·meh eh·<u>THoh</u>...
– to take photographs	**– για να βγάλουμε φωτογραφίες** yah nah <u>vghah</u>·loo·meh foh·toh·ghrah·<u>fee</u>·ehs
– to buy souvenirs	**– για να αγοράσουμε σουβενίρ** yah nah ah·ghoh·<u>rah</u>·soo·meh soo·veh·<u>neer</u>
– to use the restroom [toilet]	**– για τουαλέτα** yah too·ah·<u>leh</u>·tah
Is there access for the disabled?	**Υπάρχει πρόσβαση για άτομα με ειδικές ανάγκες;** ee·<u>pahr</u>·khee <u>prohz</u>·vah·see yah <u>ah</u>·toh·mah meh ee·THee·<u>kehs</u> ah·<u>nahn</u>·gehs

▶ For ticketing, see page 19.

Sights

Where is...?	**Πού είναι...;** poo <u>ee</u>·neh...
– the battleground	**– το πεδίο μάχης** toh peh·<u>THee</u>·oh <u>mah</u>·khees
– the botanical garden	**– ο βοτανικός κήπος** oh voh·tah·nee·<u>kohs</u> <u>kee</u>·pohs
– the castle	**– το κάστρο** toh <u>kahs</u>·troh

Where is...?	Πού είναι...; poo <u>ee</u>·neh...
– the downtown area	– το κέντρο της πόλης toh <u>kehn</u>·droh tees <u>poh</u>·lees
– the fountain	– το συντριβάνι toh seen·dree·<u>vah</u>·nee
– the library	– η βιβλιοθήκη ee veev·lee·oh·<u>thee</u>·kee
– the market	– η αγορά ee ah·ghoh·<u>rah</u>
– the museum	– το μουσείο toh moo·<u>see</u>·oh
– the old town	– η παλιά πόλη ee pah·<u>liah</u> <u>poh</u>·lee
– the palace	– τα ανάκτορα tah ah·<u>nahk</u>·toh·rah
– the park	– το πάρκο toh <u>pahr</u>·koh
– the shopping area	– η εμπορική περιοχή ee ehm·boh·ree·<u>kee</u> peh·ree·oh·<u>khee</u>
– the town hall	– το Δημαρχείο toh THee·mahr·<u>khee</u>·oh
Can you show me on the map?	Μπορείτε να μου δείξετε στο χάρτη; boh·<u>ree</u>·teh nah moo <u>THee</u>·kseh·teh stoh <u>khahr</u>·tee

▶ For directions, see page 33.

Impressions

It's...	**Είναι...** <u>ee</u>·neh...
– beautiful	– **όμορφο** <u>oh</u>·mohr·foh
– boring	– **βαρετός** vah·reh·<u>toh</u>
– interesting	– **ενδιαφέρον** ehn·THee·ah·<u>feh</u>·rohn
– magnificent	– **μεγαλοπρεπές** meh·ghah·lohp·reh·<u>pehs</u>
– romantic	– **ρομαντικό** roh·mahn·dee·<u>koh</u>
– terrible	– **απαίσιο** ah·<u>peh</u>·see·oh
– ugly	– **άσχημο** <u>ahs</u>·khee·moh
I (don't) like it.	**(Δεν) Μου αρέσει.** (THen) moo ah·<u>reh</u>·see

Religion

Where is...?	**Πού είναι...;** poo <u>ee</u>·neh...
– the church	– **η εκκλησία** ee ehk·lee·<u>see</u>·ah
– the mosque	– **το τζαμί** toh jah·<u>mee</u>
– the shrine	– **ο ιερός χώρος** oh ee·eh·<u>rohs</u> <u>khoh</u>·rohs
– the synagogue	– **η συναγωγή** ee see·nah·ghoh·<u>yee</u>
– the temple	– **ο ναός** oh nah·<u>ohs</u>
What time is *mass/ the service*?	**Τι ώρα είναι η λειτουργία;** tee <u>oh</u>·rah <u>ee</u>·neh ee lee·toor·<u>yee</u>·ah

Shopping

Essential

Where is the *market/mall [shopping centre]*?	**Πού είναι *η αγορά/το εμπορικό κέντρο*;** poo <u>ee</u>·neh ee ah·ghoh·<u>rah</u>/toh ehm·boh·ree·<u>koh</u> <u>kehn</u>·droh

I'm just looking.	**Απλώς κοιτάω.** ahp·lohs kee·tah·oh
Can you help me?	**Μπορείτε να με βοηθήσετε;** boh·ree·teh nah meh voh·ee·thee·seh·teh
I'm being helped.	**Με εξυπηρετούν.** meh eh·ksee·pee·reh·toon
How much?	**Πόσο;** poh·soh
This/That one, thanks.	**Αυτό/Εκείνο, παρακαλώ.** *ahf·toh/eh·kee·noh* pah·rah·kah·loh
That's all, thanks.	**Τίποτε άλλο, ευχαριστώ.** tee·poh·teh ah·loh ehf·khah·rees·toh
Where do I pay?	**Πού πληρώνω;** poo plee·roh·noh
I'll pay *in cash/by credit card*.	**Θα πληρώσω** *τοις μετρητοίς/με πιστωτική κάρτα.* thah plee·roh·soh *tees meht·ree·tees/ meh pees·toh·tee·kee kahr·tah*
A receipt, please.	**Μια απόδειξη, παρακαλώ.** miah ah·poh·THee·ksee pah·rah·kah·loh

Shopping can be a great pleasure in Greece. Apart from the standard department stores, you can wander through flea markets and seek out the small handicraft stores that line the narrow alleys of most islands and old towns.

Stores

Where is...?	**Πού είναι...;** poo ee·neh...
– the antiques store	– **το κατάστημα με αντίκες** toh kah·tahs·tee·mah meh ahn·tee·kehs
– the bakery	– **το αρτοποιείο** toh ahr·toh·pee·ee·oh
– the bookstore	– **το βιβλιοπωλείο** toh veev·lee·oh·poh·lee·oh
– the clothing store [clothes shop]	– **το κατάστημα ρούχων** toh kah·tahs·tee·mah roo·khohn

– the delicatessen	– **τα τυριά-αλλαντικά** tah teer·<u>yah</u> ah·lahn·dee·<u>kah</u>
– the department store	– **το πολυκατάστημα** toh poh·lee·kah·<u>tahs</u>·tee·mah
– the health food store	– **το κατάστημα με υγιεινές τροφές** toh kah·<u>tahs</u>·tee·mah meh ee·yee·ee·<u>nehs</u> troh·<u>fehs</u>
– the jeweler	– **το κοσμηματοπωλείο** toh kohz·mee·mah·toh·poh·<u>lee</u>·oh
– the liquor store [off-licence]	– **η κάβα** ee <u>kah</u>·vah
– the market	– **η αγορά** ee ah·ghoh·<u>rah</u>
– the pastry store	– **το ζαχαροπλαστείο** toh zah·khah·rohp·lahs·<u>tee</u>·oh

Where is...?	**Πού είναι...;** poo <u>ee</u>·neh...
– the pharmacy [chemist's]	**– το φαρμακείο** toh fahr·mah·<u>kee</u>·oh
– the produce [grocery] store	**– το παντοπωλείο** toh pahn·doh·poh·<u>lee</u>·oh
– the shoe store	**– το κατάστημα υποδημάτων** toh kah·<u>tahs</u>·tee·mah ee·poh·THee·<u>mah</u>·tohn
– the shopping mall [centre]	**– το εμπορικό κέντρο** toh ehm·boh·ree·<u>koh</u> <u>kehn</u>·droh
– the souvenir store	**– το κατάστημα σουβενίρ** toh kah·<u>tahs</u>·tee·mah soo·veh·<u>neer</u>
– the supermarket	**– το σουπερμάρκετ** toh <u>soo</u>·pehr <u>mahr</u>·keht
– the tobacconist	**– το καπνοπωλείο** toh kahp·noh·poh·<u>lee</u>·oh
– the toy store	**– το κατάστημα παιχνιδιών** toh kah·<u>tahs</u>·tee·mah pehkh·neeTH·<u>yohn</u>

Services

Can you recommend...?	**Μπορείτε να συστήσετε...;** boh·<u>ree</u>·teh nah sees·<u>tee</u>·seh·teh...
– a barber	**– έναν κουρέα** <u>eh</u>·nahn koo·<u>reh</u>·ah
– a dry cleaner	**– ένα καθαριστήριο** <u>eh</u>·nah kah·thah·rees·<u>tee</u>·ree·oh
– a hairdresser	**– ένα κομμωτήριο** <u>eh</u>·nah koh·moh·<u>tee</u>·ree·oh
– a nail salon	**– ένα σαλόνι νυχιών** <u>eh</u>·nah sah·<u>loh</u>·nee nee·<u>khiohn</u>
– a spa	**– ένα σπα** <u>eh</u>·nah spah
– a travel agency	**– ένα ταξιδιωτικό γραφείο** <u>eh</u>·nah tah·ksee·THee·oh·tee·<u>koh</u> ghrah·<u>fee</u>·oh((Neuter))
Can you...this?	**Μπορείτε να...αυτό;** boh·<u>ree</u>·teh nah...ahf·<u>toh</u>
– alter	**– μεταποιήσετε** meh·tah·pee·<u>ee</u>·seh·teh
– clean	**– καθαρίσετε** kah·thah·<u>ree</u>·seh·teh

108

– mend	– **επιδιορθώσετε** eh·pee·THee·ohr·<u>thoh</u>·seh·teh
– press	– **σιδερώσετε** see·THeh·<u>roh</u>·seh·teh
When will *it/they* be ready?	**Πότε θα είναι** *έτοιμο/έτοιμα*; <u>poh</u>·teh thah ee·neh <u>eh</u>·tee·moh/<u>eh</u>·tee·mah

Spa

I'd like...	**Θα ήθελα...** thah <u>ee</u>·theh·lah...
– an *eyebrow/ bikini* wax	– **χαλάουα** *στα φρύδια/στο μπικίνι* khah·<u>lah</u>·oo·ah stah <u>free</u>·yah/stoh bee·<u>kee</u>·nee
– a facial	– **έναν καθαρισμό προσώπου** <u>eh</u>·nahn kah·thah·reez·<u>moh</u> proh·<u>soh</u>·poo
– a *manicure/ pedicure*	– **ένα** *μανικιούρ/πεντικιούρ* <u>eh</u>·nah mah·nee·kee·<u>oor</u>/pehn·dee·kee·<u>oor</u>
– a (sports) massage	– **ένα (αθλητικό) μασάζ** <u>eh</u>·nah (ahth·lee·tee·<u>koh</u>) mah·<u>sahz</u>
Do you do...?	**Κάνετε...;** <u>kah</u>·neh·teh...
– acupuncture	– **βελονισμό** veh·loh·neez·<u>moh</u>
– aromatherapy	– **αρωματοθεραπεία** ah·roh·mah·toh·theh·rah·<u>pee</u>·ah
– oxygen treatment	– **οξυγονοθεραπεία** oh·ksee·ghoh·noh·theh·rah·<u>pee</u>·ah
Is there a sauna?	**Υπάρχει σάουνα;** ee·<u>pahr</u>·kee sah·oo·nah

You will find spas and wellness centers, particularly at luxury hotels, in every major city and on most islands in Greece. You can visit these spas for a full day or for one treatment, without being a guest at the hotel. You will usually have to make an appointment in advance. Tipping is customary, particularly in hair salons, where customers may choose to tip the assistants or trainees.

Hair Salon

I'd like...	**Θα ήθελα...** thah ee·theh·lah...
– an appointment for *today/tomorrow*	– **να κλείσω ένα ραντεβού για** *σήμερα/αύριο* nah klee·soh eh·nah rahn·deh·voo yah *see·meh·rah/ahv·ree·oh*
– my hair styled	– **ένα χτένισμα** eh·nah khteh·nee·smah
– a hair cut	– **ένα κούρεμα** eh·nah koo·reh·mah
Don't cut it too short.	**Μην τα κόψετε πολύ κοντά.** meen tah koh·pseh·teh poh·lee kohn·dah
Shorter here.	**Πιο κοντά εδώ.** pioh kohn·dah eh·THoh

Sales Help

When do you *open/close*?	**Τι ώρα** *ανοίγετε/κλείνετε*; tee oh·rah ah·nee·gheh·teh/klee·neh·teh
Where is...?	**Πού είναι...;** poo ee·neh...
– the cashier [cash desk]	– **το ταμείο** toh tah·mee·oh
– the escalator	– **οι κυλιόμενες σκάλες** ee kee·lee·oh·meh·nehs skah·lehs
– the elevator [lift]	– **το ασανσέρ** toh ah·sahn·sehr
– the fitting room	– **το δοκιμαστήριο** toh THoh·kee·mahs·tee·ree·oh
– the store directory [guide]	– **ο οδηγός καταστήματος** oh oh·THee·ghohs kah·tahs·tee·mah·tohs
Can you help me?	**Μπορείτε να με βοηθήσετε;** boh·ree·teh nah meh voh·ee·thee·seh·teh
I'm just looking.	**Απλώς κοιτάω.** ahp·lohs kee·tah·oh
I'm being helped.	**Εξυπηρετούμαι.** eh·ksee·pee·reh·too·meh
Do you have any...?	**Έχετε καθόλου...;** eh·kheh·teh kah·thoh·loo...
Could you show me...?	**Μπορείτε να μου δείξετε...;** boh·ree·teh nah moo THee·kseh·teh...

Can you *ship/wrap* it?	**Μπορείτε να το *στείλετε/τυλίξετε*;** boh·<u>ree</u>·teh nah toh <u>stee</u>·leh·teh/ tee·<u>lee</u>·kseh·teh
How much?	**Πόσο;** <u>poh</u>·soh
That's all, thanks.	**Τίποτε άλλο, ευχαριστώ.** <u>tee</u>·poh·teh <u>ah</u>·loh ehf·khahr·ees·<u>toh</u>

▶ For clothing items, see page 117.

▶ For food items, see page 81.

▶ For souvenirs, see page 113.

You May Hear...

Μπορώ να σας βοηθήσω; boh·<u>roh</u> nah sahs voh·ee·<u>thee</u>·soh	Can I help you?
Μισό λεπτό. mee·<u>soh</u> lehp·<u>toh</u>	Just a moment.
Τί θα θέλατε; tee thah <u>theh</u>·lah·teh	What would you like?
Τίποτε άλλο; <u>tee</u>·poh·teh <u>ah</u>·loh	Anything else?

Preferences

I want something...	**Θέλω κάτι...** <u>theh</u>·loh <u>kah</u>·tee...
– cheap	– **φτηνό** ftee·<u>noh</u>
– expensive	– **ακριβό** ahk·ree·<u>voh</u>
– larger	– **μεγαλύτερο** meh·ghah·<u>lee</u>·teh·roh
– smaller	– **μικρότερο** meek·<u>roh</u>·teh·roh
– from this region	– **από αυτό το μέρος** ah·<u>poh</u> ahf·<u>toh</u> toh <u>meh</u>·rohs
Around...euros.	**Γύρω στα...ευρώ.** <u>yee</u>·roh stah...ehv·<u>roh</u>
Is it real?	**Είναι αληθινό;** ee·neh ah·lee·thee·<u>noh</u>

| Could you show me this/that? | **Μπορείτε να μου δείξετε *αυτό/εκείνο*;** boh·<u>ree</u>·teh nah moo <u>THee</u>·kseh·teh *ahf·<u>toh</u>/ eh·<u>kee</u>·noh* |

Decisions

That's not quite what I want.	**Δεν είναι ακριβώς αυτό που θέλω.** THehn <u>ee</u>·neh ahk·ree·<u>vohs</u> ahf·<u>toh</u> poo <u>theh</u>·loh
I don't like it.	**Δεν μου αρέσει.** THehn moo ah·<u>reh</u>·see
That's too expensive.	**Είναι πολύ ακριβό.** <u>ee</u>·neh poh·<u>lee</u> ahk·ree·<u>voh</u>
I'd like to think about it.	**Θα ήθελα να το σκεφτώ.** thah <u>ee</u>·theh·lah nah toh skehf·<u>toh</u>
I'll take it.	**Θα το πάρω.** thah toh <u>pah</u>·roh

Bargaining

That's too much.	**Είναι πολλά.** <u>ee</u>·neh poh·<u>lah</u>
I'll give you...	**Θα σας δώσω...** thah sahs <u>THoh</u>·soh...
I only have...euros.	**Έχω μόνο...ευρώ.** <u>eh</u>·khoh <u>moh</u>·noh...ehv·<u>roh</u>
Can you give me a discount?	**Μπορείτε να μου κάνετε έκπτωση;** boh·<u>ree</u>·teh nah moo <u>kah</u>·neh·teh <u>ehkp</u>·toh·see

▶ For numbers, see page 158.

Paying

How much?	**Πόσο;** <u>poh</u>·soh
I'll pay...	**Θα πληρώσω...** thah plee·<u>roh</u>·soh...
– by cash	**– τοις μετρητοίς** tees meht·ree·<u>tees</u>
– by credit card	**– με πιστωτική κάρτα** meh pees·toh·tee·<u>kee</u> <u>kahr</u>·tah
– by traveler's check [cheque]	**– με ταξιδιωτική επιταγή** meh tah·ksee·THyo·tee·<u>kee</u> eh·pee·tah·<u>yee</u>

A receipt, please.	**Μια απόδειξη, παρακαλώ.** miah ah·<u>poh</u>·THee·ksee pah·rah·kah·<u>loh</u>

You May Hear...

Πώς θα πληρώσετε; pohs thah plee·<u>roh</u>·seh·teh	How are you paying?
Μόνο μετρητά, παρακαλώ. <u>moh</u>·noh meht·ree·<u>tah</u> pah·rah·kah·<u>loh</u>	Cash only, please.
Εχετε ψιλά; <u>eh</u>·kheh·teh psee·<u>lah</u>	Do you have any smaller change?

Complaints

I'd like...	**Θα ήθελα...** thah <u>ee</u>·theh·lah...
- to exchange this	**– να αλλάξω αυτό** nah ah·<u>lah</u>·ksoh ahf·<u>toh</u>
- to return this	**– να επιστρέψω αυτό** nah eh·pees·<u>treh</u>·psoh ahf·<u>toh</u>
- a refund	**– επιστροφή των χρημάτων μου** eh·pees·troh·<u>fee</u> tohn khree·<u>mah</u>·tohn moo
- to see the manager	**– να δω τον διευθυντή** nah THoh tohn THee·ehf·theen·<u>dee</u>

Souvenirs

bottle of wine	**μπουκάλι κρασί** boo·<u>kah</u>·lee krah·<u>see</u>
box of pastries	**κουτί γλυκά** koo·<u>tee</u> ghlee·<u>kah</u>
dried Corinthian currants	**κορινθιακή σταφίδα** koh·reen·thee·ah·<u>kee</u> stah·<u>fee</u>·THah
ground Greek coffee	**ελληνικός καφές** eh·lee·nee·<u>kohs</u> kah·<u>fehs</u>
halva	**χαλβά** khahl·<u>vahs</u>
key ring	**μπρελόκ** breh·<u>lohk</u>

olives	**ελιές** eh·<u>liehs</u>
olive oil	**λάδι** <u>lah</u>·THee
pistachio nuts	**φυστίκια** fees·<u>tee</u>·kiah
postcard	**καρτποστάλ** kahrt·pohs·<u>tahl</u>
T-shirt	**μπλουζάκι** bloo·<u>zah</u>·kee
thyme honey	**θυμαρίσιο μέλι** thee·mah·<u>ree</u>·sioh <u>meh</u>·lee
Turkish delight	**λουκούμι** loo·<u>koo</u>·mee
Can I see *this/ that*?	**Μπορώ να δω *αυτό/εκείνο*;** boh·<u>roh</u> nah THoh ahf·<u>toh</u>/eh·<u>kee</u>·noh
The one in the *window/display case.*	**Αυτό στη βιτρίνα.** ahf·<u>toh</u> stee veet·<u>ree</u>·nah
I'd like...	**Θα ήθελα...** thah <u>ee</u>·theh·lah...
– a battery	**– μια μπαταρία** miah bah·tah·<u>ree</u>·ah
– a bracelet	**– ένα βραχιόλι** <u>eh</u>·nah vrah·<u>khioh</u>·lee
– a brooch	**– μια καρφίτσα** ♀ miah kahr·<u>fee</u>·tsah ♀
– earrings	**– ένα ζευγάρι σκουλαρίκια** <u>eh</u>·nah zehv·<u>gah</u>·ree skoo·lah·<u>ree</u>·kiah
– a necklace	**– ένα κολλιέ** <u>eh</u>·nah koh·<u>lieh</u>
– a ring	**– ένα δαχτυλίδι** <u>eh</u>·nah THahkh·tee·<u>lee</u>·THee
– a watch	**– ένα ρολόι** <u>eh</u>·nah roh·<u>loh</u>·ee
– copper	**– χαλκό** khahl·<u>koh</u>
– crystal	**– κρύσταλλο** <u>krees</u>·tah·loh
– diamond	**– διαμάντι** THiah·<u>mahn</u>·dee
– (*white/yellow*) gold	**– λευκόχρυσο/χρυσό** lehf·<u>koh</u>·khree·soh/ khree·<u>soh</u>
– pearl	**– μαργαριτάρι** mahr·ghah·ree·<u>tah</u>·ree
– pewter	**– κασσίτερο** kah·<u>see</u>·teh·roh
– platinum	**– πλατίνα** plah·<u>tee</u>·nah

– sterling silver	**– ασήμι** ah·<u>see</u>·mee
Is this real?	**Είναι αληθινό;** <u>ee</u>·neh ah·lee·thee·<u>noh</u>
Can you engrave it?	**Μπορείτε να το χαράξετε;** boh·<u>ree</u>·teh nah toh khah·<u>rah</u>·kseh·teh

> *i* There is a vast choice of souvenirs to buy in Greece. In all major tourist locations, you will find shops selling jewelry, handmade goods and other typical souvenirs. In Athens, there are some very nice jewelry shops in Monastiraki. You can find anything from ancient Greek-style jewelry to pieces made by contemporary designers. Handicrafts range from re-creations of ancient Greek pottery to textiles, and even handmade backgammon sets.

Antiques

How old is this?	**Πόσο παλιό είναι αυτό;** <u>poh</u>·soh pah·<u>lioh</u> <u>ee</u>·neh ahf·<u>toh</u>
Will I have problems with customs?	**Θα έχω προβλήματα με το τελωνείο;** thah <u>eh</u>·khoh prohv·<u>lee</u>·mah·tah meh toh teh·loh·<u>nee</u>·oh
Is there a certificate of authenticity?	**Υπάρχει πιστοποιητικό γνησιότητας;** ee·<u>pahr</u>·khee pees·toh·pee·ee·tee·<u>koh</u> ghnee·see·<u>oh</u>·tee·tahs

Clothing

Can I try this on?	**Μπορώ να το δοκιμάσω;** boh·<u>roh</u> nah toh THoh·kee·<u>mah</u>·soh
It doesn't fit.	**Δεν μου κάνει.** THehn moo <u>kah</u>·nee
It's too...	**Είναι πολύ...** <u>ee</u>·neh poh·<u>lee</u>...
– big	**– μεγάλο** meh·<u>ghah</u>·loh
– small	**– μικρό** meek·<u>roh</u>
– short	**– κοντό** kon·<u>doh</u>
– long	**– μακρύ** mak·<u>ree</u>
Do you have this in size...?	**Το έχετε στο μέγεθος...;** toh <u>eh</u>·kheh·teh stoh <u>meh</u>·yeh·thohs...
Do you have this in a *bigger/smaller* size?	**Το έχετε σε *μεγαλύτερο/μικρότερο* μέγεθος;** toh <u>eh</u>·kheh·teh seh meh·ghah·<u>lee</u>·teh·roh/ meek·<u>roh</u>·teh·roh meh·gheh·thohs

▶ For numbers, see page 158.

You May See...

ΑΝΔΡΙΚΑ ahn·<u>THree</u>·kah	men's clothing
ΓΥΝΑΙΚΕΙΑ yee·neh·<u>kee</u>·ah	women's clothing
ΠΑΙΔΙΚΑ peh·<u>THee</u>·kah	children's clothing

Color

I'm looking for something in...	**Ψάχνω κάτι σε...** <u>psahkh</u>·noh <u>kah</u>·tee seh...
– beige	– **μπεζ** behz
– black	– **μαύρο** <u>mahv</u>·roh
– blue	– **μπλε** bleh
– brown	– **καφέ** kah·<u>feh</u>
– green	– **πράσινο** <u>prah</u>·see·noh
– gray	– **γκρι** gree
– orange	– **πορτοκαλί** pohr·toh·kah·<u>lee</u>
– pink	– **ροζ** rohz
– purple	– **μωβ** mohv
– red	– **κόκκινο** <u>koh</u>·kee·noh
– white	– **άσπρο** <u>ahs</u>·proh
– yellow	– **κίτρινο** <u>keet</u>·ree·noh

Clothes and Accessories

backpack	**το σακκίδιο** toh sah·<u>kee</u>·THee·oh
belt	**η ζώνη** ee <u>zoh</u>·nee
bikini	**το μπικίνι** toh bee·<u>kee</u>·nee
blouse	**η μπλούζα** ee <u>bloo</u>·zah
bra	**το σουτιέν** toh soo·<u>tiehn</u>
briefs [underpants] (women's)	**το κυλοτάκι** toh kee·loh·<u>tah</u>·kee
briefs [underpants] (men's and women's)	**το σλιπ** toh sleep
coat	**το παλτό** toh pahl·<u>toh</u>
dress	**το φόρεμα** toh <u>foh</u>·reh·mah
hat	**το καπέλλο** toh kah·<u>peh</u>·loh

117

jacket	**το σακάκι** toh sah·<u>kah</u>·kee
jeans	**το μπλου-τζην** toh bloo·<u>jeen</u>
pants [trousers]	**το παντελόνι** toh pahn·deh·loh·nee
pantyhose [tights]	**το καλσόν** toh kahl·<u>sohn</u>
purse [handbag]	**η τσάντα** ee <u>tsahn</u>·dah
raincoat	**το αδιάβροχο** toh ah·THee·<u>ahv</u>·roh·khoh sah·<u>kah</u>·kee
scarf	**το κασκώλ** toh kahs·<u>kohl</u>
shirt	**το πουκάμισο** toh poo·<u>kah</u>·mee·soh
shorts	**το σόρτς** toh sohrts
skirt	**η φούστα** ee <u>foos</u>·tah
socks	**οι κάλτσες** ee <u>kahl</u>·tsehs
suit (men's/ women's)	**το κουστούμι/ταγιέρ** toh koos·<u>too</u>·mee/ tah·<u>yehr</u>
sunglasses	**τα γυαλιά ηλίου** tah yah·<u>liah</u> ee·<u>lee</u>·oo
sweater	**το πουλόβερ** toh poo·<u>loh</u>·vehr
sweatshirt	**το φούτερ** toh <u>foo</u>·ter
swimming trunks/ swimsuit	**το μαγιό** toh mah·<u>yoh</u>
T-shirt	**το μπλουζάκι** toh bloo·<u>zah</u>·kee
tie	**η γραβάτα** ee ghrah·<u>vah</u>·tah
underwear	**τα εσώρουχα** tah eh·<u>soh</u>·roo·khah

Fabric

I'd like...	**Θα ήθελα...** thah <u>ee</u>·theh·lah...
– cotton	**– βαμβακερό** vahm·vah·keh·<u>roh</u>
– denim	**– τζιν** <u>deh</u>·neem jeen
– lace	**– δαντέλα** THahn·<u>teh</u>·lah
– leather	**– δερμάτινο** THehr·<u>mah</u>·tee·noh

– linen	– **λινό** lee·<u>noh</u>
– silk	– **μεταξωτό** meh·tah·ksoh·<u>toh</u>
– wool	– **μάλλινο** <u>mah</u>·lee·noh
Is it machine washable?	**Πλένεται στο πλυντήριο;** <u>pleh</u>·neh·teh stoh pleen·<u>dee</u>·ree·oh

Shoes

I'd like...	**Θα ήθελα...** thah <u>ee</u>·theh·lah...
– high-heeled/flat shoes	– **τα ψηλοτάκουνα/επίπεδα παπούτσια** tah *psee·loh·<u>tah</u>·koo·nah/<u>ee</u>·siah* pah·<u>poo</u>·tsiah
– boots	– **οι μπότες** ee <u>boh</u>·tehs
– loafers	– **τα μοκασίνια** tah moh·kah·<u>see</u>·niah
– sandals	– **τα πέδιλα** tah <u>peh</u>·THee·lah
– shoes	– **τα παπούτσια** tah pah·<u>poo</u>·tsiah
– slippers	– **οι παντόφλες** ee pahn·<u>dohf</u>·lehs
– sneakers	– **τα αθλητικά παπούτσια** tah ahth·lee·tee·<u>kah</u> pah·<u>poo</u>·tsiah
In size...	**Στο νούμερο...** stoh <u>noo</u>·meh·roh...

▶ For numbers, see page 158.

Sizes

small	**μικρό** meek·<u>roh</u>
medium	**μεσαίο** meh·<u>seh</u>·oh
large	**μεγάλο** meh·<u>gha</u>·loh
extra large	**extra large** <u>eh</u>·xtrah lahrj
petite	**μικρό νούμερο** mee·<u>kroh</u> <u>noo</u>·meh·roh
plus size	**μεγάλο νούμερο** meh·<u>ghah</u>·loh <u>noo</u>·meh·roh

Newsstand and Tobacconist

Do you sell English-language *books*/ *newspapers*?	**Πουλάτε αγγλικές *εφημερίδες*/ *περιοδικά*;** poo·lah·teh ahng·lee·kehs eh·fee·meh·ree·THes/peh·rioh·THee·kah
I'd like...	**Θα ήθελα...** thah ee·theh·lah...
– chewing gum	**– τσίχλες** tseekh·lehs
– cigars	**– πούρα** poo·rah
– a *pack*/*carton* of cigarettes	**– ένα πακέτο/ μια κούτα τσιγάρα** eh·nah pah·keh·toh/miah koo·tah tsee·ghah·rah
– a lighter	**– έναν αναπτήρα** eh·nahn ah·nahp·tee·rah
– a magazine	**– ένα περιοδικό** eh·nah peh·ree·oh·THee·koh
– matches	**– σπίρτα** speer·tah
– a newspaper	**– μια εφημερίδα** miah eh·fee·meh·ree·THah
– pen	**– ένα στυλό** eh·nah stee·loh
– postcard	**– μια καρτ ποστάλ** miah kahrt poh·stahl
– a *road*/*town* map of...	**– έναν οδικό χάρτη/έναν χάρτη της πόλης για...** eh·nahn oh·THee·koh khahr·tee/ eh·nahn khahr·tee tees poh·lees yah...
– stamps	**– γραμματόσημα** ghrah·mah·toh·see·mah

Photography

I'm looking for...camera.	**Ψάχνω για...φωτογραφική μηχανή.** psahkh·noh yah...foh·tohgh·rah·fee·kee mee·khah·nee
– an automatic	**– μια αυτόματη** miah ahf·toh·mah·tee
– a digital	**– μια ψηφιακή** miah psee·fee·ah·kee
– a disposable	**– μια μιας χρήσεως** miah miahs khree·seh·ohs
I'd like...	**Θα ήθελα...** thah ee·theh·lah...
– a battery	**– μια μπαταρία** miah bah·tah·ree·ah

– digital prints	– **ψηφιακές εκτυπώσεις** psee·fee·ah·<u>kehs</u> ehk·tee·<u>poh</u>·sees
– a memory card	– **μια κάρτα μνήμης** miah·<u>kahr</u>·tah <u>mnee</u>·mees
Can I print digital photos here?	**Μπορώ να εκτυπώσω ψηφιακές φωτογραφίες εδώ;** boh·<u>roh</u> nah ehk·tee·<u>poh</u>·soh psee·fee·ah·<u>kehs</u> foh·toh·ghrah·<u>fee</u>·ehs eh·<u>THoh</u>

Sports and Leisure

Essential

When's the game?	**Πότε είναι ο αγώνας;** <u>poh</u>·teh <u>ee</u>·neh oh ah·<u>ghoh</u>·nahs
Where's...?	**Πού είναι...;** poo <u>ee</u>·neh...
– the beach	– **η παραλία** ee pah·rah·<u>lee</u>·ah
– the park	– **το πάρκο** toh <u>pahr</u>·koh
– the pool	– **η πισίνα** ee pee·<u>see</u>·nah
Is it safe to *swim/ dive* here?	**Είναι ασφαλές εδώ για *κολύμπι/ κατάδυση*;** <u>ee</u>·neh ahs·fah·<u>lehs</u> eh·<u>THoh</u> yah koh·<u>leem</u>·bee/kah·<u>tah</u>·THee·see
Can I rent [hire] golf clubs?	**Μπορώ να νοικιάσω μπαστούνια του γκόλφ;** boh·<u>roh</u> nah nee·<u>kiah</u>·soh bahs·<u>too</u>·niah too gohlf
How much per hour?	**Πόσο χρεώνεται η ώρα;** <u>poh</u>·soh khreh·<u>oh</u>·neh·teh ee <u>oh</u>·rah
How far is it to...?	**Πόσο μακριά είναι για...;** <u>poh</u>·soh mahk·ree·<u>ah</u> <u>ee</u>·neh yah...
Can you show me on the map?	**Μπορείτε να μου δείξετε στο χάρτη;** boh·<u>ree</u>·teh nah moo <u>THee</u>·kseh·teh stoh <u>khahr</u>·tee

Spectator Sports

When's...	Πότε είναι... poh·teh ee·neh...
– the basketball game	– ο αγώνας μπάσκετ oh ah·<u>ghoh</u>·nahs <u>bahs</u>·keht
– the boxing match	– ο αγώνας μποξ oh ah·<u>ghoh</u>·nahs bohks
– the cycling race	– ο αγώνας ποδηλασίας oh ah·<u>ghoh</u>·nahs poh·THee·lah·<u>see</u>·ahs
– the golf tournament	– το τουρνουά γκολφ toh toor·noo·<u>ah</u> gohlf
– the soccer [football] game	– ο αγώνας ποδοσφαίρου oh ah·<u>ghoh</u>·nahs poh·THohs·<u>feh</u>·roo
– the tennis match	– ο αγώνας τέννις oh ah·<u>ghoh</u>·nahs <u>teh</u>·nees
– the volleyball game	– ο αγώνας βόλεϊ oh ah·<u>ghoh</u>·nahs <u>voh</u>·leh·ee
Which teams are playing?	Ποιες ομάδες παίζουν; pee·<u>ehs</u> oh·<u>mah</u>·THehs <u>peh</u>·zoon
Where's...?	Πού είναι...; poo <u>ee</u>·neh...
– the horse track	– το ιπποδρόμιο toh ee·poh·<u>THroh</u>·mee·oh
– the racetrack	– ο ιππόδρομος oh ee·<u>poh</u>·THroh·mohs
– the stadium	– το στάδιο toh <u>stah</u>·THee·oh
Where can I place a bet?	Πού μπορώ να βάλω στοίχημα; poo boh·<u>roh</u> nah <u>vah</u>·loh <u>stee</u>·khee·mah

> **i** The most popular sport in Greece is **καλαθοσφαίρηση** (kah·lah·thohs·<u>feh</u>·ree·see), basketball; even the smallest towns have their own basketball teams.
> **Ποδόσφαιρο** (poh·<u>THohs</u>·feh·roh), soccer, is also popular, and matches are usually played on Sunday.
> Water sports are very popular on the islands and in coastal areas. However, you need a special permit to dive with oxygen tanks. Winter skiing has gained popularity in the last few years—there are more than 15 ski resorts on the mainland. Contact the tourist information office for details on locations and snow conditions.

Participating

Where's...?	**Πού είναι...;** poo <u>ee</u>·neh...
– the golf course	**– το γήπεδο του γκόλφ** toh <u>yee</u>·peh·THoh too gohlf
– the gym	**– το γυμναστήριο** toh gheem·nahs·<u>tee</u>·ree·oh
– the park	**– το πάρκο** toh <u>pahr</u>·koh
Where are the tennis courts?	**Πού είναι τα γήπεδα του τέννις;** poo ee·neh tah <u>ghee</u>·peh·THah too <u>teh</u>·nees
How much per...?	**Ποιο είναι το κόστος για...;** pioh <u>ee</u>·neh toh <u>kohs</u>·tohs yah...
– day	**– την ημέρα** teen ee·<u>meh</u>·rah
– hour	**– την ώρα** teen <u>oh</u>·rah
– game	**– το παιχνίδι** toh peh·<u>khnee</u>·THee
– round	**– το παιχνίδι** toh peh·<u>khnee</u>·THee
Can I rent [hire]...?	**Μπορώ να νοικιάσω...;** boh·<u>roh</u> nah nee·<u>kiah</u>·soh...
– golf clubs	**– μπαστούνια του γκόλφ** bahs·<u>too</u>·niah too gohlf
– equipment	**– εξοπλισμό** eh·ksohp·leez·<u>moh</u>
– a racket	**– μια ρακέτα** miah rah·<u>keh</u>·tah

At the Beach/Pool

Where's the *beach/pool*?	**Πού είναι η *παραλία/πισίνα*;** poo <u>ee</u>·neh ee pah·rah·<u>lee</u>·ah/pee·<u>see</u>·nah
Is there...?	**Υπάρχει...;** ee·<u>pahr</u>·khee...
– a kiddie [paddling] pool	– **παιδική πισίνα** peh·THee·<u>kee</u> pee·<u>see</u>·nah
– an *indoor/outdoor* pool	– *εσωτερική/εξωτερική* **πισίνα** eh·soh·teh·ree·<u>kee</u>/eh·ksoh·teh·ree·<u>kee</u> pee·<u>see</u>·nah
– a lifeguard	– **ναυαγοσώστης** nah·vah·ghoh·<u>sohs</u>·tees
Is it safe...?	**Είναι ασφαλές...;** <u>ee</u>·neh ahs·fah·<u>lehs</u>...
– to swim	– **εδώ για κολύμπι** eh·<u>THoh</u> yah koh·<u>leem</u>·bee
– to dive	– **εδώ για κατάδυση** eh·<u>THoh</u> yah kah·<u>tah</u>·THee·see
– for children	– **για παιδιά** yah peh·<u>THyah</u>
I want to rent...	**Θέλω να νοικιάσω...** <u>theh</u>·loh nah nee·<u>kiah</u>·soh...
– a deck chair	– **μια σεζ-λονγκ** miah <u>sehz</u>·lohng
– a jet-ski	– **ένα τζετ-σκι** <u>eh</u>·nah jeht skee
– a motorboat	– **μια εξωλέμβιο** miah eh·ksoh·<u>lehm</u>·vee·oh
– a sailing boat	– **ένα ιστιοπλοϊκό** <u>eh</u>·nah ees·tee·oh·ploh·ee·<u>koh</u>
– a surfboard	– **μιασανίδα του σέρφινγκ** miah sah·<u>nee</u>·THah too sehrf
– a towel	– **μια πετσέτα** miah peh·<u>tseh</u>·tah
– an umbrella [sunshade]	– **μια ομπρέλλα θαλάσσης** miah ohm·<u>breh</u>·lah thah·<u>lah</u>·sees
– water skis	– **πέδιλα θαλάσσιου σκι** <u>peh</u>·THee·lah thah·<u>lah</u>·see·oo skee

▶ For travel with children, see page 134.

i Greek beaches, which are usually free of charge, often offer a range of water sports. Beaches that are run by **EOT** require an entrance fee, but they tend to have more facilities. The use of jet-skis is restricted to a few beaches only, at a certain distance from the land and at specific hours (ask for more information at your resort). At many island and mainland resorts, nude sunbathing is acceptable; be sure to ask first, though, if you don't see others topless.

Winter Sports

A lift pass for *a day/few days*, please.	**Μια άδεια για *μια ημέρα/μερικές ημέρες*, παρακαλώ.** miah <u>ah</u>·THee·ah yah *miah ee·<u>meh</u>·rah/meh·ree·<u>kehs</u>* ee·<u>meh</u>·rehs pah·rah·kah·<u>loh</u>
I'd like to rent [hire]...	**Θα ήθελα να νοικιάσω...** thah <u>ee</u>·theh·lah nah nee·<u>kiah</u>·soh...
– boots	**– μπότες του σκι** <u>boh</u>·tehs too skee
– a helmet	**– ένα κράνος** <u>eh</u>·nah <u>krah</u>·nohs
– poles	**– μπαστούνια του σκι** bahs·<u>too</u>·niah too skee
– skis	**– πέδιλα του σκι** <u>peh</u>·THee·lah too skee
– a snowboard	**– μια σανίδα snowboard** miah sah·<u>nee</u>·THah snoh·oo·<u>bohrd</u>
– snowshoes	**– παπούτσια χιονιού** pah·<u>poo</u>·tsiah khioh·<u>nioo</u>
These are too *big/small*.	**Αυτά είναι πολυ *μεγάλα/μικρά*.** ahf·<u>tah</u> ee·neh poh·<u>lee</u> *meh·<u>ghah</u>·lah/meek·<u>rah</u>*
Are there lessons?	**Γίνονται μαθήματα;** <u>yee</u>·nohn·deh mah·<u>thee</u>·mah·tah
I'm experienced.	**Είμαι έμπειρος♂/έμπειρη♀.** <u>ee</u>·meh <u>ehm</u>·bee·rohs/<u>ehm</u>·bee·ree
A trail [piste] map, please.	**Έναν χάρτη της πίστας.** <u>eh</u>·nahn <u>khahr</u>·tee tees <u>pees</u>·tahs

You May See...

ΤΕΛΕΣΚΙ teh·leh·<u>skee</u>	ski lift
ΤΕΛΕΣΕΖ teh·leh·<u>sehz</u>	chair lift
ΤΕΛΕΦΕΡΙΚ teh·leh·feh·<u>reek</u>	cable car
ΠΙΣΤΑ ΑΡΧΑΡΙΩΝ <u>pees</u>·tah ahr·khahr·<u>ee</u>·ohn	baby slope
ΜΕΣΑΙΑ ΠΙΣΤΑ meh·<u>seh</u>·ah <u>pees</u>·tah	intermediate slope
ΠΙΣΤΑ ΠΡΟΧΩΡΗΜΕΝΩΝ <u>pees</u>·tah proh·khoh·ree·<u>meh</u>·nohn	advanced slope
ΠΙΣΤΑ ΚΛΕΙΣΤΗ pees·tah klees·tee	trail closed

In the Countryside

I'd like a map of...	**Θα ήθελα ένα χάρτη...** thah <u>ee</u>·theh·lah <u>eh</u>·nah <u>khahr</u>·tee...
– this region	**– αυτής της περιοχής** ahf·<u>tees</u> tees peh·ree·oh·<u>khees</u>
– walking routes	**– των διαδρομών περιήγησης** tohn THee·ah·THroh·<u>mohn</u> peh·ree·<u>ee</u>·yee·sees
– cycle routes	**– των ποδηλατόδρομων** tohn poh·THee·lah·<u>toh</u>·THroh·mohn
– the trails	**– των μονοπατιών** tohn moh·noh·pah·<u>tiohn</u>
Is it *easy/difficult?*	**Είναι εύκολο/δύσκολο;** ee·neh <u>ehf</u>·koh·loh/ <u>ees</u>·koh·loh
Is it *far/steep?*	**Είναι μακριά/απότομο;** ee·neh mahk·ree·<u>ah</u>/ ah·<u>poh</u>·toh·moh
How far is it to...?	**Πόσο μακριά είναι για...;** <u>poh</u>·soh mahk·ree·<u>ah</u> ee·neh yah...
Can you show me on the map?	**Μπορείτε να μου δείξετε στο χάρτη;** boh·<u>ree</u>·teh nah moo THee·kseh·teh stoh <u>khahr</u>·tee
I'm lost.	**Έχω χαθεί.** <u>eh</u>·khoh khah·<u>thee</u>

Where's...?	**Πού είναι...;** poo <u>ee</u>·neh...
– the ancient temple	**– ο αρχαίος ναός** oh ahr·<u>kheh</u>·ohs nah·<u>ohs</u>
– the ancient theater	**– το αρχαίο θέατρο** toh ahr·<u>kheh</u>·oh <u>theh</u>·ah·troh
– the bridge	**– η γέφυρα** ee <u>yeh</u>·fee·rah
– the cave	**– το σπήλαιο** toh <u>spee</u>·leh·oh
– the cliff	**– ο γκρεμός** oh greh·<u>mohs</u>
– the farm	**– η φάρμα** ee <u>fahr</u>·mah
– the forest	**– το δάσος** toh <u>THah</u>·sohs
– the gorge	**– το φαράγγι** toh fah·<u>rah</u>·gee
– the lake	**– η λίμνη** ee <u>leem</u>·nee
– the mountain	**– το βουνό** toh voo·<u>noh</u>
– the nature reserve	**– ο εθνικός δρυμός** oh ehth·nee·<u>kohs</u> THree·<u>mohs</u>
– the overlook [view point]	**– η πανοραμική θέση** ee pah·noh·rah·mee·<u>kee</u> <u>theh</u>·see
– the park	**– το πάρκο** toh <u>pahr</u>·koh
– the path	**– το μονοπάτι** toh moh·noh·<u>pah</u>·tee
– the peak	**– η κορυφή** ee koh·ree·<u>fee</u>
– the picnic area	**– η περιοχή για πικ-νικ** ee peh·ree·oh·<u>khee</u> yah peek·neek
– the river	**– ο ποταμός** oh poh·tah·<u>mohs</u>
– the sea	**– η θάλασσα** ee <u>thah</u>·lah·sah
– the thermal bath	**– τα ιαματικά λουτρα** tah ee·ah·mah·tee·<u>kah</u> loot·<u>rah</u>
– the hot spring	**– τα ιαματικά λουτρα** tah ee·ah·mah·tee·<u>kah</u> loot·<u>rah</u>
– the valley	**– η κοιλάδα** ee kee·<u>lah</u>·THah
– the volcano	**– το ηφαίστειο** toh ee·<u>feh</u>·stee·oh
– the waterfall	**– ο καταρράκτης** oh kah·tah·<u>rahk</u>·tees

Culture and Nightlife

Essential

What's there to do in the evenings?	**Τι μπορώ να κάνω τα βράδια;** tee boh·<u>roh</u> nah <u>kah</u>·noh tah <u>vrahTH</u>·yah
Do you have a program of events?	**Έχετε ένα πρόγραμμα εκδηλώσεων;** <u>eh</u>·kheh·teh <u>eh</u>·nah <u>prohgh</u>·rah·mah ehk·THee·<u>loh</u>·seh·ohn
What's playing at the movies [cinema] tonight?	**Τι παίζει ο κινηματογράφος απόψε;** tee <u>peh</u>·zee oh kee·nee·mah·tohgh·<u>rah</u>·fohs ah·<u>poh</u>·pseh
Where's...?	**Πού είναι...;** poo <u>ee</u>·neh...
– the downtown area	– **το κέντρο της πόλης** toh <u>kehn</u>·droh tees <u>poh</u>·lees
– the bar	– **το μπαρ** toh bahr
– the dance club	– **η ντισκοτέκ** ee dees·koh·<u>tehk</u>
Is there a cover charge?	**Υπάρχει κουβέρ;** ee·<u>pahr</u>·hee koo·<u>vehr</u>

Entertainment

Can you recommend...?	**Μπορείτε να συστήσετε...;** boh·<u>ree</u>·teh nah sees·<u>tee</u>·seh·teh...
– a concert	– **μια συναυλία** miah see·nahv·<u>lee</u>·ah
– a movie	– **μια ταινία** miah teh·<u>nee</u>·ah
– an opera	– **μια όπερα** miah <u>oh</u>·peh·rah
– a play	– **μια θεατρική παράσταση** miah theh·aht·ree·<u>kee</u> pah·<u>rahs</u>·tah·see
When does it *start/end*?	**Πότε *αρχίζει/τελειώνει*,** <u>poh</u>·teh ahr·<u>khee</u>·zee/teh·<u>lioh</u>·nee
What's the dress code?	**Πώς πρέπει να ντυθώ;** pohs <u>preh</u>·pee nah dee·<u>thoh</u>

I like...	**Μου αρέσει...** moo ah·<u>reh</u>·see...
- classical music	- **η κλασική μουσική** ee klah·see·<u>kee</u> moo·see·<u>kee</u>
- folk music	- **η δημοτική μουσική** ee THee·moh·tee·<u>kee</u> moo·see·<u>kee</u>
- jazz	- **η τζαζ** ee jahz
- pop music	- **η ποπ μουσική** ee pohp moo·see·<u>kee</u>
- rap	- **η ραπ** ee rahp

▶ For ticketing, see page 19.

i Nightlife in Greece is excellent. There are a great number of cafes, bars and dance and music clubs throughout cities and on the islands. Greeks will often start the evening around 10 p.m.; the evening will most likely go on well into the early hours at a nightclub or at **μπουζούκια** (boo·<u>zoo</u>·kee·ah), live music clubs. Bouzoukia are a big part of Greek nightlife, where Greeks often reserve a table and spend the evening listening, throwing flowers at their favorite singers and sometimes dancing on the tables. These clubs offer a range of musical genres: from traditional Greek music to contemporary pop. A typical evening there would end at around 5 a.m., when you will often encounter traffic jams along the main club strips. Clubbing is also very popular, with open-air summer clubs operating from about April to October.

You May Hear...

Παρακαλώ απενεργοποιήστε τα κινητά σας τηλέφωνα. pah·rah·kah·<u>loh</u> ah·peh·nehr·ghoh·pee·<u>ees</u>·teh tah kee·nee·<u>tah</u> sahs tee·<u>leh</u>·foh·nah	Turn off your cell [mobile] phones, please.

Nightlife

What's there to do in the evenings?	**Τι μπορώ να κάνω τα βράδια;**	tee boh·<u>roh</u> nah <u>kah</u>·noh tah <u>vrahTH</u>·yah
Can you recommend...?	**Μπορείτε να συστήσετε...;**	boh·<u>ree</u>·teh nah sees·<u>tee</u>·seh·teh...
– a bar	**– ένα μπαρ**	<u>eh</u>·nah bahr
– a casino	**– ένα καζίνο**	eh·nah kah·<u>zee</u>·noh
– a dance club	**– μια ντισκοτέκ**	miah dees·koh·<u>tehk</u>
– a gay club	**– ένα κλαμπ για γκέι**	<u>eh</u>·nah <u>geh</u>·ee klahb
– a jazz club	**– ένα κλαμπ με τζαζ μουσική**	<u>eh</u>·nah klahb meh jahz moo·see·<u>kee</u>
– a club with local music	**– ένα κλαμπ με τοπική μουσική**	<u>eh</u>·nah klahb meh toh·pee·<u>kee</u> moo·see·<u>kee</u>
Is there live music?	**Παίζει live μουσική;**	<u>peh</u>·zee <u>lah</u>·eev moo·see·<u>kee</u>
How do I get there?	**Πώς πάω εκεί;**	pohs <u>pah</u>·oh eh·<u>kee</u>
Is there a cover charge?	**Το κουβέρ χρεώνεται;**	toh koo·<u>vehr</u> khreh·<u>oh</u>·neh·teh
Let's go dancing.	**Πάμε για χορό.**	<u>pah</u>·meh yah khoh·<u>roh</u>

---

i The Athens Festival takes place every summer and includes various concerts and theatrical performances particularly in the Odeion of Herod Atticus and the Epidaurus Ancient Theater, among other venues. Look out for feast days, especially on the islands. Some smaller villages or towns will often hold an amazing party with food, drink and music to celebrate the feast day of the patron saint of the local church or of the town.
Very useful information in English can be found in the Athens News, a newspaper which includes TV, movie, theater and other cultural listings. Athens News also includes information on where to buy tickets for various events.

▼ Special Needs

Business Travel

Essential

I'm here on business.	**Είμαι εδώ για δουλειά.** ee·meh eh·<u>THoh</u> yah THoo·lee·<u>ah</u>
Here's my business card.	**Ορίστε η κάρτα μου.** oh·<u>rees</u>·teh ee <u>kahr</u>·tah moo
Can I have your card?	**Μου δίνετε την κάρτα σας;** moo <u>THee</u>·neh·teh teen <u>kahr</u>·tah sahs
I have a meeting with...	**Έχω μια συνάντηση με...** <u>eh</u>·khoh miah see·<u>nahn</u>·dee·see me...
Where's...?	**Πού είναι...;** poo <u>ee</u>·neh...
– the business center	**– το επαγγελματικό κέντρο** toh eh·pah·gehl·mah·tee·<u>koh</u> <u>kehn</u>·droh
– the convention hall	**– η αίθουσα συνεδριάσεων** ee <u>eh</u>·thoo·sah see·nehTH·ree·<u>ah</u>·seh·ohn
– the meeting room	**– η αίθουσα συσκέψεων** ee <u>eh</u>·thoo·sah sees·<u>keh</u>·pseh·ohn

Business Communication

I'm here to attend...	**Είμαι εδώ για να συμμετάσχω...** <u>ee</u>·meh eh·<u>THoh</u> yah nah see·meh·<u>tahs</u>·khoh...
– a seminar	**– σε ένα σεμινάριο** seh <u>eh</u>·nah seh·mee·<u>nah</u>·ree·oh
– a conference	**– σε μια σύσκεψη** seh miah <u>sees</u>·keh·psee
– a meeting	**– σε μια συνάντηση** seh miah see·<u>nahn</u>·dee·see
My name is...	**Λέγομαι...** <u>leh</u>·ghoh·meh...
May I introduce my colleague...?	**Να σας συστήσω τον♂/την♀ συνάδελφό μου...;** nah sahs sees·<u>tee</u>·soh tohn♂/teen♀ see·<u>nah</u>·THehl·<u>foh</u> moo...

I'm sorry I'm late.	**Συγγνώμη που άργησα.** seegh·<u>noh</u>·mee poo <u>ahr</u>·ghee·sah
I'd like an interpreter.	**Θα ήθελα έναν♂/μια♀ διερμηνέα.** thah <u>ee</u>·theh·lah <u>eh</u>·nahn♂/miah♀ THee·ehr·mee·<u>neh</u>·ah
You can reach me at the...Hotel.	**Μπορείτε να με βρείτε στο...Ξενοδοχείο.** boh·<u>ree</u>·teh nah meh <u>vree</u>·teh stoh...kseh·noh·THoh·<u>khee</u>·oh
I'm here until...	**Θα είμαι εδώ μέχρι...** thah <u>ee</u>·meh eh·<u>THoh</u> mekh·ree...
I need to...	**Χρειάζομαι να...** khree·<u>ah</u>·zoh·meh nah...
– make a call...	**– κάνω ένα τηλέφωνο...** <u>kah</u>·noh <u>eh</u>·nah tee·<u>leh</u>·foh·noh...
– make a photocopy	**– βγάλω μια φωτοτυπία** <u>vghah</u>·loh miah foh·toh·tee·<u>pee</u>·ah

I need to...	**Χρειάζομαι να...** khree·<u>ah</u>·zoh·meh nah...
– send an e-mail	**– στείλω ένα e-mail** <u>stee</u>·loh <u>eh</u>·nah ee·<u>meh</u>·eel
– send a fax	**– στείλω ένα φαξ** <u>stee</u>·loh <u>eh</u>·nah fahks
– send a package (overnight)	**– στείλω ένα πακέτο (αυθημερόν)** <u>stee</u>·loh <u>eh</u>·nah pah·<u>keh</u>·toh (ahf·thee·meh·<u>rohn</u>)
Nice to meet you.	**Χαίρω πολύ.** <u>kheh</u>·roh poh·<u>lee</u>

▶ For internet and communications, see page 47.

You May Hear...

Έχετε ραντεβού; <u>eh</u>·kheh·teh rahn·deh·<u>voo</u>	Do you have an appointment?
Με ποιον; meh piohn	With whom?
Είναι σε συνάντηση. <u>ee</u>·neh seh see·<u>nahn</u>·dee·see	*He/She* is in a meeting.
Μισό λεπτό. mee·<u>soh</u> lehp·<u>toh</u>	One moment, please.
Ευχαριστώ που ήρθατε. ehf·khah·rees·<u>toh</u> poo <u>eer</u>·thah·teh	Thank you for coming.

Travel with Children

Essential

Is there a discount for children?	**Υπάρχει μειωμένο εισιτήριο για παιδιά;** ee·<u>pahr</u>·khee mee·oh·<u>meh</u>·noh ee·see·<u>tee</u>·ree·oh yah peh·<u>THyah</u>
Can you recommend a babysitter?	**Μπορείτε να συστήσετε μια υπεύθυνη μπέιμπυ-σίτερ;** boh·<u>ree</u>·teh nah sees·<u>tee</u>·seh·teh miah ee·<u>pehf</u>·thee·nee <u>beh</u>·ee·bee <u>see</u>·tehr

Could I have a child's seat/highchair?	**Μπορούμε να έχουμε ένα παιδικό καθισματάκι/ μια καρέκλα μωρού;** boh·<u>roo</u>·meh nah <u>eh</u>·khoo·meh eh·nah peh·THee·<u>koh</u> kah·theez·mah·<u>tah</u>·kee/miah kah·<u>reh</u>·klah moh·<u>roo</u>
Where can I change the baby?	**Πού μπορώ να αλλάξω το μωρό;** poo boh·<u>roh</u> nah ah·<u>lah</u>·ksoh toh moh·<u>roh</u>

Fun with Kids

Can you recommend something for the kids?	**Μπορείτε να μας συστήσετε κάτι για τα παιδιά;** boh·<u>ree</u>·teh nah mahs sees·<u>tee</u>·seh·teh <u>kah</u>·tee yah tah peh·<u>THyah</u>
Where's...?	**Πού είναι...;** poo <u>ee</u>·neh...
– the amusement park	**– το πάρκο ψυχαγωγίας** toh <u>pahr</u>·koh psee·khah·ghoh·<u>yee</u>·ahs
– the arcade	**– η αίθουσα ψυχαγωγίας** ee <u>eh</u>·thoo·sah psee·khah·ghoh·<u>yee</u>·ahs
– the kiddie [paddling] pool	**– η παιδική πισίνα** ee peh·THee·<u>kee</u> pee·<u>see</u>·nah
– the park	**– το πάρκο** toh <u>pahr</u>·koh
– the playground	**– η παιδική χαρά** ee peh·THee·<u>kee</u> khah·<u>rah</u>
– the zoo	**– ο ζωολογικός κήπος** oh zoh·oh·loh·yee·<u>kohs</u> <u>kee</u>·pohs
Are kids allowed?	**Επιτρέπονται τα παιδιά;** eh·pee·<u>treh</u>·pohn·deh tah peh·<u>THyah</u>
Is it safe for kids?	**Είναι ασφαλές για παιδιά;** <u>ee</u>·neh ahs·fah·<u>lehs</u> yah tah peh·<u>THyah</u>
Is it suitable for...year olds?	**Είναι κατάλληλο για παιδιά...ετών;** <u>ee</u>·neh kah·<u>tah</u>·lee·loh yah peh·<u>THyah</u>...eh·<u>tohn</u>

▶ For numbers, see page 158.

You May Hear...

Τι όμορφο! tee <u>oh</u>·mohr·foh   How cute!

Πως *τον/την* λένε; pohs *tohn/teen* <u>leh</u>·neh   What's *his/her* name?

Πόσο χρονών είναι; <u>poh</u>·soh khroh·<u>nohn</u> ee·neh   How old is *he/she*?

Basic Needs for Kids

Do you have...?	Έχετε...; <u>eh</u>·kheh·teh...
– a baby bottle	– ένα μπιμπερό <u>eh</u>·nah bee·beh·<u>roh</u>
– baby wipes	– υγρά μαντηλάκια eegh·<u>rah</u> mahn·dee·<u>lah</u>·kiah
– a car seat	– ένα παιδικό κάθισμα <u>eh</u>·nah peh·THee·<u>koh</u> <u>kah</u>·thee·smah
– a children's menu	– έναν παιδικό κατάλογο <u>eh</u>·nahn peh·THee·<u>koh</u> kah·<u>tah</u>·loh·ghoh
– a child's portion	– μια παιδική μερίδα miah peh·THee·<u>kee</u> meh·<u>ree</u>·THah
– a *child's seat/ highchair*	– ένα παιδικό *κάθισμα/καρεκλάκι* <u>eh</u>·nah peh·ee·<u>koh</u> <u>kah</u>·theez·mah/kah·rehk·<u>lah</u>·kee moh·<u>roo</u>
– a *crib/cot*	– μια *κούνια/ένα παιδικό κρεβάτι* miah <u>koo</u>·niah/<u>eh</u>·nah peh·THee·<u>koh</u> kreh·<u>vah</u>·tee
– diapers [nappies]	– πάνες μωρού ee <u>pah</u>·nehs moh·<u>roo</u>
– formula	– βρεφικό γάλα vreh·fee·<u>koh</u> ghah·lah
– a pacifier [soother]	– μια πιπίλα miah pee·<u>pee</u>·lah
– a playpen	– ένα παιδικό παρκάκι <u>eh</u>·nah peh·THee·<u>koh</u> pahr·<u>kah</u>·kee
– a stroller [pushchair]	– ένα καροτσάκι <u>eh</u>·nah kah·roh·<u>tsah</u>·kee

| Can I breastfeed the baby here? | **Μπορώ να θηλάσω το μωρό εδώ;** boh·<u>roh</u> nah thee·<u>lah</u>·soh toh moh·<u>roh</u> eh·<u>THoh</u> |
| Where can I change the baby? | **Πού μπορώ να αλλάξω το μωρό;** poo boh·<u>roh</u> nah ah·<u>lah</u>·ksoh toh moh·<u>roh</u> |

▶ For dining with kids, see page 62.

Babysitting

Can you recommend a reliable babysitter?	**Μπορείτε να συστήσετε μια υπεύθυνη μπέιμπυ-σίτερ;** boh·<u>ree</u>·teh nah sees·<u>tee</u>·seh·teh miah ee·<u>pehf</u>·thee·nee <u>beh</u>·ee·bee <u>see</u>·tehr
What's the charge?	**Ποιό είναι το κόστος;** pioh <u>ee</u>·neh toh <u>kohs</u>·tohs
I'll pick them up at...	**Θα τα πάρω στις...** thah tah <u>pah</u>·roh stees...

▶ For time, see page 160.

| I can be reached at... | **Θα με βρείτε στο...** thah meh <u>vree</u>·teh stoh... |

Health and Emergency

Can you recommend a pediatrician?	**Μπορείτε να συστήσετε έναν παιδίατρο;** boh·<u>ree</u>·teh nah sees·<u>tee</u>·seh·teh eh·nahn peh·<u>THee</u>·aht·roh
My child is allergic to...	**Το παιδί μου είναι αλλεργικό σε...** toh peh·<u>THee</u> moo <u>ee</u>·neh ah·lehr·ghee·<u>koh</u> seh...
My child is missing.	**Λείπει το παιδί μου.** <u>lee</u>·pee toh peh·<u>THee</u> moo
Have you seen a boy/girl?	**Είδατε ένα *αγόρι/κορίτσι*;** <u>ee</u>·THah·teh eh·nah ah·<u>ghoh</u>·ree/koh·<u>ree</u>·tsee

▶ For food items, see page 81.

▶ For health, see page 143.

▶ For police, see page 141.

For the Disabled

Essential

Is there...?	**Υπάρχει...;** ee·<u>pahr</u>·khee...
– access for the disabled	**– πρόσβαση για άτομα με ειδικές ανάγκες;** <u>prohz</u>·vah·see yah ah·toh·mah meh ee·THee·<u>kehs</u> ah·<u>nahn</u>·gehs
– a wheelchair ramp	**– ράμπα για αναπηρικό καρότσι** <u>rahm</u>·bah yah ah·nah·pee·ree·<u>koh</u> kah·<u>roh</u>·tsee
– a handicapped- [disabled-] accessible toilet	**– προσβάσιμη τουαλέτα για ανάπηρους** prohs·<u>vah</u>·see·mee too·ah·<u>leh</u>·tah yah ah·<u>nah</u>·pee·roos
I need...	**Χρειάζομαι...** khree·<u>ah</u>·zoh·meh...
– assistance	**– βοήθεια** voh·<u>ee</u>·thiah
– an elevator [lift]	**– ασανσέρ** ah·sahn·<u>sehr</u>
– a ground-floor room	**– ισόγειο** ee·<u>soh</u>·yee·oh

Getting Help

I'm disabled. **Είμαι ανάπηρος.** ee-meh ah-<u>nah</u>-pee-rohs

I'm deaf. **Είμαι κουφός.** <u>ee</u>-meh koo-<u>fohs</u>

I'm *visually/ hearing* impaired. **Έχω προβλήματα *όρασης/ακοής.*** <u>eh</u>-khoh prohv-<u>lee</u>-mah-tah *<u>oh</u>-rah-sees/ah-koh-ees*

I'm unable to *walk far/use the stairs.* **Δεν μπορώ να *περπατήσω/χρησιμοποιήσω τις σκάλες.*** thehn boh-<u>roh</u> nah *pehr-pah-<u>tee</u>-soh/khree-see-moh-pee-<u>ee</u>-soh tees <u>skah</u>-lehs*

Can I bring my wheelchair? **Μπορώ να φέρω την αναπηρική μου καρέκλα;** boh-<u>roh</u> nah <u>feh</u>-roh teen ah-nah-pee-ree-<u>kee</u> moo kah-<u>rehk</u>-lah

Are guide dogs permitted? **Επιτρέπονται οι σκύλοι οδηγοί;** eh-peet-<u>reh</u>-pohn-deh ee <u>skee</u>-lee oh-THee-<u>ghee</u>

Can you help me? **Μπορείτε να με βοηθήσετε;** boh-<u>ree</u>-teh nah meh voh-ee-<u>thee</u>-seh-teh

Please *open/hold* the door. **Παρακαλώ *ανοίξτε/κρατείστε* την πόρτα.** pah-rah-kah-<u>loh</u> *ah-<u>nee</u>-ksteh/krah-<u>tee</u>-steh* teen <u>pohr</u>-tah

▼ Resources

Emergencies

Essential

Help!	**Βοήθεια!** voh·<u>ee</u>·thee·ah
Go away!	**Φύγετε!** <u>fee</u>·yeh·teh
Stop, thief!	**Σταματήστε τον κλέφτη!** stah·mah·<u>tees</u>·teh tohn <u>klehf</u>·tee
Get a doctor!	**Φωνάξτε ένα γιατρό!** foh·<u>nahks</u>·teh <u>eh</u>·nah yaht·<u>roh</u>
Fire!	**Φωτιά!** foh·<u>tiah</u>
I'm lost.	**Έχω χαθεί.** <u>eh</u>·khoh khah·<u>thee</u>
Can you help me?	**Μπορείτε να με βοηθήσετε;** boh·<u>ree</u>·teh nah meh voh·ee·<u>thee</u>·seh·teh

Police

Essential

Call the police!	**Φωνάξτε την αστυνομία!** foh·<u>nahks</u>·teh teen ahs·tee·noh·<u>mee</u>·ah
Where's the nearest police station?	**Πού είναι το κοντινότερο αστυνομικό τμήμα;** poo <u>ee</u>·neh toh kohn·dee·<u>noh</u>·teh·roh ahs·tee·noh·mee·<u>koh</u> tmee·mah
There has been an accident.	**Έγινε ένα ατύχημα.** <u>eh</u>·yee·neh eh·nah ah·<u>tee</u>·khee·mah
My child is missing.	**Λείπει το παιδί μου.** <u>lee</u>·pee toh peh·<u>THee</u> moo
I need...	**Χρειάζομαι...** khree·<u>ah</u>·zoh·meh...
– an interpreter	**– έναν διερμηνέα** <u>eh</u>·nahn THee·ehr·mee·<u>neh</u>·ah

I need...	**Χρειάζομαι...** khree·<u>ah</u>·zoh·meh...
– to contact my lawyer	**– να επικοινωνήσω με τον δικηγόρο μου** nah eh·pee·kee·noh·<u>nee</u>·soh meh tohn THee·kee·<u>ghoh</u>·roh moo
– to make a phone call	**– να κάνω ένα τηλέφωνο** nah <u>kah</u>·noh eh·nah tee·<u>leh</u>·foh·noh
I'm innocent.	**Είμαι αθώος♂/αθώα♀.** ee·meh ah·<u>thoh</u>·ohs♂/ah·<u>thoh</u>·ah♀

You May Hear...

Παρακαλώ συμπληρώστε αυτό το έντυπο. pah·rah·kah·<u>loh</u> sehm·blee·<u>rohs</u>·teh ahf·<u>toh</u> toh <u>ehn</u>·tee·poh	Please fill out this form.
Την ταυτότητά σας, παρακαλώ. teen tahf·<u>toh</u>·tee·<u>tah</u> sahs pah·rah·kah·<u>loh</u>	Your identification, please.
Πότε/Πού έγινε; <u>poh</u>·teh/poo eh·yee·neh	*When/Where did it happen?*
Πώς είναι εμφανισιακά; pohs <u>ee</u>·neh ehm·fah·nee·see·ah·<u>kah</u>	What does *he/she* look like?

Lost Property and Theft

I want to report...	**Θέλω να αναφέρω...** <u>theh</u>·loh nah ah·nah·<u>feh</u>·roh...
– a mugging	**– μια ληστεία** miah lehs·<u>tee</u>·ah
– a rape	**– έναν βιασμό** <u>eh</u>·nahn vee·ahs·<u>moh</u>
– a theft	**– μια κλοπή** miah kloh·<u>pee</u>
I've been *robbed/mugged*.	**Με έκλεψαν/λήστεψαν.** meh <u>ehk</u>·leh·psahn/<u>lees</u>·teh·psahn
I've lost my...	**Έχασα...** <u>eh</u>·khah·sah...

My...has/have been stolen.	**Μου έκλεψαν...μου.** moo ehk·leh·psahn...moo
– knapsack	– **τον σάκκο** tohn sah·koh
– bicycle	– **το ποδήλατο** toh poh·THee·lah·toh
– camera	– **τη φωτογραφική μηχανή** tee foh·tohgh·rah·fee·kee mee·khah·nee
– car	– **το αυτοκίνητο ι** toh ahf·toh·kee·nee·toh
– computer	– **τον υπολογιστή** tohn ee·poh·loh·yees·tee
– credit cards	– **τις πιστωτικές κάρτες** tees pees·toh·tee·kehs kahr·tehs
– jewelry	– **τα κοσμήματα** tah kohs·mee·mah·tah
– money	– **τα χρήματα** tah khree·mah·tah
– passport	– **το διαβατήριο** toh THiah·vah·tee·ree·oh
– purse	– **την τσάντα** teen tsahn·dah
– traveler's checks [cheques]	– **τις ταξιδιωτικές επιταγές** tees tah·ksee·THee·oh·tee·kehs eh·pee·tah·yehs
– wallet	– **το πορτοφόλι** toh pohr·toh·foh·lee

Health

Essential

I'm sick [ill].	**Είμαι άρρωστος.** ee·meh ah·rohs·tohs
I need an English-speaking doctor.	**Χρειάζομαι έναν γιατρό που να μιλάει αγγλικά.** khree·ah·zoh·meh eh·nahn yaht·roh poo nah mee·lah·ee ang·lee·kah
It hurts here.	**Με πονάει εδώ.** meh poh·nah·ee eh·THoh
I have a stomachache.	**Έχω στομαχόπονο.** eh·khoh stoh·mah·khoh·poh·noh

Finding a Doctor

Can you recommend a *doctor/dentist*?	**Μπορείτε να συστήσετε έναν *γιατρό/ οδοντίατρο*;** boh·<u>ree</u>·teh nah sees·<u>tee</u>·seh·teh eh·nahn *yaht·<u>roh</u>/oh·THohn·<u>dee</u>·aht·roh*
Could the doctor come to see me here?	**Μπορεί να έρθει να με δει εδώ ο γιατρός;** boh·<u>ree</u> nah <u>ehr</u>·thee nah meh THee eh·<u>THoh</u> oh yaht·<u>rohs</u>
I need an English-speaking doctor.	**Χρειάζομαι έναν γιατρό που να μιλάει αγγλικά.** khree·<u>ah</u>·zoh·meh <u>eh</u>·nahn yaht·<u>roh</u> poo nah mee·<u>lah</u>·ee ahng·lee·<u>kah</u>
What are the office hours?	**Ποιες ώρες δέχεται;** piehs <u>oh</u>·rehs <u>THeh</u>·kheh·teh
Can I make an appointment for...?	**Μπορώ να κλείσω ένα ραντεβού για...;** boh·<u>roh</u> nah <u>klee</u>·soh <u>eh</u>·nah rahn·deh·<u>voo</u> yah...
– today	**– σήμερα** <u>see</u>·meh·rah
– tomorrow	**– αύριο** <u>ahv</u>·ree·oh
– as soon as possible	**– όσο το δυνατό πιο σύντομα** <u>oh</u>·soh toh THee·nah·<u>toh</u> pioh <u>seen</u>·doh·mah
It's urgent.	**Είναι επείγον.** <u>ee</u>·neh eh·<u>pee</u>·ghohn

Symptoms

I'm...	**Έχω...** <u>eh</u>·khoh...
– bleeding	**– αιμορραγία** eh·moh·rah·<u>yee</u>·ah
– constipated	**– δυσκοιλιότητα** THees·kee·lee·<u>oh</u>·tee·tah
– dizzy	**– ζαλάδες** zah·<u>lah</u>·THehs
– nauseous	**– ναυτία** nahf·<u>tee</u>·ah
– vomiting	**– εμετούς** eh·meh·<u>toos</u>
It hurts here.	**Με πονάει εδώ.** meh poh·<u>nah</u>·ee eh·<u>THoh</u>
I have...	**Έχω...** <u>eh</u>·khoh...
– an allergic reaction	**– αλλεργική αντίδραση** ah·lehr·yee·<u>kee</u> ahn·<u>dee</u>·THrah·see

– a chest pain	– **πόνο στο στήθος** <u>poh</u>·noh stoh <u>stee</u>·thohs
– an earache	– **πόνο στο αυτί** <u>poh</u>·noh stoh ahf·<u>tee</u>
– a fever	– **πυρετό** pee·reh·<u>toh</u>
– a pain	– **πόνο** <u>poh</u>·noh
– a rash	– **εξάνθημα** eh·<u>ksahn</u>·thee·mah
– a sprain	– **διάστρεμμα** THee·<u>ahs</u>·treh·mah
– some swelling	– **πρήξιμο** <u>pree</u>·ksee·moh
– stomachache	– **στομαχόπονο** stoh·mah·<u>khoh</u>·poh·noh
– sunstroke	– **ηλίαση** ee·<u>lee</u>·ah·see
I've been sick [ill] for...days.	**Αισθάνομαι άρρωστος εδώ και...ημέρες.** ehs·<u>thah</u>·noh·meh <u>ah</u>·rohs·tohs eh·<u>THoh</u> keh...ee·<u>meh</u>·rehs

▶ For numbers, see page 158.

Health Conditions

I'm...	**Έχω...** <u>eh</u>·khoh...
– anemic	– **αναιμία** ah·neh·<u>mee</u>·ah
– asthmatic	– **άσθμα** <u>ahs</u>·thmah
– diabetic	– **διαβήτη** THiah·<u>vee</u>·tee
I'm allergic to *antibiotics/ penicillin*.	**Είμαι αλλεργικός *στα αντιβιωτικά/στην πενικιλίνη*.** <u>ee</u>·meh ah·lehr·yee·<u>kohs</u> stah ahn·dee·vee·oh·tee·<u>kah</u>/steen peh·nee·kee·<u>lee</u>·nee

▶ For food items, see page 81.

I have *arthritis/ (high/low) blood pressure*.	**Έχω *αρθρίτιδα/(υψηλή/χαμηλή) πίεση*.** <u>eh</u>·khoh ahr·<u>three</u>·tee·THah/(ee·psee·<u>lee</u>/khah·mee·<u>lee</u>) <u>pee</u>·eh·see
I have a heart condition.	**Έχω πρόβλημα καρδιάς.** <u>eh</u>·khoh <u>prohv</u>·lee·mah kahrTH·<u>yahs</u>
I'm on...	**Παίρνω...** <u>pehr</u>·noh...

You May Hear...

Τι συμβαίνει; tee seem·<u>veh</u>·nee — What's wrong?

Πού πονάει; poo poh·<u>nah</u>·ee — Where does it hurt?

Παίρνετε άλλα φάρμακα; <u>pehr</u>·neh·teh <u>ah</u>·lah <u>fahr</u>·mah·kah — Are you taking any other medication?

Είστε αλλεργικός♂/αλλεργική♀ σε κάτι; <u>ees</u>·teh ah·lehr·yeek·<u>ohs</u>♂/ah·lehr·yeek·<u>ee</u>♀ seh <u>kah</u>·tee — Are you allergic to anything?

Ανοίξτε το στόμα σας. ah·<u>nee</u>·ksteh toh <u>stoh</u>·mah sahs — Open your mouth.

Πάρτε μια βαθιά αναπνοή. <u>pahr</u>·teh miah vah·<u>thiah</u> ah·nahp·noh·<u>ee</u> — Breathe deeply.

Θέλω να πάτε στο νοσοκομείο. <u>theh</u>·loh nah <u>pah</u>·teh stoh noh·soh·koh·<u>mee</u>·oh — I want you to go to the hospital.

Hospital

Please notify my family.
Παρακαλώ ειδοποιήστε την οικογένειά μου. pah·rah·kah·<u>loh</u> ee·THoh·pee·<u>ees</u>·teh teen ee·koh·<u>yeh</u>·nee·<u>ah</u> moo

I'm in pain.
Πονάω. poh·<u>nah</u>·oh

I need a *doctor/ nurse.*
Χρειάζομαι *έναν γιατρό/μια νοσοκόμα.* khree·<u>ah</u>·zoh·meh *eh·nahn yaht·<u>roh</u>/miah noh·soh·<u>koh</u>·mah*

When are visiting hours?
Ποιες είναι οι ώρες επισκεπτηρίου; pee·<u>ehs</u> <u>ee</u>·neh ee <u>oh</u>·rehs eh·pees·kehp·tee·<u>ree</u>·oo

I'm visiting...
Επισκέπτομαι... eh·pees·<u>kehp</u>·toh·meh...

Dentist

I've broken a tooth.	**Έσπασα ένα δόντι.**	ehs·pah·sah eh·nah THohn·dee
I'm lost a filling.	**Μου έφυγε ένα σφράγισμα.**	moo eh·fee·gheh eh·nah sfrah·yees·mah
This tooth hurts.	**Αυτό το δόντι με πονάει.**	ahf·toh toh THohn·dee meh poh·nah·ee
Can you fix this denture?	**Μπορείτε να φτιάξετε αυτή την τεχνητή οδοντοστοιχία;**	boh·ree·teh nah ftee·ah·kseh·teh ahf·tee teen tehkh·nee·tee oh·THohn·dohs·tee·khee·ah

Gynecologist

I have menstrual cramps/a vaginal infection.	**Έχω *πόνους περιόδου/κολπική μόλυνση*.**	eh·khoh *poh·noos peh·ree·oh·THoo/ kohl·pee·kee moh·leen·see*
I missed my period.	**Έχω καθυστέρηση.**	eh·khoh kah·thees·teh·ree·see
I'm on the Pill.	**Παίρνω αντισυλληπτικό χάπι.**	pehr·noh ahn·dee·see·leep·tee·koh khah·pee
I'm (not) pregnant.	**(Δεν) Είμαι έγκυος.**	(THehn) ee·meh ehn·gee·ohs
I haven't had my period for...months.	**Δεν έχω περίοδο εδώ και...μήνες.**	THehn eh·khoh peh·ree·oh·THoh eh·THoh keh...mee·nehs

▶ For numbers, see page 158.

Optician

I've lost...	**Έχασα...**	eh·khah·sah...
- a contact lens	**– έναν φακό επαφής**	eh·nahn fah·koh eh·pah·fees
- my glasses	**– τα γυαλιά μου**	tah yah·lee·ah moo
- a lens	**– έναν φακό**	eh·nahn fah·koh

Payment and Insurance

How much?	**Πόσο;** <u>poh</u>·soh
Can I pay by credit card?	**Μπορώ να πληρώσω με αυτή την πιστωτική κάρτα;** boh·<u>roh</u> nah plee·<u>roh</u>·soh meh ahf·<u>tee</u> teen pees·toh·tee·<u>kee</u> kahr·tah
I have insurance.	**Έχω ασφάλεια.** <u>eh</u>·khoh ahs·<u>fah</u>·lee·ah
Can I have a receipt for my insurance?	**Μπορώ να έχω μια απόδειξη για την ασφάλεια υγείας μου;** boh·<u>roh</u> nah <u>eh</u>·khoh miah ah·<u>poh</u>·THee·ksee yah teen ahs·<u>fah</u>·lee·ah ee·<u>yee</u>·ahs moo

Pharmacy [Chemist]

Essential

Where's the nearest pharmacy [chemist]?	**Πού είναι το κοντινότερο φαρμακείο;** poo <u>ee</u>·neh toh kohn·dee·<u>noh</u>·teh·roh fahr·mah·<u>kee</u>·oh
What time does the pharmacy [chemist] *open/close*?	**Τι ώρα *ανοίγει/κλείνει* το φαρμακείο;** tee <u>oh</u>·rah ah·<u>nee</u>·yee/<u>klee</u>·nee toh fahr·mah·<u>kee</u>·oh
What would you recommend for...?	**Τι συνιστάτε για...;** tee see·nees·<u>tah</u>·teh yah...
How much should I take?	**Πόσο πρέπει να πάρω;** <u>poh</u>·soh <u>preh</u>·pee nah <u>pah</u>·roh
Can you fill [make up] this prescription for me?	**Μπορείτε να μου φτιάξετε αυτή τη συνταγή;** boh·<u>ree</u>·teh nah moo <u>ftiah</u>·kseh·teh ahf·<u>tee</u> tee seen·dah·<u>yee</u>
I'm allergic to...	**Είμαι αλλεργικός♂/αλλεργική♀ σε ...** <u>ee</u>·meh ah·lehr·yeek·<u>ohs</u>♂/ah·lehr·yeek·<u>ee</u>♀ seh...

Many medications that are prescription-only in other countries can be bought over the counter in Greece. Pharmacies are open during normal working hours and on a rotating basis at all other times, so that there will always be one open 24 hours a day in any given area. Read the list on display in all pharmacy windows to find the one nearest to you.

Dosage Instructions

How much should I take?	**Πόσο πρέπει να πάρω;** <u>poh</u>·soh <u>preh</u>·pee nah <u>pah</u>·roh
How many times a day should I take it?	**Πόσες φορές την ημέρα πρέπει να το παίρνω;** <u>poh</u>·sehs foh·<u>rehs</u> teen ee·<u>meh</u>·rah <u>preh</u>·pee nah toh <u>pehr</u>·noh
Is it suitable for children?	**Είναι κατάλληλο για παιδιά;** <u>ee</u>·neh kah·<u>tah</u>·lee·loh yah peh·<u>THyah</u>
I'm taking...	**Παίρνω...** <u>pehr</u>·noh...
Are there side effects?	**Έχει παρενέργειες;** <u>eh</u>·khee pah·reh·<u>nehr</u>·yee·ehs

You May See...

ΧΑΠΙ(Α) <u>khah</u>·pee(ah)	tablet(s)
ΣΤΑΓΟΝΕΣ stah·<u>ghoh</u>·nehs	drops
ΠΡΙΝ/ΜΕΤΑ/ΜΕ ΤΟ ΓΕΥΜΑ preen/me·<u>tah</u>/ meh toh <u>yehv</u>·mah	before/after/with meals
ΜΕ ΑΔΕΙΟ ΣΤΟΜΑΧΙ meh <u>ah</u>·THioh stoh·<u>mah</u>·khee	on an empty stomach
ΜΟΝΟ ΓΙΑ ΕΞΩΤΕΡΙΚΗ ΧΡΗΣΗ <u>moh</u>·noh ya eh·ksoh·teh·ree·<u>kee</u> <u>khree</u>·see	for external use only
ΜΙΑ/ΔΥΟ/ΤΡΕΙΣ ΦΟΡΕΣ ΤΗΝ ΗΜΕΡΑ miah/ <u>ee</u>·oh/trees foh·<u>rehs</u> teen ee·<u>meh</u>·rah	once/twice/three times a day

Health Problems

I'd like some medicine for...	**Θα ήθελα ένα φάρμακο για...** thah <u>ee</u>·theh·lah <u>eh</u>·nah <u>fahr</u>·mah·koh yah...
– a cold	– **το κρυολόγημα** toh kree·oh·<u>loh</u>·yee·mah
– a cough	– **το βήχα** toh <u>vee</u>·khah
– diarrhea	– **τη διάρροια** tee THee·<u>ah</u>·ree·ah
– hay fever	– **την αλλεργία σε γύρη** teen ah·lehr·<u>yee</u>·ah seh <u>yee</u>·ree
– insect bites	– **το τσίμπημα από έντομο** toh <u>tseem</u>·bee·mah ah·<u>poh</u> <u>ehn</u>·doh·moh
– motion [travel] sickness	– **τη ναυτία** tee nahf·<u>tee</u>·ah
– a sore throat	– **τον πονόλαιμο** tohn poh·<u>noh</u>·leh·moh
– sunburn	– **τα εγκαύματα από τον ήλιο** tah eh·<u>gkahv</u>·mah·tah ahpoh tohn <u>ee</u>·lioh
– an upset stomach	– **το στομαχόπονο** toh stoh·mah·<u>khoh</u>·poh·noh

Basic Needs

I'd like...	**Θα ήθελα...** thah <u>ee</u>·theh·lah...
– acetaminophen [paracetamol]	– **παρακεταμόλη** pah·rah·keh·tah·<u>moh</u>·lee
– antiseptic cream	– **μια αντισηπτική κρέμα** miah ahn·dee·seep·tee·<u>kee</u> <u>kreh</u>·mah
– aspirin	– **ασπιρίνη** ahs·pee·<u>ree</u>·nee
– bandages	– **επιδέσμους** eh·pee·<u>THehz</u>·moos
– a comb	– **μια χτένα** miah <u>khteh</u>·nah
– condoms	– **προφυλακτικά** proh·fee·lahk·tee·<u>kah</u>
– contact lens solution	– **ένα υγρό καθαρισμού φακών επαφής** eegh·<u>roh</u> kah·thah·rees·<u>moo</u> fah·<u>kohn</u> eh·pah·<u>fees</u>
– deodorant	– **ένα αποσμητικό** <u>eh</u>·nah ah·pohz·mee·tee·<u>koh</u>
– a hairbrush	– **μια βούρτσα** miah <u>voor</u>·tsah
– hair spray	– **μια λακ** miah lahk
– ibuprofen	– **ιμπουπροφέν** ee·boo·proh·<u>fehn</u>
– insect repellent	– **εντομοαπωθητικό** ehn·doh·moh·ah·poh·thee·tee·<u>koh</u>
– a nail file	– **μια λίμα για τα νύχια** miah <u>lee</u>·mah yah tah <u>nee</u>·khiah
– a (disposable) razor	– **ένα ξυραφάκι (μιας χρήσης)** <u>eh</u>·nah ksee·rah·<u>fah</u>·kee (miahs <u>khree</u>·sees)
– razor blades	– **ξυραφάκια** ksee·rah·<u>fah</u>·kiah
– sanitary napkins [pads]	– **σερβιέτες** sehr·vee·<u>eh</u>·tehs
– shampoo conditioner	– **σαμπουάν/γαλάκτωμα για τα μαλλιά** sahm·poo·<u>ahn</u>/ghah·<u>lahk</u>·toh·mah yah tah mah·<u>liah</u>
– soap	– **ένα σαπούνι** <u>eh</u>·nah sah·<u>poo</u>·nee

I'd like...	**Θα ήθελα...** thah ee·theh·lah...
- sunscreen	– **αντιηλιακό** ahn·dee·ee·lee·ah·<u>koh</u>
- tampons	– **ταμπόν** tahm·<u>bohn</u>
- tissues	– **χαρτομάντηλα** khahr·toh·<u>mahn</u>·dee·lah
- toilet paper	– **χαρτί υγείας** khahr·<u>tee</u> ee·<u>yee</u>·ahs
- a toothbrush	– **οδοντόβουρτσα** oh·THoh·<u>ndoh</u>·voor·tsah
- toothpaste	– **μια οδοντόπαστα** miah oh·THohn·<u>doh</u>·pah·stah

▶ For baby products, see page 136.

Reference

Greeks generally use **εσείς** (eh·<u>sees</u>) the plural form of "you" with people they do not know well. The familiar, singular form **εσύ** (eh·<u>see</u>), is used among friends and with children, but don't worry too much - you will not be considered rude, just friendly!

Grammar

Verbs

Below are three of the main categories of regular verbs in the present tense. Using the endings indicated after the dash, you can use a large number of verbs competently.

Greek verbs are divided in categories that are formed by using certain endings and are conjugated accordingly. Some of the most popular endings are:

– **ω** oh	– **έρνω** <u>ehr</u>·noh
– **νω** noh	– **αίνω** <u>eh</u>·noh
– **άζω** <u>ah</u>·zoh	– **ένω** <u>eh</u>·noh

– άω ah·oh	– άσκω <u>as</u>·koh
– ήνω ee·noh	– όμαι <u>oh</u>·meh
– ώνω <u>oh</u>·noh	– άμαι <u>ah</u>·meh
– έλνω <u>ehl</u>·noh	– έμαι <u>eh</u>·meh

Είμαι (to be)	Present
I am	**Εγώ είμαι** eh·<u>goh</u> <u>ee</u>·meh
You are	**Εσύ είσαι** eh·<u>see</u> <u>ee</u>·seh
He is	**Αυτός είναι** ahf·<u>tohs</u> <u>ee</u>·neh
She is	**Αυτή είναι** ahf·<u>tee</u> <u>ee</u>·neh
We are	**Εμείς είμαστε** eh·<u>mees</u> <u>eem</u>·ah·steh
You are	**Εσείς είστε** eh·<u>sees</u> <u>ee</u>·steh
They are	**Αυτοί είναι** ahf·<u>tee</u> <u>ee</u>·neh

Αφήνω (to let)	Present
I let	**Εγώ αφήνω** ah·<u>fee</u>·noh
You let	**Εσύ αφήνεις** ah·<u>fee</u>·nees
He lets	**Αυτός αφήνει** ah·<u>fee</u>·nee
She lets	**Αυτή αφήνει** ah·<u>fee</u>·nee
We let	**Εμείς αφήνουμε** ah·<u>fee</u>·noo·meh
You let	**Εσείς αφήνετε** ah·<u>fee</u>·neh·teh
They let	**Αυτοί αφήνουν** ah·<u>fee</u>·noon

Φέρνω (to bring)	Present
I bring	**Εγώ φέρνω** <u>fehr</u>·noh
You bring	**Εσύ φέρνεις** <u>fehr</u>·nees
He brings	**Αυτός φέρνει** <u>feh</u>·rnee
She brings	**Αυτή φέρνει** <u>fehr</u>·nee

sing. = singular, pl. = plural, form. = formal

Φέρνω (to bring)	Present
We bring	**Εμείς φέρνουμε** <u>feh</u>·rnoo·meh
You bring	**Εσείς φέρνετε** <u>feh</u>·neh·teh
They bring	**Αυτοί φέρνουν** <u>fehr</u>·noon

The infinitive/first person of most Greek verbs end in –ω:
to do   **κάνω**   <u>kah</u>·noh

To conjugate this verb, drop the final **ω**, and add the appropriate ending:

Κάνω (to do)	Present
I do	**Εγώ κάνω** eh·<u>goh</u> <u>kahn</u>·oh
You do (familiar or sing.)	**Εσύ κάνεις** eh·<u>see</u> <u>kahn</u>·ees
He does	**Αυτός κάνει** ahf·<u>tohs</u> <u>kahn</u>·ee
She does	**Αυτή κάνει** ahf·<u>tee</u> <u>kahn</u>·ee
We do	**Εμείς κάνουμε** eh·<u>mees</u> <u>kahn</u>·oo·meh
You do (form., pl.)	**Εσείς κάνετε** eh·<u>sees</u> <u>kahn</u>·eh·teh
They do	**Αυτοί κάνουν** ahf·<u>tee</u> <u>kahn</u>·oun

So, by applying this rule you can conjugate another verb ending in –ω:

Γράφω (to write)	Present
I write	**Εγώ γράφω** eh·<u>goh</u> <u>grahf</u>·oh
You write	**Εσύ γράφεις** eh·<u>see</u> <u>grahf</u>·ees
He writes	**Αυτός γράφει** ahf·<u>tohs</u> <u>grahf</u>·ee
She writes	**Αυτή γράφει** ahf·<u>tee</u> <u>grahf</u>·ee
We write	**Εμείς γράφουμε** eh·<u>mees</u> <u>grahf</u>·oo·meh
You write	**Εσείς γράφετε** eh·<u>sees</u> <u>grahf</u>·eh·teh
They write	**Αυτοί γράφουν** ahf·<u>ee</u> <u>grahf</u>·oon

Nouns and Articles

There are three genders in Greek: masculine, feminine and neuter;

all nouns in Greek are assigned a specific gender. The gender of the article changes based on the gender of the noun it modifies. For example:

She is tall.	**Είναι ψηλή.** <u>ee</u>·neh psee·<u>lee</u>	
He is tall.	**Είναι ψηλός.** <u>ee</u>·neh psee·<u>lohs</u>	

The article **o** (oh) is used with masculine nouns, **η** (ee) with feminine nouns and **το** (toh) with neuter nouns.

masculine	**ο καφές** oh kah·<u>fehs</u>	the coffee
feminine	**η μπίρα** ee <u>bee</u>·rah	the beer
neuter	**το τρένο** toh <u>treh</u>·noh	the train

Greek nouns have four cases: nominative, genitive, accusative and vocative. A simple way to explain their use would be that the nominative indicates the subject, the genitive indicates possession, the accusative indicates the object and the vocative is used to address someone. Don't worry too much about this. In most cases, people will understand what you are saying even if you use a noun with the wrong case. The words in the dictionary are in nominative.

There is no easy way to form the plural. Beginner speakers of Greek should clearly state the number along with the noun to be easily understood.

Word Order

Syntax in Greek, especially in everyday spoken language, is very flexible. The standard word order is subject-verb-object, but you can change the order of sentence components to shift emphasis.
Example:
Το τρένο φεύγει τώρα.   toh <u>treh</u>·noh <u>fehv</u>·ghee toh·rah
The train leaves now.
You can say the same thing by placing the verb at the beginning of the sentence:
Φεύγει το τρένο τώρα.   <u>fehv</u>·ghee toh <u>treh</u>·noh <u>toh</u>·rah
The train leaves now.

Also, use an interrogatory intonation to turn this sentence into a question. The question form can work both with the verb in the beginning and at the end of the sentence.

Τώρα φεύγει το τραίνο;   toh·rah <u>fehv</u>·ghee toh <u>treh</u>·noh

Is the train leaving now?

Note that, in Greek, the equivalent of a semi-colon (;) is used in place of a question mark.

Negation

To form a negative sentence in Greek, add the word **δεν** (THehn) before the verb.

Example:

Θέλω	<u>theh</u>·loh	I want
Δεν θέλω	THehn <u>theh</u>·loh	I don't want

Imperatives

Imperative sentences are formed by adding the appropriate ending to the stem of the verb. The endings used to form the imperative of a verb are mainly **–α** (ah), **–ε** (eh), **–ήσου** (<u>ee</u>·soo), **–άσου** (<u>ah</u>·soo).

Examples:	**πηγαίνω**	pee·<u>yeh</u>·noh	to go
	Πήγαινε!	<u>pee</u>·yeh·neh	Go!
	βιάζομαι	<u>viah</u>·zoh·meh	to hurry
	Βιάσου!	<u>viah</u>·soo	Hurry!

Comparative and Superlative

The comparative form of adjectives is usually formed by adding the word **πιο** (pioh) before the adjective. Also, in certain cases, the comparative may be formed by adding the ending **–ερος**♂ (eh·rohs), **–ερη**♀ (eh·ree), **–ερο** (eh·roh) (neuter) to the stem of an adjective, respectively. To form the superlative of an adjective, add the ending **–ατος**♂ (ah·tohs), **–ατη**♀ (ah·tee), **–ατο** (ah·tee) (neuter) to the stem of the adjective.

Possessive Pronouns

mine	μου	moo
yours	σου	soo
his/her/its	του/της/του	too/tees/too
ours	μας	mahs
yours	σας	sahs
theirs	τους	toos

Example:

Το βιβλίο είναι δικό μου. toh veev·<u>lee</u>·oh ee·neh thee·<u>koh</u> moo
This book is mine.

Adjectives and Adverbs

Adjectives agree with the noun they describe in gender, case and number. The most common ending for a feminine adjective is **–η** (ee), for a masculine adjective it is **–ος** (ohs) and for the neuter **o** (oh).
Example:

Είναι γρήγορος οδηγός. <u>ee</u>·neh <u>ghree</u>·ghoh·rohs oh·THee·<u>ghohs</u>
He is a fast driver.

Είναι γρήγορη οδηγός. <u>ee</u>·neh <u>ghree</u>·ghoh·ree oh·THee·<u>ghohs</u>
She is a fast driver.

Είναι γρήγορο αυτοκίνητο. <u>ee</u>·neh <u>ghree</u>·ghoh·roh ah·ftoh·<u>kee</u>·nee·toh
This is a fast car.

Adverbs are used to describe the action of verbs. Almost all adverbs are formed by adding the ending **–α** (ah) to the stem of the adjective.
Example:

Οδηγεί γρήγορα. oh·THee·<u>yee</u> <u>ghree</u>·ghoh·rah
He drives quickly.

Essential

0	**μηδέν** mee·<u>THEh</u>n
1	**ένας** <u>eh</u>·nahs
2	**δύο** <u>THee</u>·oh
3	**τρεις** trees
4	**τέσσερις** <u>teh</u>·seh·rees
5	**πέντε** <u>pehn</u>·deh
6	**έξι** <u>eh</u>·ksee
7	**επτά** eh·<u>ptah</u>
8	**οκτώ** oh·<u>ktoh</u>
9	**εννέα** eh·<u>neh</u>·ah
10	**δέκα** <u>THeh</u>·kah
11	**έντεκα** <u>ehn</u>·deh·kah
12	**δώδεκα** <u>THoh</u>·THEh·kah
13	**δεκατρία** THeh·kah·<u>tree</u>·ah
14	**δεκατέσσερα** THeh·kah·<u>teh</u>·seh·rah
15	**δεκαπέντε** THeh·kah·<u>pehn</u>·deh
16	**δεκαέξι** THeh·kah·<u>eh</u>·ksee
17	**δεκαεπτά** THeh·kah·eh·<u>ptah</u>
18	**δεκαοκτώ** THeh·kah·oh·<u>ktoh</u>
19	**δεκαεννέα** THeh·kah·eh·<u>neh</u>·ah
20	**είκοσι** <u>ee</u>·koh·see
21	**είκοσι ένα** <u>ee</u>·koh·see <u>eh</u>·nah
22	**είκοσι δύο** <u>ee</u>·koh·see <u>THee</u>·oh

30	**τριάντα** tree·<u>ahn</u>·dah
31	**τριάντα ένα** tree·<u>ahn</u>·dah <u>eh</u>·nah
40	**σαράντα** sah·<u>rahn</u>·dah
50	**πενήντα** peh·<u>neen</u>·dah
60	**εξήντα** eh·<u>kseen</u>·dah
70	**εβδομήντα** ehv·THoh·<u>meen</u>·dah
80	**ογδόντα** ohgh·<u>THohn</u>·dah
90	**ενενήντα** eh·neh·<u>neen</u>·dah
100	**εκατό** eh·kah·<u>toh</u>
101	**εκατόν ένα** eh·kah·<u>tohn</u> <u>eh</u>·nah
200	**διακόσια** THee·ah·<u>koh</u>·siah
500	**πεντακόσια** pehn·dah·<u>koh</u>·siah
1,000	**χίλια** <u>khee</u>·liah
10,000	**δέκα χιλιάδες** <u>THeh</u>·kah khee·<u>liah</u>·THehs
1,000,000	**ένα εκατομμύριο** <u>eh</u>·nah eh·kah·toh·<u>mee</u>·ree·oh

Ordinal Numbers

first	**πρώτος** <u>proh</u>·tohs
second	**δεύτερος** <u>THehf</u>·teh·rohs
third	**τρίτος** <u>tree</u>·tohs
fourth	**τέταρτος** <u>teh</u>·tahr·tohs
fifth	**πέμπτος** <u>pehm</u>·ptohs
once	**μια φορά** miah foh·<u>rah</u>
twice	**δύο φορές** <u>THee</u>·oh foh·<u>rehs</u>
three times	**τρεις φορές** trees foh·<u>rehs</u>

Time

Essential

What time is it?	**Τι ώρα είναι;** tee <u>oh</u>·rah <u>ee</u>·neh
It's noon [midday].	**Είναι μεσημέρι.** <u>ee</u>·neh meh·see·<u>meh</u>·ree
At midnight.	**Τα μεσάνυχτα.** tah meh·<u>sah</u>·neekh·tah
From nine o'clock to five o'clock.	**Από τις εννέα ως τις πέντε.** ah·<u>poh</u> tees eh·<u>neh</u>·ah ohs tees <u>pehn</u>·deh
Twenty after [past] four.	**Τέσσερις και είκοσι.** <u>teh</u>·seh·rees keh <u>ee</u>·koh·see
A quarter to nine.	**Εννέα παρά τέταρτο.** eh·<u>neh</u>·ah pah·<u>rah</u> <u>teh</u>·tahr·toh
5:30 *a.m./p.m.*	**Πεντέμιση *π.μ./μ.μ.*** pehn·<u>deh</u>·mee·see *proh meh·seem·<u>vree</u>·ahs/meh·<u>tah</u> meh·seem·<u>vree</u>·ahs*

Days

Essential

Monday	**Δευτέρα** THehf·<u>teh</u>·rah
Tuesday	**Τρίτη** <u>tree</u>·tee
Wednesday	**Τετάρτη** teh·<u>tahr</u>·tee
Thursday	**Πέμπτη** <u>pehm</u>·tee
Friday	**Παρασκευή** pah·rahs·keh·<u>vee</u>
Saturday	**Σάββατο** <u>sah</u>·vah·toh
Sunday	**Κυριακή** keer·yah·<u>kee</u>

Dates

yesterday	**χτες** khtehs
today	**σήμερα** <u>see</u>·meh·rah
tomorrow	**αύριο** <u>ahv</u>·ree·oh
day	**ημέρα** ee·<u>meh</u>·rah
week	**εβδομάδα** ehv·THoh·<u>mah</u>·THah
month	**μήνας** <u>mee</u>·nahs
year	**χρόνος** <u>khroh</u>·nohs

Months

January	**Ιανουάριος** ee·ah·noo·<u>ah</u>·ree·ohs
February	**Φεβρουάριος** fehv·roo·<u>ah</u>·ree·ohs
March	**Μάρτιος** <u>mahr</u>·tee·ohs
April	**Απρίλιος** ahp·<u>ree</u>·lee·ohs
May	**Μάιος** <u>mah</u>·ee·ohs
June	**Ιούνιος** ee·<u>oo</u>·nee·ohs

July	**Ιούλιος** ee·<u>oo</u>·lee·ohs
August	**Αύγουστος** <u>ahv</u>·ghoo·stohs
September	**Σεπτέμβριος** sehp·<u>tehm</u>·vree·ohs
October	**Οκτώβριος** ohk·<u>toh</u>·vree·ohs
November	**Νοέμβριος** noh·<u>ehm</u>·vree·ohs
December	**Δεκέμβριος** THeh·<u>kehm</u>·vree·ohs

Seasons

spring	**η άνοιξη** ee <u>ah</u>·nee·ksee
summer	**το καλοκαίρι** toh kah·loh·<u>keh</u>·ree
fall [autumn]	**το φθινόπωρο** toh fthee·<u>noh</u>·poh·roh
winter	**ο χειμώνας** oh khee·<u>moh</u>·nahs

Holidays

January 1, New Year's Day	**Πρωτοχρονιά** proh·toh·hroh·<u>niah</u>
January 6, Epiphany	**Θεοφάνεια** theh·oh·<u>fah</u>·nee·ah
March 25, Annunciation/ National Holiday (Proclamation of the Greek War of Independence)	**Ευαγγελισμός/Εθνική εορτή** eh·vahn·geh·lee·<u>smohs</u>/ehth·nee·<u>kee</u> eh·ohr·<u>tee</u>
May 1, May Day	**Πρωτομαγιά** proh·toh·mah·<u>yah</u>
August 15, Assumption	**Κοίμηση της Θεοτόκου** <u>kee</u>·mee·see tees theh·oh·<u>toh</u>·koo
October 28, The OXI day	**Εθνική εορτή** ehth·nee·<u>kee</u> eh·ohr·<u>tee</u>
December 25, Christmas	**Χριστούγεννα** khrees·<u>too</u>·yeh·nah

Moveable Holidays

Easter	**Πάσχα** <u>pahs</u>·khah
Greek Orthodox Shrove Monday	**Καθαρή Δευτέρα** kah·thah·<u>ree</u> THeh·<u>fteh</u>·rah
Pentecost	**Αγίου Πνεύματος** ah·<u>yee</u>·oo <u>pnehv</u>·mah·tohs

i Each city and town has a patron saint. The saint's holy day, also known as a name day, is a local public holiday.

i The most important holidays in Greece are religious celebrations such as Easter and Christmas, with Easter being the most sacred holiday. The traditional celebrations usually start on Good Friday with a procession of the Epitaph (Bier) symbolizing the tomb of Christ. On Holy Saturday evening, the resurrection mass takes place when everyone goes to church at around 11 p.m. with unlit candles. At midnight the bells are rung and the priest comes out of the church to pass the Holy Light to the congregation. This is the largest religious gathering. In most places, the crowds fill the streets outside the church, traffic is blocked and there are usually fireworks right after midnight. After this, it is customary to eat a soup called **μαγειρίτσα** (mah·ghee·ree·tsah), made from the lamb's internal organs. On Sunday the celebration is usually taken outdoors. Whole families come together to roast a lamb on the spit, a big feast lasting the whole day. If you are in the countryside you will see large parties of people roasting the lamb and you could be invited to join them. Even in the big cities, don't be surprised if you see people doing the same on their rooftops!
Another major holiday is March 25th, which is a day of remembrance of the start of the Greek War of Independence. On this day there is a military parade in every major city.

Conversion Tables

Mileage

1 km – 0.62 mi	20 km – 12.4 mi
5 km – 3.10 mi	50 km – 31.0 mi
10 km – 6.20 mi	100 km – 61.0 mi

Measurement

1 gram	**γραμμάριο** ghrah·<u>mah</u>·ree·oh	= 0.035 oz.
1 kilogram (kg)	**κιλό** kee·<u>loh</u>	= 2.2 lb
1 liter (l)	**λίτρο** <u>lee</u>·troh	= 1.06 U.S./0.88 Brit. quarts
1 centimeter (cm)	**εκατοστό** eh·kah·toh·<u>stoh</u>	= 0.4 inch
1 meter (m)	**μέτρο** <u>meh</u>·troh	= 3.28 feet
1 kilometer (km)	**χιλιόμετρο** khee·<u>lioh</u>·meh·troh	= 0.62 mile

Temperature

-40° C – -40° F	-1° C – 30° F	20° C – 68° F
-30° C – -22° F	0° C – 32° F	25° C – 77° F
-20° C – -4° F	5° C – 41° F	30° C – 86° F
-10° C – 14° F	10° C – 50° F	35° C – 95° F
-5° C – 23° F	15° C – 59° F	

Oven Temperature

100° C – 212° F	177° C – 350° F
121° C – 250° F	204° C – 400° F
149° C – 300° F	260° C – 500° F

Useful Websites

www.grhotels.gr
Hellenic Chamber of Hotels site

www.hihostels.com
Hostelling International website

www.olympicairlines.com
*Olympic Airlines, the Greek
national airline*

www.ose.gr
*OSE, the national railway of
Greece*

www.diakopes.gr
*Official website of a major Greek
travel magazine*

www.isap.gr
Athens Urban Electric Railway

www.ametro.gr
Athens subway website

www.greekhotels.gr
*Guide for hotels, villas and
apartments in Greece*

www.greekferries.gr
Greek ferry website

www.aegeanair.com
Aegean Air website

www.oasa.gr
*Athens Urban Transport
Organization website*

www.ktel.org
*KTEL, the national bus service
of Greece*

www.gnto.gr
*Greek National Tourist
Organization*

www.tramsa.gr
Athens tram system website

www.berlitzpublishing.com
Berlitz Publishing website

English–Greek Dictionary

A

access *n* **πρόσβαση** prohz·vah·see
accessory **αξεσουάρ**
  ah·kseh·soo·ahr
accident **ατύχημα** ah·tee·khee·mah
accompany **συνοδεύω**
  see·noh·THeh·voh
account *n* **λογαριασμός**
  loh·ghahr·yahz·mohs
adaptor **προσαρμοστής**
  proh·sahr·moh·stees
address *n* **διεύθυνση**
  THee·ehf·theen·see
admission **είσοδος** ee·soh·Thohs
adult **ενήλικας** eh·nee·lee·kahs
advance **προκαταβολή**
  proh·kah·tah·voh·lee
after **μετά** meh·tah
afternoon **απόγευμα**
  ah·poh·yehv·mah
after-sun lotion **λοσιόν μετά την**
  ηλιοθεραπεία loh·siohn meh·tah
  teen ee·lioh·theh·rah·pee·ah
age *n* **ηλικία** ee·lee·kee·ah
agree **συμφωνώ** seem·foh·noh
air conditioning **κλιματισμός**
  klee·mah·teez·mohs
air pump *n* **αντλία αέρος**
  ahn·dlee·ah ah·eh·rohs

airline **αεροπορική εταιρία**
  ah·eh·roh·poh·ree·kee
  eh·the·ree·ah
airmail **αεροπορικώς**
  ah·eh·roh·poh·ree·kohs
airport **αεροδρόμιο**
  ah·eh·roh·THroh·mee·oh
aisle seat **διάδρομος**
  THee·ah·Throh·mohs
allergic **αλλεργικός**
  ahl·ehr·yee·kohs
allergy **αλλεργία** ah·lehr·yee·ah
alone **μόνος** moh·nohs
aluminum foil **αλουμινόχαρτο**
  ah·loo·mee·noh·khah·rtoh
amazing **καταπληκτικός**
  kah·tahp·leek·tee·kohs
ambassador **πρεσβευτής**
  prehz·vehf·tees
amber **κεχριμπάρι**
  kchkh·reem·bah·ree
ambulance **αυθενοφόρο**
  ahs·theh·noh·foh·roh
American *adj* **αμερικάνικος**
  ah·meh·ree·kah·nee·kohs;
  (nationality) **Αμερικανός**
  ah·meh·ree·kah·nohs
amount *n* **ποσό** poh·soh
amusement park **πάρκο**
  ψυχαγωγίας pahr·koh
  psee·khah·ghoh·yee·ahs
animal **ζώο** zoh·oh
another **άλλος** ah·lohs
antibiotic **αντιβιοτικό**
  ahn·dee·vee·oh·tee·koh

---

adj adjective   **adv** adverb   **BE** British English   **n** noun   **v** verb

antiques store **κατάστημα με αντίκες** kah·<u>tah</u>·stee·mah meh ahn·<u>tee</u>·kehs

antiseptic cream **αντισηπτική κρέμα** ahn·dee·seep·tee·<u>kee</u> <u>kreh</u>·mah

anything **οτιδήποτε** oh·tee·<u>THee</u>·poh·teh

apartment **διαμέρισμα** THee·ah·<u>meh</u>·reez·mah

apologize **ζητώ συγγνώμη** zee·<u>toh</u> seegh·<u>noh</u>·mee

appendix **σκωληκοειδίτιδα** skoh·lee·koh·ee·<u>THee</u>·tee·THah

appointment **ραντεβού** rahn·deh·<u>voo</u>

architecture **αρχιτεκτονική** ahr·khee·teh·ktoh·nee·<u>kee</u>

area code **κωδικός περιοχής** koh·THee·<u>kohs</u> peh·ree·oh·<u>khees</u>

arm n **χέρι** <u>kheh</u>·ree

arrange **κανονίζω** kah·noh·<u>nee</u>·zoh

arrest v **συλλαμβάνω** see·lahm·<u>vah</u>·noh

arrive **φτάνω** <u>ftah</u>·noh

art **τέχνη** <u>tekh</u>·nee

art gallery **γκαλερί τέχνης** gah·leh·<u>ree</u> <u>tekh</u>·nees

ashtray **σταχτοδοχείο** stakh·toh·THoh·<u>khee</u>·oh

ask **ζητώ** zee·<u>toh</u>

aspirin **ασπιρίνη** ahs·pee·<u>ree</u>·nee

asthmatic **ασθματικός** ahsth·mah·tee·<u>kohs</u>

ATM **ATM** ehee·tee·<u>ehm</u>

attack n **επίθεση** eh·<u>pee</u>·theh·see; v **επιτίθεμαι** eh·pee·<u>tee</u>·theh·meh

attractive **ελκυστικός** ehl·kees·tee·<u>kohs</u>

authenticity **αυθεντικότητα** ahf·thehn·dee·<u>koh</u>·tee·tah

B

baby **μωρό** moh·<u>roh</u>

baby food **βρεφική τροφή** vreh·fee·<u>kee</u> troh·<u>fee</u>

baby seat **καρέκλα μωρού** kah·<u>reh</u>·klah moh·<u>roo</u>

babysitter **μπέιμπι σίτερ** <u>beh</u>·ee·bee <u>see</u>·tehr

back n **πλάτη** <u>plah</u>·tee

back ache **πόνος στην πλάτη** <u>poh</u>·nohs steen <u>plah</u>·tee

backgammon **τάβλι** <u>tah</u>·vlee

bad **κακός** kah·<u>kohs</u>

baggage **αποσκευές** ah·pohs·keh·<u>vehs</u>

baggage check **φύλαξη αποσκευών** <u>fee</u>·lah·ksee ah·poh·skeh·<u>vohn</u>

baggage reclaim **παραλαβή αποσκευών** pah·rah·lah·<u>vee</u> ah·poh·skeh·<u>vohn</u>

bakery **αρτοποιείο** ah·rtoh·pee·<u>ee</u>·oh

balcony **μπαλκόνι** bahl·<u>koh</u>·nee

ballet **μπαλέτο** bah·<u>leh</u>·toh

bandage **γάζα** <u>ghah</u>·zah

bank **τράπεζα** <u>trah</u>·peh·zah

bank account **λογαριασμός τραπέζης** loh·ghahr·yahz·<u>mohs</u> trah·<u>peh</u>·zees

bank loan **τραπεζικό δάνειο** trah·peh·zee·<u>koh</u> <u>THah</u>·nee·oh bar **μπαρ** bahr

barber **κουρείο** koo·<u>ree</u>·oh

basket **καλάθι** kah·<u>lah</u>·THee

basketball **μπάσκετ** bah·skeht

bathing suit **μαγιό** mah·<u>yoh</u>

bathroom **μπάνιο** bah·nioh

battery **μπαταρία** bah·tah·<u>ree</u>·ah

beach **παραλία** pah·rah·<u>lee</u>·ah

beautiful **όμορφος** oh·mohr·fohs

bed **κρεβάτι** kreh·<u>vah</u>·tee

bed and breakfast **διαμονή με πρωινό** THiah·moh·<u>nee</u> meh proh·ee·<u>noh</u>

bedding **σεντόνια** sehn·<u>doh</u>·niah

bedroom **υπνοδωμάτιο** eep·noh·THoh·<u>mah</u>·tee·oh

before **πριν** preen

beginner **αρχάριος** ahr·<u>khah</u>·ree·ohs

belong **ανήκω** ah·<u>nee</u>·koh

belt **ζώνη** <u>zoh</u>·nee

bicycle **ποδήλατο** poh·<u>THee</u>·lah·toh

big **μεγάλος** meh·<u>ghah</u>·lohs

bikini **μπικίνι** bee·<u>kee</u>·nee

bird **πουλί** poo·<u>lee</u>

bite n (insect) **τσίμπημα** <u>tsee</u>·bee·mah

bladder **ουροδόχος κύστη** oo·roh·<u>THoh</u>·khohs <u>kee</u>·stee

blanket **κουβέρτα** koo·<u>veh</u>·rtah

bleed n **αιμορραγία** eh·moh·rah·<u>yee</u>·ah; v **αιμορραγώ** eh·moh·rah·<u>yoh</u>

blinds **περσίδες** peh·<u>rsee</u>·THehs

blister **φουσκάλα** foo·<u>skah</u>·lah

blood **αίμα** <u>eh</u>·mah

blood group **ομάδα αίματος** oh·<u>mah</u>·THah <u>eh</u>·mah·tohs

blood pressure **πίεση** <u>pee</u>·eh·see

blouse **μπλούζα** <u>bloo</u>·zah

boarding card **κάρτα επιβίβασης** <u>kah</u>·rtah eh·pee·<u>vee</u>·vah·sees

boat **βάρκα** <u>vahr</u>·kah

boat trip **ταξίδι με πλοίο** tah·<u>ksee</u>·THee meh <u>plee</u>·oh

body **σώμα** <u>soh</u>·mah

bone **οστό** oh·<u>stoh</u>

book n **βιβλίο** veev·<u>lee</u>·oh; v **κάνω κράτηση** <u>kah</u>·noh <u>krah</u>·tee·see

bookstore **βιβλιοπωλείο** veev·lee·oh·poh·<u>lee</u>·oh

boot **μπότα** <u>boh</u>·tah

border (country) **σύνορο** <u>see</u>·noh·roh

boring **βαρετός** vah·reh·<u>tohs</u>

borrow **δανείζομαι** THah·<u>nee</u>·zoh·meh

botanical garden **βοτανικός κήπος** voh·tah·nee·<u>kohs</u> <u>kee</u>·pohs

bottle **μπουκάλι** boo·<u>kah</u>·lee

bottle opener **τιρμπουσόν** teer·boo·<u>sohn</u>

bowel **έντερο** <u>ehn</u>·deh·roh

box office **ταχυδρομική θυρίδα** tah·khee·THroh·mee·<u>kee</u> THee·<u>ree</u>·THah

boxing n **μποξ** bohks

boy **αγόρι** ah·<u>ghoh</u>·ree

boyfriend **φίλος** <u>fee</u>·lohs

bra **σουτιέν** soo·<u>tiehn</u>

break n **διάλειμμα** THee·<u>ah</u>·lee·mah; v **σπάω** <u>spah</u>·oh

breakdown n (car) **βλάβη** <u>vlah</u>·vee

breakfast **πρωινό** proh·ee·<u>noh</u>

break-in n **διάρρηξη** THee·<u>ah</u>·ree·ksee

breast **στήθος** <u>stee</u>·THohs

breathe **αναπνέω** ah·nahp·<u>neh</u>·oh

breathtaking **φαντασμαγορικός**
fahn·dahz·mah·ghoh·ree·<u>kohs</u>

bridge n (over water) **γέφυρα**
<u>yeh</u>·fee·rah; (card game) **μπριτζ**
breetz

briefcase **χαρτοφύλακας**
khah·rtoh·<u>fee</u>·lah·kahs

briefs (men's, women's) **σλιπ**
sleep (women's); **κυλοτάκι**
kee·loh·<u>tah</u>·kee

bring **φέρνω** <u>fehr</u>·noh

Britain **Βρετανία** vreh·tah·<u>nee</u>·ah

British adj **βρετανικός**
vreh·tah·nee·<u>kohs</u>; (nationality)
Βρετανός vreh·tah·<u>nohs</u>

brochure **φυλλάδιο**
fee·<u>lah</u>·THee·oh

broken **σπασμένος**
spahz·<u>meh</u>·nohs

broom n **σκούπα** <u>skoo</u>·pah

browse **ξεφυλλίζω**
kseh·fee·<u>lee</u>·zoh

bruise n **μελανιά** meh·lah·<u>niah</u>

brush n **βούρτσα** <u>voor</u>·tsah;
v **βουρτσίζω** voor·<u>tsee</u>·zoh

build **κτίζω** <u>ktee</u>·zoh

building **κτίριο** <u>ktee</u>·ree·oh

burn n **έγκαυμα** <u>eh</u>·gahv·mah

bus **λεωφορείο** leh·oh·foh·<u>ree</u>·oh

bus route **διαδρομή λεωφορείων**
THee·ah·THroh·<u>mee</u>
leh·oh·foh·<u>ree</u>·ohn

bus station **σταθμός λεωφορείων**
stahTH·<u>mohs</u> leh·oh·foh·<u>ree</u>·ohn

bus stop **στάση λεωφορείου**
<u>stah</u>·see leh·oh·foh·<u>ree</u>·oo

business class **μπίζνες θέση**
bee·znehs <u>theh</u>·see

business trip **επαγγελματικό
ταξίδι** eh·pah·gehl·mah·tee·<u>koh</u>
tah·<u>ksee</u>·THee

busy (occupied) **απασχολημένος**
ah·pahs·khoh·lee·<u>meh</u>·nohs

but **αλλά** ah·<u>lah</u>

butane gas **υγραέριο**
eegh·rah·<u>eh</u>·ree·oh

butcher shop **κρεοπωλείο**
kreh·oh·poh·<u>lee</u>·oh

button **κουμπί** koo·<u>bee</u>

buy **αγοράζω** ah·ghoh·<u>rah</u>·zoh

C

cabaret **καμπαρέ** kah·bah·<u>reh</u>

cabin **καμπίνα** kah·<u>bee</u>·nah

cable car **τελεφερίκ**
teh·leh·feh·<u>reek</u>

cafe **καφετέρια**
kah·feh·<u>teh</u>·ree·ah

calendar **ημερολόγιο**
ee·meh·roh·<u>loh</u>·yee·oh

call collect **με χρέωση του
καλούμενου** meh <u>khreh</u>·oh·see too
kah·<u>loo</u>·meh·noo

call n **κλήση** <u>klee</u>·see; v **καλώ**
kah·<u>loh</u>

camcorder **φορητή
βιντεοκάμερα** foh·ree·<u>tee</u>
vee·deh·oh·<u>kah</u>·meh·rah

camera **φωτογραφική μηχανή**
foh·tohgh·rah·fee·<u>kee</u>
mee·khah·<u>nee</u>

camera case **θήκη μηχανής**
<u>thee</u>·kee mee·khah·<u>nees</u>

camera store **κατάστημα με φωτογραφικά είδη** kah·<u>tah</u>·stee·mah meh foh·<u>tohgh</u>·rah·fee·<u>kah</u> ee·<u>THee</u>

camp bed **κρεβάτι εκστρατείας** kreh·<u>vah</u>·tee ehk·strah·<u>tee</u>·ahs

camping **κάμπινγκ** <u>kah</u>·mpeeng

camping equipment **εξοπλισμός κάμπιγκ** eh·ksohp·leez·<u>mohs</u> <u>kah</u>·mpeeng

campsite **χώρος κάμπινγκ** <u>khoh</u>·rohs <u>kah</u>·mpeeng

can opener **ανοιχτήρι** ah·neekh·<u>tee</u>·ree

Canada **Καναδάς** kah·nah·<u>THahs</u>

canal **κανάλι** kah·<u>nah</u>·lee

cancel v **ακυρώνω** ah·kee·<u>roh</u>·noh

cancer (disease) **καρκίνος** kahr·<u>kee</u>·nohs

candle **κερί** keh·<u>ree</u>

canoe **κανό** kah·<u>noh</u>

car **αυτοκίνητο** ahf·toh·<u>kee</u>·nee·toh

car park [BE] **χώρος στάθμευσης** <u>khoh</u>·rohs <u>stahth</u>·mehf·sees

car rental **ενοικίαση αυτοκινήτων** eh·nee·<u>kee</u>·ah·see ahf·toh·kee·<u>nee</u>·tohn

car wash **πλύσιμο αυτοκινήτου** <u>plee</u>·see·moh ahf·toh·kee·<u>nee</u>·too

carafe **καράφα** kah·<u>rah</u>·fah

caravan **τροχόσπιτο** troh·<u>khohs</u>·pee·toh

cards **χαρτιά** khahr·<u>tiah</u>

carpet (fitted) **μοκέτα** moh·<u>keh</u>·tah

carton **κουτί** koo·<u>tee</u>

cash desk [BE] **ταμείο** tah·<u>mee</u>·oh

cash n **μετρητά** meht·ree·<u>tah</u>; v **εξαργυρώνω** eh·ksahr·ghee·<u>roh</u>·noh

casino **καζίνο** kah·<u>see</u>·noh

castle **κάστρο** <u>kahs</u>·troh

catch v (bus) **παίρνω** <u>pehr</u>·noh

cathedral **καθεδρικός ναός** kah·theh·<u>THree</u>·<u>kohs</u> nah·<u>ohs</u>

cave n **σπήλαιο** <u>spee</u>·leh·oh

CD **σι ντι** see dee

cell phone **κινητό** kee·nee·<u>toh</u>

change n **αλλαγή** ah·lah·<u>yee</u>; v **αλλάζω** ah·<u>lah</u>·zoh

cheap **φτηνός** ftee·<u>nohs</u>

check n (bank) **επιταγή** eh·pee·tah·<u>yee</u>; (bill) **λογαριασμός** loh·ghahr·yahz·<u>mohs</u>

choose **διαλέγω** THiah·<u>leh</u>·ghoh

clean **καθαρός** kah·thah·<u>rohs</u>

cling film [BE] **διαφανή μεμβράνη** THee·ah·fah·<u>nee</u> mehm·<u>vrah</u>·nce

clothing store **κατάστημα ρούχων** kah·<u>tahs</u>·tee·mah <u>roo</u>·khohn

cold adj (temperature) **κρύος** <u>kree</u>·ohs; n (chill) **κρυολόγημα** kree·oh·<u>loh</u>·yee·mah

collapse v **καταρρέω** kah·tah·<u>reh</u>·oh

collect v **παίρνω** <u>peh</u>·rnoh

color n **χρώμα** <u>khroh</u>·mah

comb n **χτένα** <u>khteh</u>·nah; v **χτενίζω** khteh·<u>nee</u>·zoh

come **έρχομαι** <u>ehr</u>·khoh·meh

come back v (return) **επιστρέφω** eh·pees·<u>treh</u>·foh

commission n (agent fee) **προμήθεια** proh·<u>mee</u>·thee·ah

company *n* (business) **εταιρία**
eh·teh·<u>ree</u>·ah; (companionship)
παρέα pah·<u>reh</u>·ah

complain **παραπονιέμαι**
pah·rah·poh·<u>nieh</u>·meh

computer **υπολογιστής**
ee·poh·loh·yee·<u>stees</u>

concert **συναυλία** see·nahv·<u>lee</u>·ah

concert hall **αίθουσα συναυλιών**
<u>eh</u>·thoo·sah see·nahv·lee·<u>ohn</u>

conditioner (hair) **γαλάκτωμα για τα**
μαλλιά ghah·<u>lah</u>·ktoh·mah yah tah
mah·<u>liah</u>

condom **προφυλακτικό**
proh·fee·lah·ktee·<u>koh</u>

conference **συνέδριο**
see·<u>neh</u>·THree·oh

confirm **επιβεβαιώνω**
eh·pee·veh·veh·<u>oh</u>·noh

constipation **δυσκοιλιότητα**
thees·kee·lee·<u>oh</u>·tee·tah

Consulate **Προξενείο**
proh·kseh·<u>nee</u>·oh

consult *v* **συμβουλεύομαι**
seem·voo·<u>leh</u>·voh·meh

contact *v* **επικοινωνώ**
eh·pee·kee·noh·<u>noh</u>

contact fluid **υγρό για φακούς**
επαφής eegh·<u>roh</u> yah fah·<u>koos</u>
eh·pah·<u>fees</u>

contact lens **φακός επαφής**
fah·<u>kohs</u> eh·pah·<u>fees</u>

contagious **μεταδοτικός**
meh·tah·THoh·tee·<u>kohs</u>

contain **περιέχω** peh·ree·<u>eh</u>·khoh

contraceptive pill **αντισυλληπτικό**
χάπι ahn·dee·see·leep·tee·<u>koh</u>
khah·pee

cook *n* (chef) **μάγειρας**
<u>mah</u>·yee·rahs; *v* **μαγειρεύω**
mah·yee·<u>reh</u>·voh

copper **χαλκός** khahl·<u>kohs</u>

corkscrew **τιρμπουσόν**
teer·boo·<u>sohn</u>

corner **γωνία** ghoh·<u>nee</u>·ah

correct *v* **διορθώνω**
THee·ohr·<u>thoh</u>·noh

cosmetics **καλλυντικά**
kah·leen·dee·<u>kah</u>

cot [BE] **παιδικό κρεβάτι**
peh·THee·<u>koh</u> kreh·<u>vah</u>·tee

cotton **βαμβάκι** vahm·<u>vah</u>·kee

cough *n* **βήχας** <u>vee</u>·khahs; *v* **βήχω**
<u>vee</u>·khoh

counter **ταμείο** tah·<u>mee</u>·oh

country (nation) **χώρα** <u>khoh</u>·rah

countryside **εξοχή** eh·ksoh·<u>khee</u>

couple *n* (pair) **ζευγάρι**
zehv·<u>ghah</u>·ree

courier *n* (messenger) **κούριερ**
<u>koo</u>·ree·ehr

court house **δικαστήριο**
THee·kahs·<u>tee</u>·ree·oh

cramp *n* **κράμπα** <u>krahm</u>·bah

credit card **πιστωτική κάρτα**
pees·toh·tee·<u>kee</u> <u>kahr</u>·tah

crib [cot BE] **παιδικό κρεβάτι**
peh·THee·<u>koh</u> kreh·<u>vah</u>·tee

crown *n* (dental, royal) **κορώνα**
koh·<u>roh</u>·nah

cruise *n* **κρουαζιέρα**
kroo·ahz·<u>yeh</u>·rah

crutch *n* (walking support) **δεκανίκι**
THeh·kah·<u>nee</u>·kee

crystal *n* **κρύσταλλο** <u>kree</u>·stah·loh

cup **φλυτζάνι** flee·<u>jah</u>·nee

cupboard **ντουλάπα** doo·<u>lah</u>·pah
currency **νόμισμα** <u>noh</u>·meez·mah
currency exchange office **γραφείο
ανταλλαγής συναλλάγματος**
ghrah·<u>fee</u>·oh ahn·dah·lah·<u>yees</u>
see·nah·<u>lahgh</u>·mah·tohs
customs (tolls) **τελωνείο**
teh·loh·<u>nee</u>·oh
customs declaration (tolls)
τελωνειακή δήλωση
teh·loh·nee·ah·<u>kee</u> THee·loh·see
cut n (wound) **κόψιμο**
<u>koh</u>·psee·moh
cut glass n **σκαλιστό γυαλί**
skah·lees·<u>toh</u> yah·<u>lee</u>
cycle helmet **κράνος ποδηλάτη**
<u>krah</u>·nohs poh·THee·<u>lah</u>·tee
cyclist **ποδηλάτης**
poh·THee·<u>lah</u>·tees
Cypriot adj **κυπριακός**
keep·ree·ah·<u>kohs</u>; (nationality)
Κύπριος <u>kee</u>·pree·ohs
Cyprus **Κύπρος** <u>kee</u>·prohs

D

damage n **ζημιά** zee·<u>miah</u>;
v **καταστρέφω** kah·tah·<u>streh</u>·foh
dance v **χορεύω** khoh·<u>reh</u>·voh
dangerous **επικίνδυνος**
eh·pee·<u>keen</u>·THee·nohs
dark adj (color) **σκούρος** <u>skoo</u>·rohs
dawn n **ξημερώματα**
ksee·meh·<u>roh</u>·mah·tah
day trip **ημερήσια εκδρομή**
ee·meh·<u>ree</u>·see·ah
ehk·THroh·<u>mee</u>
deaf **κουφός** koo·<u>fohs</u>

decide **αποφασίζω**
ah·poh·fah·<u>see</u>·zoh
deck n **κατάστρωμα**
kah·<u>tah</u>·stroh·mah
deck chair **σεζ-λονγκ** sehz <u>lohng</u>
declare **δηλώνω** THee·<u>loh</u>·noh
deduct (money) **αφαιρώ**
ah·feh·<u>roh</u>
defrost **ξεπαγώνω**
kseh·pah·<u>ghoh</u>·noh
degrees (temperature) **βαθμοί**
vahth·<u>mee</u>
delay n **καθυστέρηση**
kah·thee·<u>steh</u>·ree·see;
v **καθυστερώ** kah·thee·steh·<u>roh</u>
delicious **νόστιμος** <u>nohs</u>·tee·mohs
deliver **παραδίδω**
pah·rah·<u>THee</u>·THoh
dental floss **οδοντικό νήμα**
oh·THohn·dee·<u>koh</u> <u>nee</u>·mah
dentist **οδοντίατρος**
oh·THohn·<u>dee</u>·ah·trohs
deodorant **αποσμητικό**
ah·pohz·mee·tee·<u>koh</u>
department store **πολυκατάστημα**
poh·lee·kah·<u>tahs</u>·tee·mah
departure (travel) **αναχώρηση**
ah·nah·<u>khoh</u>·ree·see
departure lounge **αίθουσα
αναχωρήσεων** <u>eh</u>·thoo·sah
ah·nah·khoh·<u>ree</u>·seh·ohn
depend **εξαρτώμαι**
eh·ksahr·<u>toh</u>·meh
deposit n (down
payment) **προκαταβολή**
proh·kah·tah·voh·<u>lee</u>
describe **περιγράφω**
peh·reegh·<u>rah</u>·foh

designer **σχεδιαστής**
skheh·THee·ahs·<u>tees</u>

detergent **απορρυπαντικό**
ah·poh·ree·pahn·dee·<u>koh</u>

develop (photos) **εμφανίζω**
ehm·fah·<u>nee</u>·zoh

diabetes **διαβήτης**
THee·ah·<u>vee</u>·tees

diabetic **διαβητικός**
THee·ah·vee·tee·<u>kohs</u>

diagnosis **διάγνωση**
THee·<u>ahgh</u>·noh·see

dialing code **κωδικός**
koh·THee·<u>kohs</u>

diamond n **διαμάντι**
THiah·<u>mahn</u>·dee

diaper **πάνα μωρού** <u>pah</u>·nah
moh·<u>roo</u>

diarrhea **διάρροια** THee·<u>ah</u>·ree·ah

dice n **ζάρια** <u>zah</u>·riah

dictionary **λεξικό** leh·ksee·<u>koh</u>

diesel **ντήζελ** <u>dee</u>·zehl

diet n **δίαιτα** <u>THee</u>·eh·tah

difficult **δύσκολος** <u>THee</u>·skoh·lohs

dining room **τραπεζαρία**
trah·peh·zah·<u>ree</u>·ah

dinner **βραδινό** vrah·THee·<u>noh</u>

direct v **κατευθύνω**
kah·tehf·<u>thee</u>·noh

direction n (instruction) **οδηγία**
oh·THee·<u>yee</u>·ah

dirty adj **βρώμικος** <u>vroh</u>·mee·kohs

disabled **άτομο με ειδικές ανάγκες**
<u>ah</u>·toh·moh meh ee·THee·<u>kehs</u>
ah·<u>nahn</u>·gehs

discounted ticket **μειωμένο**
εισιτήριο mee·oh·<u>meh</u>·noh
ee·see·<u>tee</u>·ree·oh

dishwashing liquid **λίγο υγρό πιάτων**
<u>lee</u>·ghoh ee·<u>ghroh</u> piah·tohn

district **περιφέρεια**
peh·ree·<u>feh</u>·ree·ah

disturb **ενοχλώ** eh·noh·<u>khloh</u>

diving equipment
καταδυτικός εξοπλισμός
kah·tah·THee·tee·<u>kohs</u>
eh·ksoh·pleez·<u>mohs</u>

divorced **διαζευγμένος**
THee·ah·zehv·<u>ghmeh</u>·nohs

dock **προκυμαία** proh·kee·<u>meh</u>·ah

doctor **γιατρός** yah·<u>trohs</u>

doll **κούκλα** <u>kook</u>·lah

dollar **δολάριο** THoh·<u>lah</u>·ree·oh

door **πόρτα** <u>pohr</u>·tah

dosage **δοσολογία**
THoh·soh·loh·<u>yee</u>·ah

double adj **διπλός** THeep·<u>lohs</u>

double bed **διπλό κρεβάτι**
THeep·<u>loh</u> kreh·<u>vah</u>·tee

double room **δίκλινο δωμάτιο**
<u>THeek</u>·lee·noh THoh·<u>mah</u>·tee·oh

downtown area **κέντρο της πόλης**
<u>kehn</u>·droh tees poh·lees

dozen **ντουζίνα** doo·<u>zee</u>·nah

dress n **φόρεμα** <u>foh</u>·reh·mah

drink n **ποτό** poh·<u>toh</u>; v **πίνω**
<u>pee</u>·noh

drive v **οδηγώ** oh·THee·<u>ghoh</u>

drugstore **φαρμακείο**
fahr·mah·<u>kee</u>·oh

dry cleaner **καθαριστήριο**
kah·thah·rees·<u>tee</u>·ree·oh

dubbed **μεταγλωττισμένος**
meh·tahgh·loh·teez·<u>meh</u>·nohs

dusty **σκονισμένος**
skoh·neez·<u>meh</u>·nohs

duty (customs) **φόρος** <u>foh</u>·rohs; (obligation) **καθήκον** kah·<u>thee</u>·kohn

duty-free goods **αφορολόγητα είδη** ah·foh·roh·<u>loh</u>·yee·tah ee·THee

duty-free shop **κατάστημα αφορολόγητων** kah·<u>tahs</u>·tee·mah ah·foh·roh·<u>loh</u>·yee·tohn

E

each **κάθε ένα** <u>kah</u>·theh <u>eh</u>·nah

ear **αυτί** ahf·<u>tee</u>

earache **πόνος στο αυτί** <u>poh</u>·nohs stoh ahf·<u>tee</u>

early **νωρίς** noh·<u>rees</u>

east **ανατολικά** ah·nah·toh·lee·<u>kah</u>

easy *adj* **εύκολος** <u>ehf</u>·koh·lohs

eat **τρώω** <u>troh</u>·oh

economical **οικονομικός** ee·koh·noh·mee·<u>kohs</u>

economy class **τουριστική θέση** too·ree·stee·<u>kee</u> <u>theh</u>·see

elastic **ελαστικός** eh·lahs·tee·<u>kohs</u>

electrical outlet **πρίζα** <u>pree</u>·zah

e-mail **ηλεκτρονικό ταχυδρομείο (e-mail)** ee·lehk·troh·nee·<u>koh</u> tah·hee·dro·<u>mee</u>·oh (ee·<u>meh</u>·eel)

embassy **πρεσβεία** prehz·<u>vee</u>·ah

emerald **σμαράγδι** zmah·<u>rahgh</u>·THee

emergency **έκτακτη ανάγκη** <u>ehk</u>·tahk·tee ah·<u>nah</u>·gee

emergency exit **έξοδος κινδύνου** <u>eh</u>·ksoh·THohs keen·THee·noo

empty *adj* **άδειος** <u>ahTH</u>·yohs

end *n* **τέλος** <u>teh</u>·lohs; *v* **τελειώνω** teh·lee·<u>oh</u>·noh

engine **μηχανή** mee·khah·<u>nee</u>

England **Αγγλία** ahng·<u>lee</u>·ah

English *adj* **αγγλικός** ahng·lee·<u>kohs</u>; (nationality) **Άγγλος** <u>ahng</u>·lohs; (language) **αγγλικά** ahng·lee·<u>kah</u>

enjoy **ευχαριστιέμαι** ehf·khah·rees·<u>tieh</u>·meh

enough **αρκετά** ahr·keh·<u>tah</u>

entertainment guide **οδηγός ψυχαγωγίας** oh·THee·<u>ghohs</u> psee·khah·ghoh·<u>yee</u>·ahs

entrance fee **τιμή εισόδου** tee·<u>mee</u> ee·<u>soh</u>·THoo

epileptic **επιληπτικός** eh·pee·leep·tee·<u>kohs</u>

error **λάθος** <u>lah</u>·thohs

escalator **κυλιόμενες σκάλες** kee·lee·<u>oh</u>·meh·nehs <u>skah</u>·lehs

essential **απαραίτητος** ah·pah·<u>reh</u>·tee·tohs

e-ticket **ηλεκτρονικό εισιτήριο** ee·lehk·troh·nee·<u>koh</u> ee·see·<u>tee</u>·ree·oh

European Union **Ευρωπαϊκή Ένωση** ehv·roh·pah·ee·<u>kee</u> <u>eh</u>·noh·see

euro **ευρώ** ehv·<u>roh</u>

evening **βράδυ** <u>vrah</u>·THee

examination (medical) **ιατρική εξέταση** ee·ah·tree·<u>kee</u> eh·<u>kseh</u>·tah·see

example **παράδειγμα** pah·<u>rah</u>·THeegh·mah

excess baggage **υπέρβαρο** ee·<u>pehr</u>·vah·roh

exchange *v* (money) **αλλάζω** ah·<u>lah</u>·zoh

174

exchange rate **τιμή συναλλάγματος** tee·mee see·nah·<u>lahgh</u>·mah·tohs

excursion **εκδρομή** ehk·THroh·<u>mee</u>

exhibition **έκθεση** <u>ehk</u>·theh·see

exit n **έξοδος** <u>eh</u>·ksoh·THohs

expensive **ακριβός** ahk·ree·<u>vohs</u>

expiration date **ημερομηνία λήξεως** ee·meh·roh·mee·<u>nee</u>·ah <u>lee</u>·kseh·ohs

exposure (photos) **στάση** <u>stah</u>·see

express (mail) **εξπρές** ehk·<u>sprehs</u>

extension (number) **εσωτερική γραμμή** eh·soh·theh·ree·<u>kee</u> ghrah·<u>mee</u>

extra (additional) **άλλο ένα** <u>ah</u>·loh <u>eh</u>·nah

eye n **μάτι** <u>mah</u>·tee

F

fabric (cloth) **ύφασμα** <u>ee</u>·fahs·mah

face n **πρόσωπο** <u>proh</u>·soh·poh

facial **καθαρισμός προσώπου** kah·thah·reez·<u>mohs</u> proh·<u>soh</u>·poo

facility **εξυπηρέτηση** eh·ksee·pee·<u>reh</u>·tee·see

faint **λιποθυμώ** lee·poh·thee·<u>moh</u>

fall v **πέφτω** <u>pehf</u>·toh

family **οικογένεια** ee·koh·<u>yeh</u>·nee·ah

famous **διάσημος** <u>THee</u>·<u>ah</u>·see·mohs

fan n (air) **ανεμιστήρας** ah·neh·mees·<u>tee</u>·rahs

far adv **μακριά** mahk·ree·<u>ah</u>

fare **εισιτήριο** ee·see·<u>tee</u>·ree·oh

farm n **φάρμα** <u>fahr</u>·mah

fast adv **γρήγορα** <u>ghree</u>·ghoh·rah

fat adj (person) **παχύς** pah·<u>khees</u>

faucet **βρύση** <u>vree</u>·see

fault **λάθος** <u>lah</u>·thohs

favorite **αγαπημένος** ah·ghah·pee·<u>meh</u>·nohs

fax facility **υπηρεσία φαξ** ee·pee·reh·<u>see</u>·ah fahks

feed v **ταΐζω** tah·<u>ee</u>·zoh

female **θηλυκός** thee·lee·<u>kohs</u>

fence n **φράχτης** <u>frahkh</u>·tees

ferry **φέρυ-μπωτ** <u>feh</u>·ree·boht

festival **φεστιβάλ** fehs·tee·<u>vahl</u>

fever **πυρετός** pee·reh·<u>tohs</u>

fiancé **αρραβωνιαστικός** ah·rah·voh·niahs·tee·<u>kohs</u>

fiancée **αρραβωνιαστικιά** ah·rah·voh·niahs·tee·<u>kiah</u>

filling (dental) **σφράγισμα** <u>sfrah</u>·yeez·mah

film n (camera) **φιλμ** feelm

filter n **φίλτρο** <u>feel</u>·troh

fine adv **καλά** kah·<u>lah</u>; n **πρόστιμο** <u>prohs</u>·tee·moh

finger n **δάχτυλο** <u>THakh</u>·tee·loh

fire n **φωτιά** foh·<u>tiah</u>

fire brigade [BE] **πυροσβεστική** pee·rohz·vehs·tee·<u>kee</u>

fire escape **έξοδος κινδύνου** <u>eh</u>·ksoh·THohs keen·<u>THee</u>·noo

fire extinguisher **πυροσβεστήρας** pee·rohz·vehs·<u>tee</u>·rahs

first class **πρώτη θέση** <u>proh</u>·tee <u>theh</u>·see

first-aid kit **κουτί πρώτων βοηθειών** koo·<u>tee</u> <u>proh</u>·tohn voh·ee·thee·<u>ohn</u>

fishing **ψάρεμα** psah·reh·mah

flag n **σημαία** see·meh·ah

flashlight **φακός** fah·kohs

flat adj **επίπεδος**
eh·pee·peh·Thohs; n **διαμέρισμα**
THee·ah·mehr·ees·mah

flea **ψύλλος** psee·lohs

flight **πτήση** ptee·see

flight number **αριθμός πτήσεως**
ah·reeth·mohs ptee·seh·ohs

flip-flops **σαγιονάρες**
sah·yoh·nah·rehs

flood n **πλημμύρα** plee·mee·rah

florist **ανθοπωλείο**
ahn·thoh·poh·lee·oh

flower n **λουλούδι** loo·loo·THee

flu **γρίππη** ghree·pee

flush **τραβώ το καζανάκι** trah·voh
toh kah·zah·nah·kee

fly n **μύγα** mee·ghah; v **πετάω**
peh·tah·oh

follow v **ακολουθώ** ah·koh·loo·thoh

foot **πόδι** poh·THee

football [BE] **ποδόσφαιρο**
poh·THohs·feh·roh

footpath **μονοπάτι** moh·noh·pah·tee

forecast n **πρόβλεψη**
prohv·leh·psee

foreign **ξένος** kseh·nohs

foreign currency **ξένο συνάλλαγμα**
kseh·noh see·nah·lahgh·mah

forest n **δάσος** THah·sohs

forget **ξεχνώ** ksehkh·noh

form n **έντυπο** ehn·dee·poh

fortunately **ευτυχώς** ehf·tee·khohs

forward **προωθώ** proh·oh·thoh

fountain **συντριβάνι**
seen·dree·vah·nee

free adj (available) **ελεύθερος**
eh·lehf·theh·rohs

freezer **κατάψυξη**
kah·tah·psee·ksee

frequent adj **συχνός** seekh·nohs

fresh adj **φρέσκος** frehs·kohs

friend n **φίλος** fee·lohs

frightened **φοβισμένος**
foh·veez·meh·nohs

from **από** ah·poh

front n **προκυμαία**
proh·kee·meh·ah

full adj **γεμάτος** yeh·mah·tohs

furniture **έπιπλα** eh·peep·lah

fuse n **ασφάλεια** ahs·fah·lee·ah

gambling **τζόγος** joh·ghohs

game (toy) **παιχνίδι** pehkh·nee·THee

garage **γκαράζ** gah·rahz

garden n **κήπος** kee·pohs

gas **βενζίνη** vehn·zee·nee

gas station **βενζινάδικο**
vehn·zee·nah·THee·koh

gastritis **γαστρίτιδα**
ghahs·tree·tee·THah

gate (airport) **έξοδος** eh·ksoh·THohs

genuine **αυθεντικός**
ahf·thehn·dee·kohs

get off (transport) **κατεβαίνω**
kah·teh·veh·noh

get out (of vehicle) **βγαίνω**
vyeh·noh

gift **δώρο** THoh·roh

gift store **κατάστημα με είδη δώρων**
kah·tahs·tee·mah meh ee·THee
THoh·rohn

girl **κορίτσι** koh·<u>ree</u>·tsee
girlfriend **φίλη** <u>fee</u>·lee
give **δίνω** <u>THee</u>·noh
glass (container) **ποτήρι**
  poh·<u>tee</u>·ree
glasses (optical) **γυαλιά** yah·<u>liah</u>
glove *n* **γάντι** <u>ghahn</u>·dee
go **πηγαίνω** pee·<u>yeh</u>·noh
gold *n* **χρυσός** khree·<u>sohs</u>
golf **γκόλφ** gohlf
golf course **γήπεδο γκολφ**
  <u>yee</u>·peh·THoh gohlf
good **καλός** kah·<u>lohs</u>
grass **γρασίδι** ghrah·<u>see</u>·THee
gratuity **φιλοδώρημα**
  fee·loh·<u>THoh</u>·ree·mah
greasy (hair, skin) **λιπαρός**
  lee·pah·<u>rohs</u>
Greece **Ελλάδα** eh·<u>lah</u>·THah
Greek *adj* **ελληνικός**
  eh·lee·nee·<u>kohs</u>; (nationality)
  Έλληνας <u>eh</u>·lee·nahs
greengrocer [BE] **οπωροπωλείο**
  oh·poh·roh·poh·<u>lee</u>·oh
ground (earth) **έδαφος**
  <u>eh</u>·THah·fohs
group *n* **γκρουπ** groop
guarantee *n* **εγγύηση**
  eh·<u>gee</u>·ee·see; *v* **εγγυώμαι**
  eh·gee·<u>oh</u>·meh
guide book **τουριστικός οδηγός**
  too·ree·stee·<u>kohs</u> oh·THee·<u>ghohs</u>
guided tour **ξενάγηση**
  kseh·<u>nah</u>·yee·see
guitar **κιθάρα** kee·<u>thah</u>·rah
gynecologist **γυναικολόγος**
  yee·neh·koh·<u>loh</u>·ghohs

hair **μαλλιά** mah·<u>liah</u>
hairbrush **βούρτσα** <u>voor</u>·tsah
hair dresser **κομμωτήριο**
  koh·moh·<u>tee</u>·ree·oh
hair dryer **σεσουάρ** seh·soo·<u>ahr</u>
half **μισός** mee·<u>sohs</u>
hammer **σφυρί** sfee·<u>ree</u>
hand *n* **χέρι** <u>kheh</u>·ree
hand luggage **αποσκευές χειρός**
  ah·pohs·keh·<u>vehs</u> khee·<u>rohs</u>
handbag **τσάντα** <u>tsahn</u>·dah
handicraft **λαϊκή τέχνη** lah·ee·<u>kee</u>
  tehkh·nee
handicapped-accessible toilet
  προσβάσιμη τουαλέτα για
  ανάπηρους prohs·<u>vah</u>·see·mee
  too·ah·<u>leh</u>·tah yah
  ah·<u>nah</u>·pee·roos
handkerchief **χαρτομάντηλο**
  khah·rtoh·<u>mahn</u>·dee·loh
handle *n* **πόμολο** <u>poh</u>·moh·loh
hanger **κρεμάστρα** kreh·<u>mahs</u>·trah
harbor *n* **λιμάνι** lee·<u>mah</u>·nee
hat **καπέλο** kah·<u>peh</u>·loh
have (possession) **έχω** <u>eh</u>·khoh
have to (obligation) **οφείλω**
  oh·<u>fee</u>·loh
head *n* **κεφάλι** keh·<u>fah</u>·lee
headache **πονοκέφαλος**
  poh·noh·<u>keh</u>·fah·lohs
health food store **κατάστημα**
  με υγιεινές τροφές
  kah·<u>tahs</u>·tee·mah meh
  ee·yee·ee·<u>nehs</u> troh·<u>fehs</u>
health insurance **ασφάλεια υγείας**
  ahs·<u>fah</u>·lee·ah ee·<u>yee</u>·ahs

177

hearing aid ακουστικό
βαρυκοΐας ah·koo·stee·koh
vah·ree·koh·<u>ee</u>·ahs

heart v **καρδιά** kahr·THee·<u>ah</u>

heart attack καρδιακό
έμφραγμα kahr·THee·ah·<u>koh</u>
<u>ehm</u>·frahgh·mah

heat wave καύσωνας
<u>kahf</u>·soh·nahs

heater (water) θερμοσίφωνας
thehr·moh·<u>see</u>·foh·nahs

heating θέρμανση <u>thehr</u>·mahn·see

heavy βαρύς vah·<u>rees</u>

height ύψος <u>ee</u>·psohs

helicopter ελικόπτερο
eh·lee·<u>kohp</u>·teh·roh

help n **βοήθεια** voh·<u>ee</u>·thee·ah;
v **βοηθώ** voh·ee·<u>thoh</u>

here εδώ eh·<u>THoh</u>

highway εθνική οδός ehth·nee·<u>kee</u>
oh·<u>THohs</u>

hike v **κάνω πεζοπορία** <u>kah</u>·noh
peh·zoh·poh·<u>ree</u>·ah

hill λόφος <u>loh</u>·fohs

hire [BE] v **νοικιάζω** nee·<u>kiah</u>·zoh

history ιστορία ee·stoh·<u>ree</u>·ah

hitchhiking οτοστόπ oh·toh·<u>stohp</u>

hobby (pastime) χόμπυ <u>khoh</u>·bee

hold on περιμένω
peh·ree·<u>meh</u>·noh

hole (in clothes) τρύπα <u>tree</u>·pah

holiday [BE] διακοπές
THee·ah·koh·<u>pehs</u>

honeymoon μήνας του μέλιτος
<u>mee</u>·nahs too <u>meh</u>·lee·tohs

horse track ιπποδρόμιο
ee·poh·<u>THroh</u>·mee·oh

hospital νοσοκομείο
noh·soh·koh·<u>mee</u>·oh

hot (weather) ζεστός zehs·<u>tohs</u>

hot spring θερμή πηγή thehr·<u>mee</u>
pee·<u>yee</u>

hotel ξενοδοχείο
kseh·noh·THoh·<u>khee</u>·oh

household articles είδη οικιακής
χρήσεως <u>ee</u>·THee ee·kee·ah·<u>kees</u>
<u>khree</u>·seh·ohs

husband σύζυγος <u>see</u>·zee·ghohs

I

ice n **πάγος** <u>pah</u>·ghohs

identification ταυτότητα
tahf·<u>toh</u>·tee·tah

illegal παράνομος
pah·<u>rah</u>·noh·mohs

illness αρρώστεια ahr·<u>ohs</u>·tee·ah

imitation απομίμηση
ah·poh·<u>mee</u>·mee·see

immediately αμέσως ah·<u>meh</u>·sohs

impressive εντυπωσιακός
ehn·dee·poh·see·ah·<u>kohs</u>

included συμπεριλαμβάνεται
seem·beh·ree·lahm·<u>vah</u>·neh·teh

indigestion δυσπεψία
THehs·peh·<u>psee</u>·ah

indoor εσωτερικός
eh·soh·teh·ree·<u>kohs</u>

indoor pool εσωτερική πισίνα
eh·soh·teh·ree·<u>kee</u> pee·<u>see</u>·nah

inexpensive φτηνός ftee·<u>nohs</u>

infected μολυσμένος
moh·leez·<u>meh</u>·nohs

inflammation φλεγμονή
flegh·moh·<u>nee</u>

information **πληροφορίες**
plee·roh·foh·<u>ree</u>·ehs

information office **γραφείο πληροφοριών** ghrah·<u>fee</u>·oh
plee·roh·foh·ree·<u>ohn</u>

injection **ένεση** <u>eh</u>·neh·see

injured **τραυματισμένος**
trahv·mah·teez·<u>meh</u>·nohs

innocent **αθώος** ah·<u>thoh</u>·ohs

insect bite **τσίμπημα από έντομο**
<u>tseem</u>·bee·mah ah·<u>poh</u>
ehn·doh·moh

insect repellent **εντομοαπωθητικό**
ehn·doh·moh·ah·poh·thee·tee·<u>koh</u>

inside **μέσα** <u>meh</u>·sah

insist **επιμένω** eh·pee·<u>meh</u>·noh

insomnia **αϋπνία** ah·eep·<u>nee</u>·ah

instruction **οδηγία** oh·THee·<u>yee</u>·ah

insulin **ινσουλίνη** een·soo·<u>lee</u>·nee

insurance **ασφάλεια**
ahs·<u>fah</u>·lee·ah

insurance certificate
πιστοποιητικό ασφάλειας
pees·toh·pee·ee·tee·<u>koh</u>
ahs·<u>fah</u>·lee·ahs

insurance claim **ασφάλεια αποζημίωσης** ahs·<u>fah</u>·lee·ah
ah·poh·zee·<u>mee</u>·oh·sees

insurance company **ασφαλιστική εταιρία** ahs·fah·lees·tee·<u>kee</u>
eh·teh·<u>ree</u>·ah

interest rate **επιτόκιο**
eh·pee·<u>toh</u>·kee·oh

interesting **ενδιαφέρων**
ehn·THee·ah·<u>feh</u>·rohn

international **διεθνής**
THee·eth·<u>nees</u>

International Student Card **διεθνής φοιτητική κάρτα** THee·ehth·<u>nees</u>
fee·tee·tee·<u>kee</u> <u>kahr</u>·tah

internet **ίντερνετ** <u>ee</u>·nteh·rnet

internet cafe **ίντερνετ καφέ**
<u>ee</u>·nteh·rnet kah·<u>feh</u>

interpreter **διερμηνέας**
THee·ehr·mee·<u>neh</u>·ahs

interval **διάλειμμα** THee·<u>ah</u>·lee·mah

introduce **συστήνω** see·<u>stee</u>·noh

introductions **συστάσεις**
see·<u>stah</u>·sees

invitation **πρόσκληση**
<u>prohs</u>·klee·see

invite v **προσκαλώ** prohs·kah·<u>loh</u>

iodine **ιώδειο** ee·<u>oh</u>·THee·oh

iron n **σίδερο** <u>see</u>·THeh·roh;
v **σιδερώνω** see·THeh·<u>roh</u>·noh

itemized bill **αναλυτικός λογαριασμός** ah·nah·lee·tee·<u>kohs</u>
loh·ghahr·yahz·<u>mohs</u>

J

jacket **σακάκι** sah·<u>kah</u>·kee

jammed **σφηνωμένος**
sfee·noh·<u>meh</u>·nohs

jar n **βάζο** <u>vah</u>·zoh

jaw **σαγόνι** sah·<u>ghoh</u>·nee

jeans **μπλου-τζην** bloo·<u>jeen</u>

jellyfish **μέδουσα** <u>meh</u>·THoo·sah

jet-ski **τζετ-σκι** jeht·skee

jeweler **κοσμηματοπωλείο**
kohz·mee·mah·toh·poh·<u>lee</u>·oh

job **δουλειά** THoo·<u>liah</u>

jogging **τζόγκιγκ** joh·geeng

joke n **ανέκδοτο** ah·<u>nehk</u>·THoh·toh

journey **ταξίδι** tah·<u>ksee</u>·THee

junction (intersection) **κόμβος**
  <u>kohm</u>·vohs

K

keep *v* **κρατώ** krah·<u>toh</u>
key *n* **κλειδί** klee·<u>THee</u>
key card **κάρτα-κλειδί**
  <u>kahr</u>·tah·klee·<u>dee</u>
key ring **μπρελόκ** breh·<u>lohk</u>
kidney **νεφρό** nehf·<u>roh</u>
kind **είδος** <u>ee</u>·THohs
king **βασιλιάς** vah·see·<u>liahs</u>
kiosk **περίπτερο** peh·<u>ree</u>·pteh·roh
kiss *n* **φιλί** fee·<u>lee</u>; *v* **φιλώ** fee·<u>loh</u>
kitchen **χαρτί κουζίνας** khah·<u>rtee</u>
  koo·<u>zee</u>·nahs
knapsack **σάκκος** <u>sah</u>·kohs
knee **γόνατο** <u>ghoh</u>·nah·toh
knife **μαχαίρι** mah·<u>kheh</u>·ree
know **γνωρίζω** ghnoh·<u>ree</u>·zoh

L

label *n* **ετικέτα** eh·tee·<u>keh</u>·tah
ladder **σκάλα** <u>skah</u>·lah
lake **λίμνη** <u>leem</u>·nee
lamp **λάμπα** <u>lahm</u>·bah
land *n* **γη** ghee; *v* **προσγειώνομαι**
  prohz·yee·<u>oh</u>·noh·meh
language course **μάθημα ξένης**
  γλώσσας <u>mah</u>·thee·mah
  <u>kseh</u>·nees ghloh·sahs
large *adj* **μεγάλος** meh·<u>ghah</u>·lohs
last **τελευταίος** teh·lehf·<u>teh</u>·ohs
late *adv* **αργά** ahr·<u>ghah</u>
laugh *v* **γελώ** yeh·<u>loh</u>

laundry facility **πλυντήριο**
  pleen·<u>dee</u>·ree·oh
lavatory **μπάνιο** <u>bah</u>·nioh
lawyer **δικηγόρος**
  THee·kee·<u>ghoh</u>·rohs
laxative **καθαρτικό**
  kah·thahr·tee·<u>koh</u>
learn **μαθαίνω** mah·<u>theh</u>·noh
leave *v* (depart) **φεύγω** <u>fehv</u>·ghoh;
  (let go) **αφήνω** ah·<u>fee</u>·noh
left *adj* **αριστερός** ah·rees·teh·<u>rohs</u>;
  adv **αριστερά** ah·rees·teh·<u>rah</u>
leg **πόδι** poh·<u>THee</u>
legal **νόμιμος** <u>noh</u>·mee·mohs
lend **δανείζω** THah·<u>nee</u>·zoh
length **μήκος** <u>mee</u>·kohs
lens **φακός** fah·<u>kohs</u>
lens cap **κάλυμμα φακού**
  <u>kah</u>·lee·mah fah·<u>koo</u>
less **λιγότερο** lee·<u>ghoh</u>·teh·roh
letter **γράμμα** <u>ghrah</u>·mah
level (even) **επίπεδο**
  eh·<u>pee</u>·peh·THoh
library **βιβλιοθήκη**
  veev·lee·oh·<u>thee</u>·kee
lie down **ξαπλώνω** ksah·<u>ploh</u>·noh
life boat **ναυαγοσωστική λέμβος**
  nah·vah·ghoh·sohs·tee·<u>kee</u>
  <u>lehm</u>·vohs
lifeguard **ναυαγοσώστης**
  nah·vah·ghoh·<u>sohs</u>·tees
life jacket **σωσίβιο** soh·<u>see</u>·vee·oh
lift [BE] *n* (elevator) **ασανσέρ**
  ah·sahn·<u>sehr</u>
lift pass **άδεια σκι** <u>ah</u>·THee·ah
  skee
light *adj* (color) **ανοιχτός**
  ah·neekh·<u>tohs</u>; *n* (electric) **φως** fohs

light bulb **λάμπα** <u>lahm</u>·bah
lighter *adj* **ανοιχτότερος**
  ah·neekh·<u>toh</u>·teh·rohs;
  n **αναπτήρας** ah·nahp·<u>tee</u>·rahs
lighthouse **φάρος** <u>fah</u>·rohs
lights (car) **φώτα** <u>foh</u>·tah
line *n* (subway) **γραμμή** ghrah·<u>mee</u>
lips **χείλη** <u>khee</u>·lee
lipstick **κραγιόν** krah·<u>yohn</u>
liter **λίτρο** <u>lee</u>·troh
little **μικρός** meek·<u>rohs</u>
liver **συκώτι** see·<u>koh</u>·tee
living room **σαλόνι** sah·<u>loh</u>·nee
local **τοπικός** toh·pee·<u>kohs</u>
location (space) **θέση** <u>theh</u>·see
lock *n* (door) **κλειδαριά**
  klee·THahr·<u>yah</u>; (river, canal)
  φράγμα <u>frahgh</u>·mah; *v* **κλειδώνω**
  klee·<u>THoh</u>·noh
long *adj* **μακρύς** mak·<u>rees</u>
long-distance bus **υπεραστικό**
  λεωφορείο ee·peh·rahs·tee·<u>koh</u>
  leh·oh·foh·<u>ree</u>·oh
long-distance call **υπεραστικό**
  τηλεφώνημα ee·pehr·ahs·tee·<u>koh</u>
  tee·leh·<u>foh</u>·nee·mah
long-sighted [BE] **πρεσβύωπας**
  prehz·<u>vee</u>·oh·pahs
look *v* **κοιτάω** kee·<u>tah</u>·oh
look for **ψάχνω** psahkh·noh
loose (fitting) **φαρδύς** fahr·<u>THees</u>
loss *n* **απώλεια** ah·<u>poh</u>·lee·ah
lotion **λοσιόν** loh·<u>siohn</u>
loud *adj* **δυνατός** THee·nah·<u>tohs</u>
love *v* **αγαπώ** ah·ghah·<u>poh</u>
lower *adj* (berth) **κάτω** <u>kah</u>·toh
lubricant **λιπαντικό**
  lee·pahn·dee·<u>koh</u>

luck **τύχη** <u>tee</u>·khee
luggage **αποσκευές**
  ah·pohs·keh·<u>vehs</u>
luggage cart **καροτσάκι**
  αποσκευών kah·roh·<u>tsah</u>·kee
  ah·pohs·keh·<u>vohn</u>
luggage locker **θυρίδα**
  thee·<u>ree</u>·THah
lukewarm **χλιαρός** khlee·ah·<u>rohs</u>
lump *n* **σβώλος** <u>svoh</u>·lohs; (medical)
  εξόγκωμα eh·<u>ksoh</u>·goh·mah
lunch *n* **μεσημεριανό**
  meh·see·mehr·yah·<u>noh</u>
lung **πνεύμονας** pnehv·moh·nahs
luxury **πολυτέλεια**
  poh·lee·<u>teh</u>·lee·ah

M

magazine **περιοδικό**
  peh·ree·oh·<u>THee</u>·koh
magnificent **μεγαλοπρεπής**
  meh·ghah·lohp·reh·<u>pees</u>
mailbox **ταχυδρομικό κουτί**
  tah·kheeTH·roh·mee·<u>koh</u>
  koo·<u>tee</u>
mail *n* **αλληλογραφία**
  ah·lee·lohgh·rah·<u>fee</u>·ah
main **κύριος** <u>kee</u>·ree·ohs
make-up **μακιγιάζ** mah·kee·<u>yahz</u>
man (male) **άνδρας** <u>ahn</u>·THrahs
manager **διευθυντής**
  THee·ehf·theen·<u>dees</u>
manicure **μανικιούρ** mah·nee·<u>kioor</u>
manual (car) **χειροκίνητος**
  khee·roh·<u>kee</u>·nee·tohs
map *n* **χάρτης** <u>khahr</u>·tees
market *n* **αγορά** ah·ghoh·<u>rah</u>

married **παντρεμένος**
pahn·dreh·<u>meh</u>·nohs

mask n (diving) **μάσκα** <u>mahs</u>·kah

mass n (church) **λειτουργία**
lee·toor·<u>yee</u>·ah

massage n **μασάζ** mah·<u>sahz</u>

match n (sport) **αγώνας**
ah·<u>ghoh</u>·nahs; (fire starter) **σπίρτο**
<u>speer</u>·toh

maybe **ίσως** ee·sohs

meal **γεύμα** <u>yehv</u>·mah

mean v **σημαίνω** see·<u>meh</u>·noh

measure v **μετρώ** meht·<u>roh</u>

measurement **μέτρηση**
<u>meh</u>·tree·see

medication **φάρμακα** <u>fahr</u>·mah·kah

meet **συναντώ** see·nahn·<u>doh</u>

memorial **μνημείο** mnee·<u>mee</u>·oh

mend **διορθώνω**
THee·ohr·<u>thoh</u>·noh

menstrual cramp **πόνος περιόδου**
<u>poh</u>·nohs peh·ree·<u>oh</u>·THoo

mention **αναφέρω** ah·nah·<u>feh</u>·roh

message n **μήνυμα** <u>mee</u>·nee·mah

metal n **μέταλλο** <u>meh</u>·tah·loh

microwave (oven) **φούρνος**
μικροκυμάτων <u>foor</u>·nohs
mee·kroh·kee·<u>mah</u>·tohn

migraine **ημικρανία**
ee·mee·krah·<u>nee</u>·ah

mileage **χιλιόμετρα**
khee·<u>lioh</u>·meh·trah

mini-bar **μίνι-μπαρ** <u>mee</u>·nee·bahr

minimart **παντοπωλείο**
pahn·doh·poh·<u>lee</u>·oh

minimum **ελάχιστος**
eh·<u>lah</u>·khees·tohs

minute n (time) **λεπτό** lehp·<u>toh</u>

mirror n **καθρέφτης** kah·<u>threhf</u>·tees

mistake **λάθος** <u>lah</u>·thohs

misunderstanding **παρεξήγηση**
pah·reh·<u>ksee</u>·yee·see

mobile phone [BE] **κινητό**
kee·nee·<u>toh</u>

modern **μοντέρνος** moh·<u>deh</u>·rnohs

moisturizer (cream) **ενυδατική**
κρέμα eh·nee·THah·tee·<u>kee</u>
<u>kreh</u>·mah

money **χρήματα** <u>khree</u>·mah·tah

money order **ταχυδρομική επιταγή**
tah·kheeTH·roh·mee·<u>kee</u>
eh·pee·tah·<u>yee</u>

money-belt **ζώνη για χρήματα**
<u>zoh</u>·nee yah <u>khree</u>·mah·tah

monument **μνημείο** mnee·<u>mee</u>·oh

moped **μοτοποδήλατο**
moh·toh·poh·<u>THee</u>·lah·toh

more **παραπάνω** pah·rah·<u>pah</u>·noh

morning **πρωί** proh·<u>ee</u>

mosquito **κουνούπι** koo·<u>noo</u>·pee

mosquito bite **τσίμπημα**
κουνουπιού <u>tseem</u>·bee·mah
koo·noo·<u>piooh</u>

motorboat **εξωλέμβιο**
eh·ksoh·<u>lehm</u>·vee·oh

motorway [BE] **εθνική οδός**
ehth·nee·<u>kee</u> oh·<u>THohs</u>

mountain **βουνό** voo·<u>noh</u>

moustache **μουστάκι**
moos·<u>tah</u>·kee

mouth n **στόμα** <u>stoh</u>·mah

move v (room) **μετακομίζω**
meh·tah·koh·<u>mee</u>·zoh

movie **ταινία** teh·<u>nee</u>·ah

movie theater **κινηματογράφος**
kee·nee·mah·tohgh·<u>rah</u>·fohs

much **πολύ** poh·<u>lee</u>
muscle *n* **μυς** mees
museum **μουσείο** moo·<u>see</u>·oh
music **μουσική** moo·see·<u>kee</u>
musician **μουσικός** moo·see·<u>kohs</u>
must *v* **πρέπει** <u>preh</u>·pee

N

nail salon **σαλόνι νυχιών**
  sah·<u>loh</u>·nee nee·<u>khiohn</u>
name *n* **όνομα** <u>oh</u>·noh·mah
napkin **πετσέτα** peh·<u>tseh</u>·tah
nappy [BE] **πάνα μωρού** <u>pah</u>·nah
  moh·<u>roo</u>
narrow **στενός** steh·<u>nohs</u>
national **εθνικός** eth·nee·<u>kohs</u>
nationality **υπηκοότητα**
  ee·pee·koh·<u>oh</u>·tee·tah
nature **φύση** <u>fee</u>·see
nature reserve **εθνικός δρυμός**
  eth·nee·<u>kohs</u> THree·<u>mohs</u>
nature trail **μονοπάτι**
  moh·noh·<u>pah</u>·tee
nausea **ναυτία** nahf·<u>tee</u>·ah
near *adv* **κοντά** kohn·<u>dah</u>
nearby **εδώ κοντά** eh·<u>THoh</u> kohn·<u>dah</u>
necessary **απαραίτητος**
  ah·pah·<u>reh</u>·tee·tohs
necklace **κολλιέ** koh·<u>lieh</u>
need *v* **χρειάζομαι**
  khree·<u>ah</u>·zoh·meh
neighbor *n* **γείτονας** <u>yee</u>·toh·nahs
nerve **νεύρο** <u>nehv</u>·roh
never **ποτέ** poh·<u>teh</u>
new **καινούργιος** keh·<u>noor</u>·yohs
newspaper **εφημερίδα**
  eh·fee·meh·<u>ree</u>·THah

newsstand **περίπτερο**
  peh·<u>ree</u>·pteh·roh
next **επόμενος** eh·<u>poh</u>·meh·nohs
next to **δίπλα** THeep·lah
night **νύχτα** <u>neekh</u>·tah
night club **νυχτερινό κέντρο**
  neekh·teh·ree·<u>noh</u> kehn·droh
noisy **θορυβώδης**
  thoh·ree·<u>voh</u>·THees
none *adj* **κανένας** kah·<u>neh</u>·nahs
non-smoking **μη καπνίζοντες** mee
  kap·<u>nee</u>·zohn·dehs
north **βόρεια** <u>voh</u>·ree·ah
nose *n* **μύτη** <u>mee</u>·tee
nudist beach **παραλία γυμνιστών**
  pah·rah·<u>lee</u>·ah yeem·nees·<u>tohn</u>
nurse *n* **νοσοκόμα**
  noh·soh·<u>koh</u>·mah

O

occupied **κατειλημένος**
  kah·tee·lee·<u>meh</u>·nohs
office **γραφείο** ghrah·<u>fee</u>·oh
old *adj* (thing) **παλιός** pah·<u>liohs</u>;
  (person) **γέρικος** <u>yeh</u>·ree·kohs
old town **παλιά πόλη** pah·<u>liah</u>
  <u>poh</u>·lee
old-fashioned **ντεμοντέ**
  deh·mohn·<u>deh</u>
once **μια φορά** miah foh·<u>rah</u>
one-way ticket **απλό εισιτήριο**
  ahp·<u>loh</u> ee·see·<u>tee</u>·ree·oh
open *adj* **ανοιχτός** ah·neekh·<u>tohs</u>;
  v **ανοίγω** ah·<u>nee</u>·ghoh
opening hours **ώρες λειτουργίας**
  <u>oh</u>·rehs lee·toor·<u>yee</u>·ahs
opera **όπερα** <u>oh</u>·peh·rah

opposite **απέναντι**
ah·<u>peh</u>·nahn·dee

optician **οφθαλμίατρος**
ohf·thahl·<u>mee</u>·aht·rohs

orchestra **ορχήστρα** ohr·<u>khees</u>·trah

order v **παραγγέλνω**
pah·rah·<u>gehl</u>·noh

organized **οργανωμένος**
ohr·ghah·noh·<u>meh</u>·nohs

others **άλλα** <u>ah</u>·lah

out adv **έξω** <u>eh</u>·ksoh

outdoor **εξωτερικός**
eh·ksoh·teh·ree·<u>kohs</u>

outside adj **έξω** <u>eh</u>·ksoh

oval **οβάλ** oh·<u>vahl</u>

oven **φούρνος** <u>foor</u>·nohs

over there **εκεί** eh·<u>kee</u>

overnight (package) **ένα βράδυ**
eh·nah <u>vrah</u>·THee

owe **χρωστώ** khroh·<u>stoh</u>

owner **κάτοχος** <u>kah</u>·toh·khohs

P

pacifier **πιπίλα** pee·<u>pee</u>·lah

pack v (baggage) **φτιάχνω τις**
βαλίτσες ftee·<u>ahkh</u>·noh tees
vah·<u>lee</u>·tsehs

paddling pool [BE] **ρηχή πισίνα**
ree·<u>khee</u> pee·<u>see</u>·nah

padlock **λουκέτο** loo·<u>keh</u>·toh

pain n **πόνος** <u>poh</u>·nohs

painkiller **παυσίπονο**
pahf·<u>see</u>·poh·noh

paint v **ζωγραφίζω**
zohgh·rah·<u>fee</u>·zoh

pair **ζευγάρι** zehv·<u>ghah</u>·ree

pajamas **πυτζάμες** pee·<u>jah</u>·mehs

palace **ανάκτορα** ah·<u>nahk</u>·toh·rah

panorama **πανόραμα**
pah·<u>noh</u>·rah·mah

pants **παντελόνι** pahn·deh·<u>loh</u>·nee

paper **χαρτί** khar·<u>tee</u>

paralysis **παραλυσία**
pah·rah·lee·<u>see</u>·ah

parcel **πακέτο** pah·<u>keh</u>·toh

parents **γονείς** ghoh·<u>nees</u>

park n **πάρκο** <u>pahr</u>·koh

parking lot **χώρος στάθμευσης**
<u>khoh</u>·rohs <u>stahth</u>·mehf·sees

parking meter **παρκόμετρο**
pahr·<u>koh</u>·meht·roh

party n (social gathering) **πάρτυ**
<u>pah</u>·rtee

pass v **περνώ** pehr·<u>noh</u>

passenger **επιβάτης**
eh·pee·<u>vah</u>·tees

passport **διαβατήριο**
THiah·vah·<u>tee</u>·ree·oh

pastry store **ζαχαροπλαστείο**
zah·khah·rohp·lahs·<u>tee</u>·oh

path **μονοπάτι** moh·noh·<u>pah</u>·tee

pay v **πληρώνω** plee·<u>roh</u>·noh

payment **πληρωμή** plee·roh·<u>mee</u>

peak n **κορυφή** koh·ree·<u>fee</u>

pearl **μαργαριτάρι**
mahr·ghah·ree·<u>tah</u>·ree

pebbly (beach) **με χαλίκια** meh
khah·<u>lee</u>·kiah

pedestrian crossing **διάβαση**
πεζών THee·<u>ah</u>·vah·see
peh·<u>zohn</u>

pedestrian zone **πεζόδρομος**
peh·<u>zohTH</u>·roh·mohs

pen n **στυλό** stee·<u>loh</u>

per **την** teen

perhaps **ίσως** ee·sohs
period (menstrual) **περίοδος**
  peh·ree·oh·THohs; (time)
  χρονική περίοδος khroh·nee·kee
  peh·ree·oh·Thohs
permit n **άδεια** ah·THee·ah
petrol [BE] **βενζίνη** vehn·zee·nee
pewter **κασσίτερος**
  kah·see·teh·rohs
phone n **τηλέφωνο** tee·leh·foh·noh
phone call **τηλεφώνημα**
  tee·leh·foh·nee·mah
phone card **τηλεκάρτα**
  tee·leh·kahr·tah
photo v **φωτογραφία**
  foh·tohgh·rah·fee·ah
photocopier **φωτοτυπικό**
  foh·toh·tee·pee·koh
phrase n **φράση** frah·see
pick up **παίρνω** pehr·noh
picnic area **περιοχή για πικνίκ**
  peh·ree·oh·khee yah peek·neek
piece **τεμάχιο** teh·mah·khee·oh
pillow **μαξιλάρι** mah·ksee·lah·ree
pillow case **μαξιλαροθήκη**
  mah·ksee·lah·roh·thee·kee
pipe (smoking) **πίπα** pee·pah
piste [BE] **μονοπάτι**
  moh·noh·pah·tee
pizzeria **πιτσαρία** pee·tsah·ree·ah
plan n **σχέδιο** skheh·THee·oh
plane n **αεροπλάνο**
  ah·eh·rohp·lah·noh
plant n **φυτό** fee·toh
plastic wrap **διαφανή μεμβράνη**
  THee·ah·fah·nee mehm·vrah·nee
platform **αποβάθρα**
  ah·poh·vahth·rah

platinum **πλατίνα** plah·tee·nah
play v (games) **παίζω** peh·zoh;
  (music) **παίζω** peh·zoh
playground **παιδική χαρά**
  peh·THee·kee khah·rah
pleasant **ευχάριστος**
  ehf·khah·rees·tohs
plug n **πρίζα** pree·zah
point n **σημείο** see·mee·oh;
  v **δείχνω** THeekh·noh
poison n **δηλητήριο**
  THee·lee·tee·ree·oh
poisonous **δηλητηριώδης**
  THee·lee·tee·ree·oh·THees
police n **αστυνομία**
  ah·stee·noh·mee·ah
police station **αστυνομικό τμήμα**
  ah·stee·noh·mee·koh tmee·mah
pond n **λιμνούλα** leem·noo·lah
popular **δημοφιλής**
  THee·moh·fee·lees
porter **αχθοφόρος**
  ahkh·thoh·foh·rohs
portion n **μερίδα** meh·ree·THah
possible **πιθανός** pee·thah·nohs
postbox [BE] **ταχυδρομικό κουτί**
  tah·kheeTH·roh·mee·koh koo·tee
post card **καρτποστάλ**
  kahrt·poh·stahl
post office **ταχυδρομείο**
  tah·kheeTH·roh·mee·oh
pottery **αγγειοπλαστική**
  ahn·gee·ohp·lahs·tee·kee
pound (sterling) **λίρα** lee·rah
pregnant **έγκυος** eh·gee·ohs
prescribe **συνταγογραφώ**
  seen·dah·ghoh·ghrah·foh

prescription **συνταγή γιατρού**
seen·dah·<u>yee</u> yaht·<u>roo</u>
present **δώρο** <u>THoh</u>·roh
press v **σιδερώνω**
see·THeh·<u>roh</u>·noh
pretty adj **όμορφος** <u>oh</u>·mohr·fohs
prison n **φυλακή** fee·lah·<u>kee</u>
private bathroom **ιδιωτικό μπάνιο**
ee·THee·oh·tee·<u>koh bah</u>·nioh
problem **πρόβλημα** <u>prohv</u>·lee·mah
program n **πρόγραμμα**
<u>prohgh</u>·rah·mah
program of events **πρόγραμμα**
θεαμάτων <u>proh</u>·ghrah·mah
theh·ah·<u>mah</u>·tohn
prohibited **απαγορευμένος**
ah·pah·ghoh·rehv·<u>meh</u>·nohs
pronounce **προφέρω** proh·<u>feh</u>·roh
public **δημόσιος**
THeh·<u>moh</u>·see·ohs
public holiday **αργία** ahr·<u>yee</u>·ah
pump n **τρόμπα** <u>troh</u>·mbah
purpose **σκοπός** skoh·<u>pohs</u>
put v **βάζω** <u>vah</u>·zoh

Q

quality **ποιότητα** pee·<u>oh</u>·tee·tah
quantity **ποσότητα** poh·<u>soh</u>·tee·tah
quarantine n **καραντίνα**
kah·rahn·<u>dee</u>·nah
quarter (quantity) **ένα τέταρτο**
<u>eh</u>·nah teh·tah·rtoh
quay **αποβάθρα** ah·poh·<u>vath</u>·rah
question n **ερώτηση**
eh·<u>roh</u>·tee·see
queue [BE] v **περιμένω στην ουρά**
peh·ree·<u>meh</u>·noh steen oo·<u>rah</u>

quick **γρήγορος** <u>ghree</u>·ghoh·rohs
quiet adj **ήσυχος** <u>ee</u>·see·khohs

R

racket (tennis, squash) **ρακέτα**
rah·<u>keh</u>·tah
radio n **ραδιόφωνο**
rah·THee·<u>oh</u>·foh·noh
railway station [BE]
σιδηροδρομικός σταθμός
see·THee·rohTH·roh·mee·<u>kohs</u>
stahth·<u>mohs</u>
rain n **βροχή** vroh·<u>khee</u>; v **βρέχει**
<u>vreh</u>·khee
raincoat **αδιάβροχο**
ah·THee·<u>ahv</u>·roh·khoh
rapids **ρεύμα ποταμού** <u>rehv</u>·mah
poh·tah·<u>moo</u>
rare (unusual) **σπάνιος**
<u>spah</u>·nee·ohs
rash n **εξάνθημα**
eh·<u>ksahn</u>·thee·mah
ravine **ρεματιά** reh·mah·<u>tiah</u>
razor **ξυραφάκι** ksee·rah·<u>fah</u>·kee
razor blade **ξυραφάκι**
ksee·rah·<u>fah</u>·kee
ready adj **έτοιμος** eh·<u>tee</u>·mohs
real (genuine) **γνήσιος**
<u>ghee</u>·see·ohs; (true) **αληθινός**
ah·lee·thee·nohs
receipt **απόδειξη** ah·<u>poh</u>·THee·kse◌
reception (hotel) **ρεσεψιόν**
reh·seh·<u>psiohn</u>
recommend **συστήνω** sees·<u>tee</u>·no◌
reduction **έκπτωση** <u>ehk</u>·ptoh·see
refund n **επιστροφή χρημάτων**
eh·pees·troh·<u>fee</u> khree·<u>mah</u>·toh◌

region **περιοχή** peh·ree·oh·<u>khee</u>
registration number **αριθμός**
κυκλοφορίας ah·reeth·<u>mohs</u>
kee·kloh·foh·<u>ree</u>·ahs
religion **θρησκεία** three·<u>skee</u>·ah
remember **θυμάμαι** thee·<u>mah</u>·meh
rent v **νοικιάζω** nee·<u>kiah</u>·zoh
repair n **επισκευή**
eh·pee·skeh·<u>vee</u>; v **επισκευάζω**
eh·pee·skeh·<u>vah</u>·zoh
repeat v **επαναλαμβάνω**
eh·pah·nah·lahm·<u>vah</u>·noh
replacement part **ανταλλακτικό**
ahn·dah·lahk·tee·<u>koh</u>
report v **αναφέρω** ah·nah·<u>feh</u>·roh
restaurant **εστιατόριο**
ehs·tee·ah·<u>toh</u>·ree·oh
restroom **τουαλέτα** too·ah·<u>leh</u>·tah
retired **συνταξιούχος**
seen·dah·ksee·<u>oo</u>·khohs
return ticket [BE] **εισιτήριο με**
επιστροφή ee·see·<u>tee</u>·ree·oh
meh eh·pee·stroh·<u>fee</u>
reverse the charges **με χρέωση του**
καλούμενου meh <u>khreh</u>·oh·see too
kah·<u>loo</u>·meh·noo
revolting **αηδιαστικός**
ah·ee·THee·ah·stee·<u>kohs</u>
rib **πλευρό** plehv·<u>roh</u>
right adj (correct) **σωστός** soh·<u>stohs</u>;
(side) **δεξιός** THeh·ksee·<u>ohs</u>
river **ποταμός** poh·tah·<u>mohs</u>
road **δρόμος** <u>THroh</u>·mohs
road assistance **οδική βοήθεια**
oh·THee·<u>kee</u> voh·<u>ee</u>·thee·ah
road sign **πινακίδα**
pee·nah·<u>kee</u>·Thah
robbery **ληστεία** lees·<u>tee</u>·ah

rock n **βράχος** <u>vrah</u>·khohs
rock climbing **αναρρίχηση**
ah·nah·<u>ree</u>·khee·see
romantic **ρομαντικός**
roh·mahn·dee·<u>kohs</u>
roof n **στέγη** <u>steh</u>·yee
room n **δωμάτιο** THoh·<u>mah</u>·tee·oh
room service **υπηρεσία**
δωματίου ee·pee·reh·<u>see</u>·ah
THoh·mah·<u>tee</u>·oo
rope n **σχοινί** skhee·<u>nee</u>
round adj **στρογγυλός**
strohn·gkee·<u>lohs</u>; n (of golf)
παιχνίδι pehkh·<u>nee</u>·THee
round-trip ticket **εισιτήριο με**
επιστροφή ee·see·<u>tee</u>·ree·oh
meh eh·pee·stroh·<u>fee</u>
route n **διαδρομή**
THee·ahTH·roh·<u>mee</u>
rowing **κωπηλασία**
koh·pee·lah·<u>see</u>·ah
rubbish [BE] **σκουπίδια**
skoo·<u>peeTH</u>·yah
rude **αγενής** ah·yeh·<u>nees</u>
rug **χαλί** khah·<u>lee</u>
run v **τρέχω** <u>treh</u>·khoh
rush hour **ώρα αιχμής** <u>oh</u>·rah
ehkh·<u>mees</u>

S

safe adj (not dangerous) **ασφαλής**
ahs·fah·<u>lees</u>
sailing boat **ιστιοπλοϊκό**
ees·tee·oh·ploh·ee·<u>koh</u>
sales tax **ΦΠΑ** fee·pee·<u>ah</u>
same **ίδιος** <u>ee</u>·THee·ohs
sand **άμμος** <u>ah</u>·mohs

sandals **πέδιλα** peh·THee·lah

sandy (beach) **με άμμο** meh ah·moh

sanitary napkin **σερβιέτα** sehr·vee·eh·tah

satin **σατέν** sah·tehn

saucepan **κατσαρόλα** kah·tsah·roh·lah

sauna **σάουνα** sah·oo·nah

scarf **κασκόλ** kahs·kohl

scissors **ψαλίδι** psah·lee·THee

scratch **γρατζουνιά** ghrah·joo·niah

screw n **βίδα** vee·THah

screwdriver **κατσαβίδι** kah·tsah·vee·THee

sea **θάλασσα** thah·lah·sah

seafront **προκυμαία** proh·kee·meh·ah

seat n **θέση** theh·see

second-hand shop **κατάστημα μεταχειρισμένων ειδών** kah·lah·stee·mah mch·tah·khee·reez·meh·nohn ee·THohn

sedative **ηρεμιστικό** ee·reh·mee·stee·koh

see **βλέπω** vleh·poh

send **στέλνω** stehl·noh

senior citizen **ηλικιωμένος** ee·lee·kee·oh·meh·nohs

separately **ξεχωριστά** kseh·khoh·ree·stah

service n (business) **υπηρεσία** ee·pee·reh·see·ah; (mass) **λειτουργία** lee·toor·yee·ah

service charge **χρέωση υπηρεσίας** khreh·oh·see ee·pee·reh·see·ahs

sewer **υπόνομος** ee·poh·noh·mohs

shade (color) **απόχρωση** ah·pohkh·roh·see; (darkness) **σκιά** skee·ah

shampoo n **σαμπουάν** sahm·poo·ahn

shape n **σχήμα** skhee·mah

shaving cream **κρέμα ξυρίσματος** kreh·mah ksee·reez·mah·tohs

shelf n **ράφι** rah·fee

ship n **πλοίο** plee·oh

shirt **πουκάμισο** poo·kah·mee·soh

shock (electric) **ηλεκτροπληξία** ee·leh·ktroh·plee·ksee·ah

shoe **παπούτσι** pah·poo·tsee

shoe polish **βερνίκι παπουτσιών** vehr·nee·kee pah·poo·tsiohn

shoe repair **επισκευή παπουτσιών** eh·pee·skeh·vee pah·poo·tsiohn

shoe store **κατάστημα υποδημάτων** kah·tah·stee·mah ee·poh·THee·mah·tohn

shop (store) **κατάστημα** kah·tah·stee·mah

shopping mall **εμπορικό κέντρο** ehm·boh·ree·koh keh·ntroh

shore n **ακτή** ahk·tee

short adj **κοντός** kohn·dohs

shorts n **σορτς** sohrts

short-sighted [BE] **μύωπας** mee·oh·pahs

shoulder n (anatomy) **ώμος** oh·mohs

show **δείχνω** THeekh·noh

shower n **ντουζ** dooz

shower gel **αφρόλουτρο για ντουζ** ahf·roh·loot·roh yah dooz

shut adj **κλειστός** klees·tohs

sick *adj* **άρρωστος** <u>ah</u>·rohs·tohs

side (of road) **μεριά** mehr·<u>yah</u>

sightseeing sight **αξιοθέατο** ah·ksee·oh·<u>theh</u>·ah·toh

sightseeing tour **ξενάγηση στα αξιοθέατα** kseh·<u>nah</u>·yee·see stah ah·ksee·oh·<u>theh</u>·ah·tah

sign (road) **σήμα** <u>see</u>·mah

silk **μετάξι** meh·<u>tah</u>·ksee

silver **ασήμι** ah·<u>see</u>·mee

simple **απλός** ahp·<u>lohs</u>

single (not married) **ελεύθερος** eh·<u>lehf</u>·theh·rohs

single room **μονόκλινο δωμάτιο** moh·<u>noh</u>·klee·noh THoh·<u>mah</u>·tee·oh

single ticket [BE] **απλό εισιτήριο** ahp·<u>loh</u> ee·see·<u>tee</u>·ree·oh

sink (bathroom) **νιπτήρας** nee·<u>ptee</u>·rahs

sit **κάθομαι** <u>kah</u>·thoh·meh

size *n* **μέγεθος** <u>meh</u>·yeh·thohs

skates **παγοπέδιλα** pah·ghoh·<u>peh</u>·THee·lah

skating rink **παγοδρόμιο** pah·ghohTH·<u>roh</u>·mee·oh

ski boots **μπότες του σκι** <u>boh</u>·tehs too skee

ski poles **μπαστούνια του σκι** bahs·<u>too</u>·niah too skee

ski school **σχολή σκι** skhoh·<u>lee</u> skee

skiing **σκι** skee

skin *n* **δέρμα** <u>Thehr</u>·mah

skirt **φούστα** <u>foo</u>·stah

sleep *v* **κοιμάμαι** kee·<u>mah</u>·meh

sleeping bag **υπνόσακκος** ee·<u>pnoh</u>·sah·kohs

sleeping car **βαγκόν-λι** vah·<u>gohn</u>·lee

sleeping pill **υπνωτικό χάπι** eep·noh·tee·<u>koh</u> khah·pee

slippers **παντόφλες** pahn·<u>dohf</u>·lehs

slope (ski) **πλαγιά** plah·<u>yah</u>

slow *adj* **αργός** ahr·<u>ghohs</u>

small **μικρός** meek·<u>rohs</u>

smell *v* **μυρίζω** mee·<u>ree</u>·zoh

smoke *v* **καπνίζω** kahp·<u>nee</u>·zoh

smoking area **περιοχή για καπνίζοντες** peh·ree·oh·<u>khee</u> yah kahp·<u>nee</u>·zohn·dehs

snack bar **κυλικείο** kee·lee·<u>kee</u>·oh

sneakers **αθλητικά παπούτσια** ath·lee·tee·<u>kah</u> pah·<u>poo</u>·tsiah

snorkeling equipment **εξοπλισμό για ελεύθερη κατάδυση** eh·ksohp·leez·<u>moh</u> yah eh·<u>lehf</u>·theh·ree kah·<u>tah</u>·THee·see

snow *v* **χιονίζει** khioh·<u>nee</u>·zee

soap *n* **σαπούνι** sah·<u>poo</u>·nee

soccer **ποδόσφαιρο** poh·<u>THohs</u>·feh·roh

socket **πρίζα** <u>pree</u>·zah

socks **κάλτσες** <u>kahl</u>·tsehs

sofa **καναπές** kah·nah·<u>pehs</u>

sole (shoes) **σόλα** <u>soh</u>·lah

something **κάτι** <u>kah</u>·tee

sometimes **μερικές φορές** meh·ree·<u>kehs</u> foh·<u>rehs</u>

soon **σύντομα** <u>seen</u>·doh·mah

soother [BE] **πιπίλα** pee·<u>pee</u>·lah

sore throat **πονόλαιμος** poh·<u>noh</u>·leh·mohs

sort *n* **είδος** ee·THohs; *v* **διαλέγω**
THiah·<u>leh</u>·ghoh
south *adj* **νότιος** <u>noh</u>·tee·ohs
souvenir **σουβενίρ** soo·veh·<u>neer</u>
souvenir store **κατάστημα σουβενίρ**
kah·<u>tahs</u>·tee·mah soo·veh·<u>neer</u>
spa **σπα** spah
space *n* (area) **χώρος** <u>khoh</u>·rohs
spare (extra) **επιπλέον**
eh·peep·<u>leh</u>·ohn
speak **μιλώ** mee·<u>loh</u>
special requirement **ειδική ανάγκη**
ee·THee·<u>kee</u> ah·<u>nahn</u>·gkee
specialist **ειδικός** ee·THee·<u>kohs</u>
specimen **δείγμα** THeegh·mah
speed *v* **τρέχω** treh·khoh
spend **ξοδεύω** ksoh·<u>THeh</u>·voh
spine **σπονδυλική στήλη**
spohn·THee·lee·<u>kee</u> stee·lee
spoon *n* **κουτάλι** koo·<u>tah</u>·lee
sport **αθλητισμός**
ahth·lee·teez·<u>mohs</u>
sporting goods store
κατάστημα αθλητικών
ειδών kah·<u>tahs</u>·tee·mah
ath·lee·tee·<u>kohn</u> ee·THohn
sports massage **αθλητικό μασάζ**
ahth·lee·tee·<u>koh</u> mah·<u>sahz</u>
sports stadium **αθλητικό στάδιο**
ahth·lee·tee·<u>koh</u> stah·THee·oh
square **τετράγωνος**
teht·<u>rah</u>·ghoh·nohs
stadium **στάδιο** <u>stah</u>·THee·oh
stain *n* **λεκές** leh·<u>kehs</u>
stairs **σκάλες** <u>skah</u>·lehs
stale **μπαγιάτικος** bah·<u>yah</u>·tee·kohs
stamp *n* (postage) **γραμματόσημο**
ghrah·mah·<u>toh</u>·see·moh

start *v* **αρχίζω** ahr·<u>khee</u>·zoh
statement (legal) **δήλωση**
THee·loh·see
statue **άγαλμα** <u>ah</u>·ghahl·mah
stay *v* **μένω** <u>meh</u>·noh
sterilizing solution **αποστειρωτικό**
διάλυμα ah·pohs·tee·roh·tee·<u>koh</u>
THee·<u>ah</u>·lee·mah
sting *n* (insect) **τσίμπημα**
<u>tsee</u>·bee·mah
stolen **κλεμένος** kleh·<u>meh</u>·nohs
stomach *n* **στομάχι** stoh·<u>mah</u>·khee
stomachache **στομαχόπονος**
stoh·mah·<u>khoh</u>·poh·nohs
stop *n* (bus) **στάση** <u>stah</u>·see;
v **σταματώ** stah·mah·<u>toh</u>
store guide [BE] **οδηγός**
καταστήματος oh·THee·<u>ghohs</u>
kah·tahs·<u>tee</u>·mah·tohs
stove **κουζίνα** koo·<u>zee</u>·nah
straight ahead **ευθεία** ehf·<u>thee</u>·ah
strange **παράξενος**
pah·<u>rah</u>·kseh·nohs
straw (drinking) **καλαμάκι**
kah·lah·<u>mah</u>·kee
stream *n* **ρυάκι** ree·<u>ah</u>·kee
street **δρόμος** THroh·mohs
string *n* (cord) **σπάγγος** <u>spah</u>·gohs
student **φοιτητής** fee·tee·<u>tees</u>
study *v* **σπουδάζω** spoo·<u>THah</u>·zoh
style *n* **στυλ** steel
subtitled **με υπότιτλους** meh
ee·<u>poh</u>·teet·loos
subway **μετρό** meh·<u>troh</u>
subway station **σταθμός μετρό**
stahth·<u>mohs</u> meh·<u>troh</u>
suggest **προτείνω** proh·<u>tee</u>·noh

suit (men's) **κουστούμι**
koos·<u>too</u>·mee; (women's) **ταγιέρ**
tah·<u>yehr</u>

suitable **κατάλληλος**
kah·<u>tah</u>·lee·lohs

sunburn *n* **έγκαυμα ηλίου**
ehn·gahv·mah ee·<u>lee</u>·oo

sunglasses **γυαλιά ηλίου** yah·<u>liah</u>
ee·<u>lee</u>·oo

sunshade [BE] **ομπρέλλα**
ohm·<u>breh</u>·lah

sunstroke **ηλίαση** ee·<u>lee</u>·ah·see

sun tan lotion **λοσιόν μαυρίσματος**
loh·<u>siohn</u> mahv·<u>rees</u>·mah·tohs

sunscreen **αντιηλιακό**
ahn·dee·ee·lee·ah·<u>koh</u>

superb **έξοχος** <u>eh</u>·ksoh·khohs

supermarket **σουπερμάρκετ**
soo·pehr·<u>mahr</u>·keht

supervision **επίβλεψη**
eh·<u>peev</u>·leh·psee

surname **επίθετο** eh·<u>pee</u>·theh·toh

sweatshirt **φούτερ** <u>foo</u>·tehr

swelling **πρήξιμο** <u>pree</u>·ksee·moh

swimming **κολύμβηση**
koh·<u>leem</u>·vee·see

swimming pool **πισίνα** pee·<u>see</u>·nah

swimming trunks **μαγιό** mah·<u>yoh</u>

swimsuit **μαγιό** mah·<u>yoh</u>

switch *n* **διακόπτης** THiah·<u>koh</u>·ptees

swollen **πρησμένος**
preez·<u>meh</u>·nohs

symptom **σύμπτωμα**
<u>seem</u>·ptoh·mah

T

table **τραπέζι** trah·<u>peh</u>·zee

tablecloth **τραπεζομάντηλο**
trah·peh·zoh·<u>mahn</u>·dee·loh

tablet **χάπι** <u>khah</u>·pee

take **παίρνω** <u>pehr</u>·noh

take a photograph **βγάζω
φωτογραφία** <u>vghah</u>·zoh
foh·tohgh·rah·<u>fee</u>·ah

take away [BE] **πακέτο για το σπίτι**
pah·<u>keh</u>·toh yah toh <u>spee</u>·tee

tall **ψηλός** psee·<u>lohs</u>

tampon **ταμπόν** tahm·<u>bohn</u>

tax *n* **φόρος** <u>foh</u>·rohs

taxi **ταξί** tah·<u>ksee</u>

taxi driver **ταξιτζής** tah·ksee·<u>jees</u>

taxi rank [BE] **πιάτσα ταξί** <u>piah</u>·tsah
tah·<u>ksee</u>

teaspoon **κουταλάκι**
koo·tah·<u>lah</u>·kee

team *n* **ομάδα** oh·<u>mah</u>·THah

teenager **έφηβος** <u>eh</u>·fee·vohs

telephone *n* **τηλέφωνο**
tee·<u>leh</u>·foh·noh

telephone booth **τηλεφωνικός
θάλαμος** tee·leh·foh·nee·<u>kohs</u>
<u>thah</u>·lah·mohs

telephone call **κλήση** <u>klee</u>·see

telephone directory **τηλεφωνικός
κατάλογος** tee·leh·foh·nee·<u>kohs</u>
kah·<u>tah</u>·loh·ghohs

telephone number **αριθμός
τηλεφώνου** ah·reeth·<u>mohs</u>
tee·leh·<u>foh</u>·noo

tell **λέω** <u>leh</u>·oh

temperature (body) **θερμοκρασία**
theh·rmohk·rah·<u>see</u>·ah

temple **ναός** nah·<u>ohs</u>

temporary **προσωρινός**
proh·soh·ree·<u>nohs</u>

tennis **τέννις** teh·nees
tennis court **γήπεδο τέννις**
  yee·peh·THoh teh·nees
tent **σκηνή** skee·nee
terrible **φοβερός** foh·veh·rohs
theater **θέατρο** theh·aht·roh
theft **κλοπή** kloh·pee
there **εκεί** eh·kee
thermal bath **ιαματικό λουτρό**
  ee·ah·mah·tee·koh loot·roh
thermos flask **θερμός** thehr·mohs
thick **χοντρός** khohn·drohs
thief **κλέφτης** klehf·tees
thin adj **λεπτός** lehp·tohs
think **νομίζω** noh·mee·zoh
thirsty **διψάω** THee·psah·oh
those **εκείνα** eh·kee·nah
throat **λαιμός** leh·mohs
thumb **αντίχειρας**
  ahn·dee·khee·rahs
ticket **εισιτήριο** ee·see·tee·ree·oh
ticket office **γραφείο εισιτηρίων**
  ghrah·fee·oh ee·see·tee·ree·ohn
tie n **γραβάτα** ghrah·vah·tah
tight adj **στενός** steh·nohs
tights [BE] n **καλσόν** kahl·sohn
timetable [BE] **δρομολόγιο**
  THroh·loh·yee·oh
tire **λάστιχο** lahs·tee·khoh
tired **κουρασμένος**
  koo·rahz·meh·nohs
tissue **χαρτομάντηλο**
  khahr·toh·mahn·dee·loh
toaster **τοστιέρα** toh·stieh·rah
tobacco **καπνός** kahp·nohs
tobacconist **καπνοπωλείο**
  kahp·noh·poh·lee·oh
toilet [BE] **τουαλέτα** too·ah·leh·tah

toilet paper **χαρτί υγείας** khahr·tee
  ee·yee·ahs
toiletries **καλλυντικά**
  kah·leen·dee·kah
tongue **γλώσσα** ghloh·sah
too (extreme) **πάρα πολύ** pah·rah
  poh·lee
tooth **δόντι** THohn·dee
toothache **πονόδοντος**
  poh·noh·THohn·dohs
toothbrush **οδοντόβουρτσα**
  oh·THohn·doh·voor·tsah
toothpaste **οδοντόπαστα**
  oh·THohn·doh·pahs·tah
top adj **πάνω** pah·noh
torn **σχισμένος** skheez·meh·nohs
tour guide **ξεναγός** kseh·nah·ghohs
tourist **τουρίστας** too·rees·tahs
towards **προς** prohs
tower **πύργος** peer·ghohs
town **πόλη** poh·lee
town hall **δημαρχείο**
  THee·mahr·khee·oh
toy store **κατάστημα**
  παιχνιδιών kah·tahs·tee·mah
  peh·khnee·THiohn
traditional **παραδοσιακός**
  pah·rah·THoh·see·ah·kohs
traffic **κίνηση** kee·nee·see
trail **μονοπάτι** moh·noh·pah·tee
trailer **τροχόσπιτο**
  troh·khohs·pee·toh
train **τρένο** treh·noh
train station **σταθμός των τρένων**
  stahth·mohs tohn treh·nohn
tram **τραμ** trahm
transfer **μεταφέρω**
  meh·tah·feh·roh

transit *n* **μεταφορά** meh·tah·foh·<u>rah</u>

translate **μεταφράζω**
meh·tah·<u>frah</u>·zoh

translation **μετάφραση**
meh·<u>tah</u>·frah·see

translator **μεταφραστής**
meh·tah·frah·<u>stees</u>

trash **σκουπίδια** skoo·<u>peeTH</u>·yah

trash can **κάδος απορριμμάτων**
<u>kah</u>·THohs ah·poh·ree·<u>mah</u>·tohn

travel agency **ταξιδιωτικό γραφείο**
tah·ksee·THyoh·tee·<u>koh</u>
ghrah·<u>fee</u>·oh

travel sickness [BE] **ναυτία**
nahf·<u>tee</u>·ah

traveler's check **ταξιδιωτική επιταγή**
tah·ksee·THee·oh·tee·<u>kee</u>
eh·pee·tah·<u>yee</u>

tray **δίσκος** <u>THees</u>·kohs

tree **δέντρο** <u>THehn</u>·droh

trim *n* **διόρθωμα**
<u>THee</u>·<u>ohr</u>·thoh·mah

trolley [BE] (cart) **καροτσάκι**
kah·roh·<u>tsah</u>·kee

trolley-bus **τρόλλεϋ** <u>troh</u>·leh·ee

trousers [BE] **παντελόνι**
pahn·deh·<u>loh</u>·nee

try on **δοκιμάζω** THoh·kee·<u>mah</u>·zoh

T-shirt **μπλουζάκι** bloo·<u>zah</u>·kee

tunnel **τούνελ** <u>too</u>·nehl

turn *v* **γυρίζω** yee·<u>ree</u>·zoh

turn down *v* (volume, heat)
χαμηλώνω khah·mee·<u>loh</u>·noh

turn off *v* **σβήνω** <u>svee</u>·noh

turn on *v* **ανάβω** ah·<u>nah</u>·voh

turn up *v* (volume, heat) **ανεβάζω**
ah·neh·<u>vah</u>·zoh

TV **τηλεόραση** tee·leh·<u>oh</u>·rah·see

twin bed **διπλό κρεβάτι** THeep·<u>loh</u>
kreh·<u>vah</u>·tee

typical **τυπικός** tee·pee·<u>kohs</u>

U

ugly **άσχημος** <u>ahs</u>·khee·mohs

unconscious **αναίσθητος**
ah·<u>nehs</u>·thee·tohs

underground [BE] **υπόγειος**
ee·<u>poh</u>·ghee·ohs

underpants [BE] **κυλοτάκι**
kee·loh·<u>tah</u>·kee

understand **καταλαβαίνω**
kah·tah·lah·<u>veh</u>·noh

uneven (ground) **ανώμαλος**
ah·<u>noh</u>·mah·lohs

unfortunately **δυστυχώς**
THees·tee·<u>khohs</u>

uniform *n* **στολή** stoh·<u>lee</u>

unique **μοναδικός**
moh·nah·THee·<u>kohs</u>

unit **μονάδα** moh·<u>nah</u>·THah

United Kingdom **Ηνωμένο Βασίλειο**
ee·noh·<u>meh</u>·noh vah·<u>see</u>·lee·oh

United States **Ηνωμένες
Πολιτείες** ee·noh·<u>meh</u>·nehs
poh·lee·<u>tee</u>·ehs

university **Πανεπιστήμιο**
pah·neh·pees·<u>tee</u>·mee·oh

unlimited mileage
απεριόριστα χιλιόμετρα
ah·peh·ree·<u>ohr</u>·ees·tah
khee·<u>lioh</u>·meht·rah

unpleasant **δυσάρεστος**
THee·<u>sah</u>·reh·stohs

upper (berth) **πάνω (κουκέτα)**
pah·noh (koo·<u>keh</u>·tah)

upstairs **επάνω** eh·pah·noh

urgent **επείγον** eh·pee·ghohn

use v **χρησιμοποιώ**
khree·see·moh·pee·oh

useful **χρήσιμος** khree·see·mohs

V

vacancy **ελεύθερο δωμάτιο**
eh·lehf·theh·roh
THoh·mah·tee·oh

vacant **ελεύθερος**
eh·lehf·theh·rohs

vacation **διακοπές**
THee·ah·koh·pehs

vacation resort **θέρετρο διακοπών**
theh·reh·troh THee·ah·koh·pohn

vaccination **εμβόλιο**
ehm·voh·lee·oh

valid **ισχύει** ee·skhee·ee

valley **κοιλάδα** kee·lah·THah

valuable **πολύτιμος**
poh·lee·tee·mohs

value n **αξία** ah·ksee·ah

VAT [BE] **ΦΠΑ** fee·pee·ah

vegetarian **χορτοφάγος**
khohr·toh·fah·ghohs

vein **φλέβα** fleh·vah

velvet **βελούδο** veh·loo·THoh

very **πολύ** poh·lee

video **βιντεοκασέτα**
vee·deh·oh·kah·seh·tah

video game **παιχνίδι βίντεο**
pehkh·nee·THee vee·deh·oh

village **χωριό** khohr·yoh

visa **βίζα** vee·zah

visit n **επίσκεψη** eh·pees·keh·psee

volleyball **βόλεϋ** voh·leh·ee

vomit v **κάνω εμετό** kah·noh
eh·meh·toh

W

wait v **περιμένω** peh·ree·meh·noh

waiter n **γκαρσόν** gahr·sohn

waitress **δεσποινίς**
THehs·pee·nees

wake v **ξυπνώ** kseep·noh

walk v **περπατώ** pehr·pah·toh

walking route **διαδρομή
περιήγησης** THee·ah·THroh·mee
peh·ree·ee·yee·sees

wall **τοίχος** tee·khohs

wallet **πορτοφόλι** pohr·toh·foh·lee

want **θέλω** theh·loh

warm **ζεστός** zehs·tohs

washing machine **πλυντήριο**
pleen·deer·ee·oh

watch n **ρολόι** roh·loh·ee

watch strap **λουρί ρολογιού** loo·ree
roh·loh·yioo

water n **νερό** neh·roh

waterfall **καταρράχτης**
kah·tah·rahkh·tees

waterproof **αδιάβροχος**
ah·THee·ahv·roh·khohs

wave n **κύμα** kee·mah

way **δρόμος** THroh·mohs

wear v **φορώ** foh·roh

weather **καιρός** keh·rohs

weather forecast **πρόβλεψη καιρού**
prohv·leh·psee keh·roo

wedding **γάμος** ghah·mohs

west **δυτικά** THee·tee·kah

wetsuit **στολή δύτη** stoh·lee
THee·tee

wheelchair **αναπηρική**
  καρέκλα ah·nah·pee·ree·<u>kee</u>
  kah·<u>rehk</u>·lah
wide **φαρδύς** fahr·<u>THees</u>
wife **σύζυγος** <u>see</u>·zee·ghohs
window **παράθυρο**
  pah·<u>rah</u>·thee·roh
window seat **θέση δίπλα στο**
  παράθυρο <u>theh</u>·see <u>THeep</u>·lah
  stoh pah·<u>rah</u>·thee·roh
winery **οινοποιείο**
  ee·noh·pee·<u>ee</u>·oh
wireless internet **ασύρματο ίντερνετ**
  ah·<u>see</u>·rmah·toh <u>ee</u>·nteh·rnet
with **με** meh
withdraw **κάνω ανάληψη** <u>kah</u>·noh
  ah·<u>nah</u>·lee·psee
without **χωρίς** khoh·<u>rees</u>
witness **μάρτυρας** <u>mahr</u>·tee·rahs
wood (forest) **δάσος** <u>THah</u>·sohs;
  (material) **ξύλο** <u>ksee</u>·loh
work **δουλεύω** THoo·<u>leh</u>·voh
worry **ανησυχώ** ah·nee·see·<u>khoh</u>
worse **χειρότερος**
  khee·<u>roh</u>·teh·rohs
wound (cut) **πληγή** plee·<u>yee</u>
write (down) **γράφω** <u>ghrah</u>·foh
wrong **λάθος** <u>lah</u>·thohs

X

x-ray **ακτινογραφία**
  ahk·tee·nohgh·rah·<u>fee</u>·ah

Y

yacht **γιωτ** yoht
yellow **κίτρινος** <u>keet</u>·ree·nohs

young **νέος** <u>neh</u>·ohs
youth hostel **ξενώνας νεότητας**
  kseh·<u>noh</u>·nahs neh·<u>oh</u>·tee·tahs

Z

zoo **ζωολογικός κήπος**
  zoh·oh·loh·yee·<u>kohs</u> <u>kee</u>·pohs

Greek–English Dictionary

ATM ehee·tee·<u>ehm</u> ATM

άγαλμα <u>ah</u>·ghahl·mah statue

αγαπημένος ah·ghah·pee·<u>meh</u>·nohs favorite

αγαπώ ah·ghah·<u>poh</u> v love

αγγειοπλαστική ahn·gee·ohp·lahs·tee·<u>kee</u> pottery

Αγγλία ahng·<u>lee</u>·ah England

αγγλικά ahng·lee·<u>kah</u> English language

αγγλικός ahng·lee·<u>kohs</u> adj English

Άγγλος <u>ahng</u>·lohs English (nationality)

αγενής ah·yeh·<u>nees</u> rude

αγορά ah·ghoh·<u>rah</u> n market

αγοράζω ah·ghoh·<u>rah</u>·zoh buy

αγόρι ah·<u>ghoh</u>·ree boy

αγώνας ah·<u>ghoh</u>·nahs n match (sport)

άδεια <u>ah</u>·THee·ah n permit

άδεια σκι <u>ah</u>·THee·ah skee lift pass

άδειος <u>ahTH</u>·yohs adj empty

αδιάβροχο ah·THee·<u>ahv</u>·roh·khoh raincoat

αδιάβροχος ah·THee·<u>ahv</u>·roh·khohs waterproof

αδύναμος ah·<u>THee</u>·nah·mohs weak

αεροδρόμιο ah·eh·roh·<u>THroh</u>·mee·oh airport

αεροπλάνο ah·eh·rohp·<u>lah</u>·noh n plane

αεροπορική εταιρία ah·eh·roh·poh·ree·<u>kee</u> eh·teh·<u>ree</u>·ah airline

αεροπορικώς ah·eh·roh·poh·ree·<u>kohs</u> airmail

αηδιαστικός ah·ee·THee·ah·stee·<u>kohs</u> revolting

αθλητικά παπούτσια ath·lee·tee·<u>kah</u> pah·<u>poo</u>·tsiah sneakers

αθλητικό στάδιο ahth·lee·tee·<u>koh</u> <u>stah</u>·THee·oh sports stadium

αθλητικός όμιλος ahth·lee·tee·<u>kohs</u> <u>oh</u>·mee·lohs sports club

αθλητισμός ahth·lee·teez·<u>mohs</u> sport

αθώος ah·<u>thoh</u>·ohs innocent

αιμορραγία eh·moh·rah·<u>yee</u>·ah n bleed

αιμορραγώ eh·moh·rah·<u>yoh</u> v bleed

αίθουσα συναυλιών <u>eh</u>·thoo·sah see·nahv·lee·<u>ohn</u> concert hall

ακολουθώ ah·koh·loo·<u>thoh</u> v follow

ακουστικό βαρυκοΐας ah·koo·stee·<u>koh</u> vah·ree·koh·<u>ee</u>·ahs hearing aid

ακριβός ahk·ree·<u>vohs</u> expensive

ακτή ahk·<u>tee</u> *n* shore
ακτινογραφία
ahk·tee·nohgh·rah·<u>fee</u>·ah x-ray
ακυρώνω ah·kee·<u>roh</u>·noh *v* cancel
αληθινός ah·lee·thee·<u>nohs</u> real
(genuine)
αλλά ah·<u>lah</u> *conj* but
άλλα <u>ah</u>·lah others
αλλαγή ah·lah·<u>yee</u> *n* change
αλλάζω ah·<u>lah</u>·zoh *v* exchange
(money)
αλλεργικός ahl·ehr·yee·<u>kohs</u>
allergic
αλληλογραφία
ah·lee·lohgh·rah·<u>fee</u>·ah *n* mail
άλλο ένα <u>ah</u>·loh eh·nah extra
(additional)
άλλος <u>ah</u>·lohs another
αλουμινόχαρτο
ah·loo·mee·<u>noh</u>·khah·rtoh
aluminum foil
Αμερικανός ah·meh·ree·kah·<u>nohs</u>
n American
αμέσως ah·<u>meh</u>·sohs immediately
άμμος <u>ah</u>·mohs sand
ανάβω ah·<u>nah</u>·voh *v* turn on
αναίσθητος ah·<u>nehs</u>·thee·tohs
unconscious
ανάκτορα ah·<u>nahk</u>·toh·rah palace
αναλυτικός λογαριασμός
ah·nah·lee·tee·<u>kohs</u>
loh·ghahr·yahz·<u>mohs</u> itemized
bill
αναπηρική καρέκλα
ah·nah·pee·ree·<u>kee</u> kah·<u>rehk</u>·lah
wheelchair

αναπνευστήρας
ah·nahp·nehf·<u>stee</u>·rahs snorkel
αναπνέω ah·nahp·<u>neh</u>·oh breathe
αναπτήρας ah·nahp·<u>tee</u>·rahs
n lighter (cigarette)
αναρρίχηση ah·nah·<u>ree</u>·khee·see
rock climbing
ανατολικά ah·nah·toh·lee·<u>kah</u>
east
αναφέρω ah·nah·<u>feh</u>·roh mention
(report)
αναχώρηση ah·nah·<u>khoh</u>·ree·see
departure (travel)
άνδρας <u>ahn</u>·THrahs *n* male (man)
ανεμιστήρας
ah·neh·mees·<u>tee</u>·rahs *n* fan (air)
ανεβάζω ah·neh·<u>vah</u>·zoh *v* turn up
(volume, heat)
ανέκδοτο ah·<u>nehk</u>·THoh·toh
n joke
ανησυχώ ah·nee·see·<u>khoh</u> worry
ανθοπωλείο ahn·thoh·poh·<u>lee</u>·oh
florist
ανοίγω ah·<u>nee</u>·ghoh *v* open
ανοιχτήρι ah·neekh·<u>tee</u>·ree can
opener
ανοιχτός ah·neekh·<u>tohs</u> *adj* light
(color), open
ανοιχτότερος ah·neekh·<u>toh</u>·teh·rohs
adj lighter (color)
ανταλλακτικό
ahn·dah·lahk·tee·<u>koh</u>
replacement part
αντιβιοτικό
ahn·dee·vee·oh·tee·<u>koh</u>
antibiotic

αντιηλιακό ahn·dee·ee·lee·ah·<u>koh</u>
sunscreen

αντισηπτική κρέμα
ahn·dee·seep·tee·<u>kee</u> <u>kreh</u>·mah
antiseptic cream

αντίχειρας ahn·<u>dee</u>·khee·rahs
thumb

ανώμαλος ah·<u>noh</u>·mah·lohs
uneven (ground)

αξεσουάρ ah·kseh·soo·<u>ahr</u>
accessory

αξία ah·<u>ksee</u>·ah *n* value

αξιοθέατο
ah·ksee·oh·<u>theh</u>·ah·tah
sightseeing sight

απαγορευμένος
ah·pah·ghoh·rehv·<u>meh</u>·nohs
prohibited

απαραίτητος ah·pah·<u>reh</u>·tee·tohs
essential, necessary

απασχολημένος
ah·pahs·khoh·lee·<u>meh</u>·nohs
adj busy (occupied)

απέναντι ah·<u>peh</u>·nahn·dee
opposite

απεριόριστα χιλιόμετρα
ah·peh·ree·<u>ohr</u>·ees·tah
khee·<u>lioh</u>·meht·rah unlimited
mileage

απλό εισιτήριο ahp·<u>loh</u>
ee·see·<u>tee</u>·ree·oh one-way
[single BE] ticket

απλός ahp·<u>lohs</u> simple

από ah·<u>poh</u> from

απομίμηση ah·poh·<u>mee</u>·mee·see
imitation

αποβάθρα ah·poh·<u>vahth</u>·rah
platform, quay

απόγευμα ah·<u>poh</u>·yehv·mah
afternoon

απόδειξη ah·<u>poh</u>·THee·ksee
receipt

απορρυπαντικό
ah·poh·ree·pahn·dee·<u>koh</u>
detergent

αποσμητικό ah·pohz·mee·tee·<u>koh</u>
deodorant

αποσκευές ah·pohs·keh·<u>vehs</u>
baggage [BE]

αποσκευές χειρός
ah·pohs·keh·<u>vehs</u> khee·<u>rohs</u>
hand luggage

αποστειρωτικό διάλυμα
ah·pohs·tee·roh·tee·<u>koh</u>
THee·<u>ah</u>·lee·mah sterilizing
solution

απόχρωση ah·<u>pohkh</u>·roh·see
shade (color)

απώλεια ah·<u>poh</u>·lee·ah *n* loss

αργά ahr·<u>ghah</u> *adv* late

αργία ahr·<u>yee</u>·ah public holiday

αργός ahr·<u>ghohs</u> *adj* slow

αριθμός κυκλοφορίας
ah·reeth·<u>mohs</u>
kee·kloh·foh·<u>ree</u>·ahs registration
number

αριθμός πτήσεως ah·reeth·<u>mohs</u>
ptee·seh·ohs flight number

αριθμός τηλεφώνου
ah·reeth·<u>mohs</u> tee·leh·<u>foh</u>·noo
telephone number

αριστερός ah·rees·teh·<u>rohs</u> left (*adj*)

αριστερά ah·rees·teh·<u>rah</u> left (*adv*)

αρκετά ahr·keh·<u>tah</u> enough

αρραβωνιαστικιά
ah·rah·voh·niahs·tee·<u>kiah</u> fiancée

αρραβωνιαστικός
ah·rah·voh·niahs·tee·<u>kohs</u>
fiancé

αρρώστεια ahr·<u>ohs</u>·tee·ah illness

άρρωστος <u>ah</u>·rohs·tohs *adj* sick

αρτοποιείο ah·rtoh·pee·<u>ee</u>·oh
bakery

αρχάριος ahr·<u>khah</u>·ree·ohs
beginner

αρχίζω *v* ahr·<u>khee</u>·zoh start

ασανσέρ ah·sahn·<u>sehr</u> *n* lift
(elevator)

ασήμι ah·<u>see</u>·mee silver

ασύρματο ίντερνετ
ah·<u>see</u>·rmah·toh ee·nteh·rnet
wireless internet

ασθενοφόρο ahs·theh·noh·<u>foh</u>·roh
ambulance

ασθματικός ahsth·mah·tee·<u>kohs</u>
asthmatic

ασπιρίνη ahs·pee·<u>ree</u>·nee aspirin

αστυνομία ah·stee·noh·<u>mee</u>·ah
n police

αστυνομικό τμήμα
ah·stee·noh·mee·<u>koh</u> tmee·mah
police station

ασφάλεια ahs·<u>fah</u>·lee·ah *n* fuse;
insurance

ασφάλεια αποζημίωσης
ahs·<u>fah</u>·lee·ah
ah·poh·zee·<u>mee</u>·oh·sees
insurance claim

ασφάλεια υγείας ahs·<u>fah</u>·lee·ah
ee·<u>yee</u>·ahs health insurance

ασφαλής ahs·fah·<u>lees</u> *adj* safe
(not dangerous)

ασφαλιστική εταιρία
ahs·fah·lees·tee·<u>kee</u>
eh·teh·<u>ree</u>·ah insurance
company

άσχημος <u>ahs</u>·khee·mohs ugly

άτομο με ειδικές ανάγκες
<u>ah</u>·toh·moh meh ee·THee·<u>kehs</u>
ah·<u>nahn</u>·gehs disabled

ατύχημα ah·<u>tee</u>·khee·mah
accident

αυθεντικός ahf·thehn·dee·<u>kohs</u>
genuine

αυθεντικότητα
ahf·thehn·dee·<u>koh</u>·tee·tah
authenticity

αϋπνία ah·eep·<u>nee</u>·ah insomnia

αυτοκίνητο ahf·toh·<u>kee</u>·nee·toh
car

αυχένας ahf·<u>kheh</u>·nahs neck (part
of body)

αφήνω ah·<u>fee</u>·noh *v* leave (let go)

αφορολόγητα είδη
ah·foh·roh·<u>loh</u>·yee·tah ee·THee
duty-free goods

αφρόλουτρο για ντουζ
ahf·<u>roh</u>·loot·roh yah dooz shower
gel

αχθοφόρος ahkh·thoh·<u>foh</u>·rohs
porter

B

βαμβάκι vahm·<u>vah</u>·kee cotton

βαγκόν-λι vah·<u>gohn</u>·lee sleeping car

βάζο <u>vah</u>·zoh n jar

βάζω <u>vah</u>·zoh v put

βαλές vah·<u>lehs</u> jack

βαρετός vah·reh·<u>tohs</u> boring

βάρκα <u>vahr</u>·kah boat

βαρύς vah·<u>rees</u> heavy

βασιλιάς vah·see·<u>liahs</u> king

βγαίνω <u>vyeh</u>·noh get out (of vehicle)

βελούδο veh·<u>loo</u>·THoh velvet

βενζινάδικο vehn·zee·<u>nah</u>·THee·koh gas [petrol BE] station

βενζίνη vehn·<u>zee</u>·nee gasoline [petrol BE]

βερνίκι παπουτσιών vehr·<u>nee</u>·kee pah·poo·<u>tsiohn</u> shoe polish

βήχας <u>vee</u>·khahs n cough

βήχω <u>vee</u>·khoh v cough

βιβλίο veev·<u>lee</u>·oh n book

βιβλιοθήκη veev·lee·oh·<u>thee</u>·kee library

βιβλιοπωλείο veev·lee·oh·poh·<u>lee</u>·oh bookstore

βίδα <u>vee</u>·THah n screw

βίζα <u>vee</u>·zah visa

βιντεοκασέτα vee·deh·oh·kah·<u>seh</u>·tah video

βλάβη <u>vlah</u>·vee breakdown n (car)

βλέπω <u>vleh</u>·poh see

βοήθεια voh·<u>ee</u>·thee·ah n help

βοηθώ voh·ee·<u>thoh</u> v help

βόλεϋ <u>voh</u>·leh·ee volleyball

βόρεια <u>voh</u>·ree·ah north

βοτανικός κήπος voh·tah·nee·<u>kohs</u> kee·pohs botanical garden

βουνό voo·<u>noh</u> mountain

βουρτσίζω voor·<u>tsee</u>·zoh v brush

βραδινό vrah·THee·<u>noh</u> dinner

βράδυ <u>vrah</u>·THee evening

βράζω <u>vrah</u>·zoh boil

βράχος <u>vrah</u>·khohs n rock

βρετανικός vreh·tah·nee·<u>kohs</u> British adj

Βρετανός vreh·tah·<u>nohs</u> British (nationality)

βρέχει <u>vreh</u>·khee v rain

βροχή vroh·<u>khee</u> n rain

βρύση <u>vree</u>·see faucet

βρώμικος <u>vroh</u>·mee·kohs adj dirty

Γ

γάμος <u>ghah</u>·mohs wedding

γάζα <u>ghah</u>·zah bandage

γαλάκτωμα για τα μαλλιά ghah·<u>lah</u>·ktoh·mah yah tah mah·<u>liah</u> conditioner (hair)

γάντι <u>ghahn</u>·dee n glove

γαστρίτιδα ghahs·<u>tree</u>·tee·THah gastritis

γεμάτος yeh·<u>mah</u>·tohs adj full

γείτονας <u>yee</u>·toh·nahs n neighbor

γελώ yeh·<u>loh</u> v laugh

γέρικος <u>yeh</u>·ree·kohs old (person)

γεύμα <u>yehv</u>·mah **meal**

γέφυρα <u>yeh</u>·fee·rah *n* **bridge** (over water)

γη ghee *n* **land**

γήπεδο γκολφ <u>yee</u>·peh·THoh gohlf **golf course**

γήπεδο τέννις <u>yee</u>·peh·THoh <u>teh</u>·nees **tennis court**

γιατρός yah·<u>trohs</u> **doctor**

γιωτ yoht **yacht**

γκαράζ gah·<u>rahz</u> **garage**

γκαρσόν gahr·<u>sohn</u> **waiter**

γκόλφ gohlf **golf**

γκρουπ groop *n* **group**

γλώσσα <u>ghloh</u>·sah **tongue**

γνωρίζω ghnoh·<u>ree</u>·zoh **know**

γόνατο <u>ghoh</u>·nah·toh **knee**

γονείς ghoh·<u>nees</u> **parents**

γράμμα <u>ghrah</u>·mah **letter**

γραμματόσημο ghrah·mah·<u>toh</u>·see·moh *n* **stamp** (postage)

γραμμή ghrah·<u>mee</u> *n* **line** (subway)

γραβάτα ghrah·<u>vah</u>·tah *n* **tie**

γρασίδι ghrah·<u>see</u>·THee **grass**

γραφείο ghrah·<u>fee</u>·oh **office**

γραφείο ανταλλαγής συναλλάγματος ghrah·<u>fee</u>·oh ahn·dah·lah·<u>yees</u> see·nah·<u>lahgh</u>·mah·tohs **currency exchange office**

γραφείο εισιτήριων ghrah·<u>fee</u>·oh ee·see·tee·<u>ree</u>·ohn **ticket office**

γραφείο πληροφοριών ghrah·<u>fee</u>·oh plee·roh·foh·ree·<u>ohn</u> **information office**

γράφω <u>ghrah</u>·foh **write** (down)

γρήγορα <u>ghree</u>·ghoh·rah *adv* **fast**

γρήγορος <u>ghree</u>·ghoh·rohs **quick**

γρίππη <u>ghree</u>·pee **flu**

γυαλιά yah·<u>liah</u> **glasses** (optical)

γυαλιά ηλίου yah·<u>liah</u> ee·<u>lee</u>·oo **sun glasses**

γυναικολόγος yee·neh·koh·<u>loh</u>·ghohs **gynecologist**

γυρίζω yee·<u>ree</u>·zoh *v* **turn**

γωνία ghoh·<u>nee</u>·ah **corner**

Δ

δανείζω THah·<u>nee</u>·zoh **lend**

δάσος <u>THah</u>·sohs *n* **forest** (wood)

δάχτυλο <u>THakh</u>·tee·loh *n* **finger**

δείγμα <u>THeegh</u>·mah **specimen**

δείχνω <u>THeekh</u>·noh *v* **point** (show)

δέντρο <u>THehn</u>·droh **tree**

δεξιός THeh·ksee·<u>ohs</u> *adj* **right** (not left)

δέρμα <u>THehr</u>·mah *n* **skin**

δημαρχείο THee·mahr·<u>khee</u>·oh **town hall**

δημοφιλής THee·moh·fee·<u>lees</u> **popular**

δηλητήριο THee·lee·<u>tee</u>·ree·oh *n* **poison**

δηλητηριώδης THee·lee·tee·ree·<u>oh</u>·THees **poisonous**

δηλώνω THee·<u>loh</u>·noh **declare**

δήλωση <u>THee</u>·loh·see **statement** (legal)

δημόσιος THee·<u>moh</u>·see·ohs public

διαμάντι THiah·<u>mahn</u>·dee *n* diamond

διαμέρισμα THee·ah·<u>meh</u>·reez·mah apartment

διάβαση πεζών THee·<u>ah</u>·vah·see peh·<u>zohn</u> pedestrian crossing

διαβατήριο THiah·vah·<u>tee</u>·ree·oh passport

διαβητικός THee·ah·vee·tee·<u>kohs</u> diabetic

διαδρομή THee·ahTH·roh·<u>mee</u> *n* route

διάδρομος THee·<u>ah</u>·THroh·mohs aisle seat

διαζευγμένος THee·ah·zehv·<u>ghmeh</u>·nohs divorced

διακοπές THee·ah·koh·<u>pehs</u> vacation [holiday BE]

διακόπτης THiah·<u>koh</u>·ptees *n* switch

διαμέρισμα THee·ah·mehr·ees·mah *n* flat

διάρροια THee·<u>ah</u>·ree·ah diarrhea

διάσημος THee·<u>ah</u>·see·mohs famous

διεθνής THee·eth·<u>nees</u> international

διεθνής φοιτητική κάρτα THee·ehth·<u>nees</u> fee·tee·tee·<u>kee</u> <u>kahr</u>·tah International Student Card

διερμηνέας THee·ehr·mee·<u>neh</u>·ahs interpreter

διεύθυνση THee·<u>ehf</u>·theen·see *n* address

διευθυντής THee·ehf·theen·<u>dees</u> manager

δικηγόρος THee·kee·<u>ghoh</u>·rohs lawyer

δίκλινο δωμάτιο <u>THeek</u>·lee·noh THoh·<u>mah</u>·tee·oh double room

δίνω THee·noh give

διόρθωμα THee·<u>ohr</u>·thoh·mah *n* trim

δίπλα <u>THeep</u>·lah next to

διπλό κρεβάτι THeep·<u>loh</u> kreh·<u>vah</u>·tee twin bed

δίσκος <u>THees</u>·kohs tray

διψάω THee·<u>psah</u>·oh thirsty

δοκιμάζω THoh·kee·<u>mah</u>·zoh try on

δολάριο THoh·<u>lah</u>·ree·oh dollar

δόντι <u>THohn</u>·dee tooth

δοσολογία THoh·soh·loh·<u>yee</u>·ah dosage

δουλειά THoo·<u>liah</u> job

δουλεύω THoo·<u>leh</u>·voh work

δρομολόγιο THroh·moh·<u>loh</u>·yee·oh time table

δρόμος <u>THroh</u>·mohs road, street, way

δυνατός THee·nah·<u>tohs</u> *adj* loud

δυσάρεστος THee·<u>sah</u>·reh stohs unpleasant

δύσκολος <u>THee</u>·skoh·lohs difficult

δυσπεψία THes·peh·<u>psee</u>·ah indigestion

δυστυχώς THees·tee·khohs
unfortunately

δυτικά THee·tee·kah west

δωμάτιο THoh·mah·tee·oh
n room

δώρο THoh·roh gift

E

εμβόλιο ehm·voh·lee·oh
vaccination

εμπορικό κέντρο ehm·boh·ree·koh
keh·ntroh shopping mall
[centre BE]

εγγύηση eh·gee·ee·see
n guarantee

εγγυώμαι eh·gee·oh·meh
v guarantee

έγκαυμα ηλίου ehn·gahv·mah
ee·lee·oo n sun burn

έγκυος eh·gee·ohs pregnant

έδαφος eh·THah·fohs ground
(earth)

εδώ eh·THoh here

εδώ κοντά eh·THoh kohn·dah
nearby

εθνική οδός ehth·nee·kee
oh·THohs highway, motorway

εθνικός eth·nee·kohs national

εθνικός δρυμός eth·nee·kohs
THree·mohs nature reserve

είμαι ee·meh be

είμαι κουφός koo·fohs deaf

είδη οικιακής χρήσεως ee·THee
ee·kee·ah·kees khree·seh·ohs
household articles

ειδική ανάγκη ee·THee·kee
ah·nahn·gkee special
requirement

ειδικός ee·THee·kohs specialist

είδος ee·THohs kind (sort)

εισιτήριο ee·see·tee·ree·oh fare
(ticket)

εισιτήριο με επιστροφή
ee·see·tee·ree·oh meh
eh·pee·stroh·fee roundtrip
[return BE] ticket

εκδρομή ehk·THroh·mee excursion

εκεί eh·kee there, over there

εκείνα eh·kee·nah those

έκθεση ehk·theh·see exhibition

έκπτωση ehk·ptoh·see reduction

έκτακτη ανάγκη ehk·tahk·tee
ah·nah·gee emergency

ελάχιστος eh·lah·khees·tohs
minimum

ελεύθερο δωμάτιο
eh·lehf·theh·roh
THoh·mah·tee·oh vacancy

ελεύθερος eh·lehf·theh·rohs
adj free, single, vacant

ελικόπτερο eh·lee·kohp·teh·roh
helicopter

Ελλάδα eh·lah·THah Greece

Έλληνας eh·lee·nahs Greek
(nationality)

ελληνικός eh·lee·nee·kohs
adj Greek

ένα βράδυ eh·nah vrah·THee
overnight

ένα τέταρτο eh·nah teh·tah·rtoh
quarter (quantity)

ενδιαφέρων en·THee·ah·<u>feh</u>·rohn interesting

ένεση eh·neh·see injection

ενήλικας eh·<u>nee</u>·lee·kahs adult

ενοχλώ eh·noh·<u>khloh</u> disturb

έντομο <u>ehn</u>·doh·moh insect

εντομοαπωθητικό ehn·doh·moh·ah·poh·thee·tee·<u>koh</u> insect repellent

έντυπο <u>ehn</u>·dee·poh *n* form

εντυπωσιακός ehn·dee·poh·see·ah·<u>kohs</u> impressive

ενυδατική κρέμα eh·nee·THah·tee·<u>kee</u> <u>kreh</u>·mah moisturizer (cream)

εξάνθημα eh·<u>ksahn</u>·thee·mah *n* rash

εξαργυρώνω eh·ksahr·ghee·<u>roh</u>·noh *v* cash

εξόγκωμα eh·<u>ksoh</u>·goh·mah *n* lump (medical)

έξοδος <u>eh</u>·ksoh·THohs *n* gate (airport); exit

έξοδος κινδύνου <u>eh</u>·ksoh·THohs keen·<u>THee</u>·noo emergency, fire exit

εξοχή eh·ksoh·<u>khee</u> countryside

έξοχος <u>eh</u>·ksoh·khohs superb

εξπρές ehk·<u>sprehs</u> express (mail)

εξυπηρέτηση eh·ksee·pee·<u>reh</u>·tee·see facility

έξω <u>eh</u>·ksoh *adv* out

έξω <u>eh</u>·ksoh *adj* outside

εξωλέμβιο eh·ksoh·<u>lehm</u>·vee·oh motorboat

εξωτερικός eh·ksoh·teh·ree·<u>kohs</u> outdoor

επαναλαμβάνω eh·pah·nah·lahm·<u>vah</u>·noh *v* repeat

επάνω eh·<u>pah</u>·noh upstairs

επείγον eh·<u>pee</u>·ghohn urgent

επιμένω eh·pee·<u>meh</u>·noh insist

επιβάτης eh·pee·<u>vah</u>·tees passenger

επιβεβαιώνω eh·pee·veh·veh·<u>oh</u>·noh confirm

επίβλεψη eh·<u>peev</u>·leh·psee supervision

επίθεση eh·<u>pee</u>·theh·see *n* attack

επίθετο eh·<u>pee</u>·theh·toh surname

επικοινωνώ eh·pee·kee·noh·<u>noh</u> *v* contact

επιληπτικός eh·pee·leep·tee·<u>kohs</u> epileptic

επίπεδο eh·<u>pee</u>·peh·THoh level (even)

επίπεδος eh·<u>pee</u>·peh·THohs *adj* flat

έπιπλα <u>eh</u>·peep·lah furniture

επιπλέον eh·peep·<u>leh</u>·ohn spare (extra)

επισκευάζω eh·pee·skeh·<u>vah</u>·zoh *v* repair

επισκευή eh·pee·skeh·<u>vee</u> *n* repair

επισκευή παπουτσιών eh·pee·skeh·<u>vee</u> pah·poo·<u>tsiohn</u> shoe repair

επίσκεψη eh·<u>pees</u>·keh·psee *n* visit

204

επιστροφή χρημάτων
eh·pees·troh·<u>fee</u> khree·<u>mah</u>·tohn
n refund

επιταγή eh·pee·tah·<u>yee</u> *n* check
[cheque BE] (bank)

επιτίθεμαι eh·pee·<u>tee</u>·theh·meh
v attack

επιτόκιο eh·pee·<u>toh</u>·kee·oh
interest rate

επόμενος eh·<u>poh</u>·meh·nohs next

έρχομαι <u>ehr</u>·khoh·meh come

ερώτηση eh·<u>roh</u>·tee·see
n question

εστιατόριο ehs·tee·ah·<u>toh</u>·ree·oh
restaurant

εσωτερική γραμμή
eh·soh·theh·ree·<u>kee</u> ghrah·<u>mee</u>
extension (number)

εσωτερική πισίνα
eh·soh·teh·ree·<u>kee</u> pee·<u>see</u>·nah
indoor pool

εσωτερικός eh·soh·teh·ree·<u>kohs</u>
indoor

ετικέτα eh·tee·<u>keh</u>·tah *n* label

έτοιμος eh·tee·mohs *adj* ready

ευθεία ehf·<u>thee</u>·ah straight ahead

εύκολος <u>ehf</u>·koh·lohs *adj* easy

ευρώ ehv·<u>roh</u> euro

Ευρωπαϊκή Ένωση
ehv·roh·pah·ee·<u>kee</u> <u>eh</u>·noh·see
European Union

ευτυχώς ehf·tee·<u>khohs</u> fortunately

ευχαριστιέμαι
ehf·khah·rees·<u>tieh</u>·meh enjoy

ευχάριστος ehf·<u>khah</u>·rees·tohs
pleasant

εφημερίδα eh·fee·meh·<u>ree</u>·THah
newspaper

έφηβος <u>eh</u>·fee·vohs teenager

έχω <u>eh</u>·khoh have (possession)

Z

ζαχαροπλαστείο
zah·khah·rohp·lahs·<u>tee</u>·oh
pastry store

ζεστός zes·<u>tohs</u> hot, warm
(weather)

ζημιά zee·<u>miah</u> *n* damage

ζητώ zee·<u>toh</u> ask

ζωγραφίζω zohgh·rah·<u>fee</u>·zoh
v paint

ζωγράφος zohgh·<u>rah</u>·fohs painter

ζώνη <u>zoh</u>·nee belt

ζώνη για χρήματα <u>zoh</u>·nee yah
<u>khree</u>·mah·tah money-belt

H

ημερομηνία λήξεως
ee·meh·roh·mee·<u>nee</u>·ah
<u>lee</u>·kseh·ohs expiration date

ημερολόγιο ee·meh·roh·<u>loh</u>·yee·oh
calendar

ημικρανία ee·mee·krah·<u>nee</u>·ah
migraine

ηλεκτρικός ee·lehk·tree·<u>kohs</u>
electric

ηλεκτρονικό εισιτήριο
ee·leh·ktroh·nee·<u>koh</u>
ee·see·<u>tee</u>·ree·oh e-ticket

ηλεκτρονικό ταχυδρομείο (e-mail) ee·lehk·troh·nee·koh tah·hee·dro·<u>mee</u>·oh (<u>ee</u>·meh·eel)

ηλεκτροπληξία ee·leh·ktroh·plee·<u>ksee</u>·ah shock (electric)

ηλίαση ee·<u>lee</u>·ah·see sun stroke

ηλικιωμένος ee·lee·kee·oh·<u>meh</u>·nohs senior citizen

Ηνωμένες Πολιτείες ee·noh·<u>meh</u>·nehs poh·lee·<u>tee</u>·ehs United Sstates

Ηνωμένο Βασίλειο ee·noh·<u>meh</u>·noh vah·<u>see</u>·lee·oh United Kingdom

ηρεμιστικό ee·reh·mee·stee·<u>koh</u> sedative

ήσυχος ee·<u>see</u>·khohs *adj* quiet

Θ

θάλασσα <u>thah</u>·lah·sah sea

θέατρο <u>theh</u>·aht·roh theater

θέλω <u>theh</u>·loh want

θέρμανση <u>thehr</u>·mahn·see heating

θερμή πηγή thehr·<u>mee</u> pee·<u>yee</u> hot spring

θερμόμετρο thehr·<u>moh</u>·meht·roh thermometer

θερμοκρασία theh·rmohk·rah·<u>see</u>·ah temperature (body)

θερμός thehr·<u>mohs</u> thermos flask

θέρετρο διακοπών <u>theh</u>·reh·troh THee·ah·koh·<u>pohn</u> vacation resort

θέση <u>theh</u>·see *n* location (space), seat

θέση δίπλα στο παράθυρο <u>theh</u>·see THeep·lah stoh pah·<u>rah</u>·thee·roh window seat

θηλυκός thee·lee·<u>kohs</u> female

θορυβώδης thoh·ree·<u>voh</u>·THees noisy

θρησκεία three·<u>skee</u>·ah religion

θυμάμαι thee·<u>mah</u>·meh remember

θυρίδα thee·<u>ree</u>·THah luggage locker (lock-up)

Ι

ιατρική εξέταση ee·ah·tree·<u>kee</u> eh·<u>kseh</u>·tah·see examination (medical)

ίδιος <u>ee</u>·THee·ohs same

ιδιωτικό μπάνιο ee·THee·oh·tee·<u>koh</u> bah·nioh private bathroom

ιερέας ee·eh·<u>reh</u>·ahs priest

ινσουλίνη een·soo·<u>lee</u>·nee insulin

ίντερνετ <u>ee</u>·nteh·rnet internet

ίντερνετ καφέ <u>ee</u>·nteh·rnet kah·<u>feh</u> internet cafe

ιπποδρομία ee·poh·THroh·<u>mee</u>·ah horse racing

ιστιοπλοϊκό ees·tee·oh·ploh·ee·<u>koh</u> sailing boat

ιστορία ee·stoh·<u>ree</u>·ah history

ισχύει ee·<u>skhee</u>·ee valid

ίσως <u>ee</u>·sohs maybe, perhaps

ιώδειο ee·<u>oh</u>·THee·oh iodine

κάδος απορριμμάτων <u>kah</u>·THohs ah·poh·ree·<u>mah</u>·tohn trash can

καθαρισμός προσώπου kah·thah·reez·<u>mohs</u> proh·<u>soh</u>·poo facial

καθαρός kah·thah·<u>rohs</u> clean

καθαρτικό kah·thahr·tee·<u>koh</u> laxative

καθεδρικός ναός kah·theh·THree·<u>kohs</u> nah·<u>ohs</u> cathedral

καθήκον kah·<u>thee</u>·kohn duty (obligation)

κάθομαι <u>kah</u>·thoh·meh sit

καθρέφτης kah·<u>threhf</u>·tees *n* mirror

καθυστέρηση kah·thee·<u>steh</u>·ree·see *n* delay

καθυστερώ kah·thee·steh·<u>roh</u> *v* delay

καινούργιος keh·<u>noor</u>·yohs new

καιρός keh·<u>rohs</u> weather

καλά kah·<u>lah</u> *adv* fine (well)

καλαμάκι kah·lah·<u>mah</u>·kee straw (drinking)

καλάθι kah·<u>lah</u>·THee basket

καλός kah·<u>lohs</u> good

καλσόν kahl·<u>sohn</u> *n* tights

κάλτσες <u>kahl</u>·tsehs socks

κάλυμμα φακού <u>kah</u>·lee·mah fah·<u>koo</u> lens cap

καλώ kah·<u>loh</u> *v* call

κάμπινγκ <u>kah</u>·mpeeng camping

καναπές kah·nah·<u>pehs</u> sofa

κανένας kah·<u>neh</u>·nahs *adj* none

κάνω ανάληψη <u>kah</u>·noh ah·<u>nah</u>·lee·psee withdraw

κάνω εμετό <u>kah</u>·noh eh·meh·<u>toh</u> *v* vomit

κάνω κράτηση <u>kah</u>·noh <u>krah</u>·tee·see *v* book

κάνω πεζοπορία <u>kah</u>·noh peh·zoh·poh·<u>ree</u>·ah *v* hike

καπέλο kah·<u>peh</u>·loh hat

καπνίζω kahp·<u>nee</u>·zoh *v* smoke

καπνοπωλείο kahp·noh·poh·<u>lee</u>·oh tobacconist

καπνός kahp·<u>nohs</u> tobacco

καραντίνα kah·rahn·<u>dee</u>·nah *n* quarantine

καράφα kah·<u>rah</u>·fah carafe

καρδιά kahr·THee·<u>ah</u> *v* heart

καρδιακό έμφραγμα kahr·THee·ah·<u>koh</u> ehm·frahgh·mah heart attack

καροτσάκι kah·roh·<u>tsah</u>·kee trolley (cart)

καροτσάκια αποσκευών kah·roh·<u>tsah</u>·kiah ah·pohs·keh·<u>vohn</u> baggage [BE] carts [trolleys]

κάρτα-κλειδί <u>kahr</u>·tah klee·<u>dee</u> key card

καρτποστάλ kahrt·poh·<u>stahl</u> post card

κασκόλ kahs·<u>kohl</u> scarf

κασσίτερος kah·<u>see</u>·teh·rohs pewter

κάστρο <u>kahs</u>·troh castle

καταδυτικός εξοπλισμός
kah·tah·THee·tee·<u>kohs</u>
eh·ksoh·pleez·<u>mohs</u> diving
equipment

καταλαβαίνω kah·tah·lah·<u>veh</u>·noh
understand

κατάλληλος kah·<u>tah</u>·lee·lohs
suitable

καταρράχτης kah·tah·<u>rahkh</u>·tees
waterfall

κατάστημα kah·<u>tah</u>·stee·mah shop
(store)

κατάστημα με αντίκες
kah·<u>tah</u>·stee·mah meh
ahn·<u>tee</u>·kehs antiques store

κατάστημα με είδη δώρων
kah·<u>tahs</u>·tee·mah meh <u>ee</u>·THee
<u>THoh</u>·rohn gift store

κατάστημα με υγιεινές τροφές
kah·<u>tahs</u>·tee·mah meh
ee·yee·ee·<u>nehs</u> troh·<u>fehs</u> health
food store

κατάστημα μεταχειρισμένων
ειδών kah·<u>tah</u>·stee·mah
meh·tah·khee·reez·<u>meh</u>·nohn
ee·<u>THohn</u> second-hand shop

κατάστημα αθλητικών
ειδών kah·<u>tahs</u>·tee·mah
ath·lee·tee·<u>kohn</u> ee·<u>THohn</u>
sporting goods store

κατάστημα ρούχων
kah·<u>tahs</u>·tee·mah <u>roo</u>·khohn
clothing store

κατάστημα σουβενίρ
kah·<u>tahs</u>·tee·mah soo·veh·<u>neer</u>
souvenir store

κατάστημα υποδημάτων
kah·<u>tah</u>·stee·mah
ee·poh·THee·<u>mah</u>·tohn shoe
store

καταστρέφω kah·tah·<u>streh</u>·foh
v damage

κατάψυξη kah·<u>tah</u>·psee·ksee
freezer

κατεβαίνω kah·teh·<u>veh</u>·noh get off
(transport)

κατειλημένος
kah·tee·lee·<u>meh</u>·nohs occupied

κάτι <u>kah</u>·tee something

κάτοχος <u>kah</u>·toh·khohs owner

κατσαβίδι kah·tsah·<u>vee</u>·THee
screwdriver

κατσαρόλα kah·tsah·<u>roh</u>·lah
saucepan

κάτω <u>kah</u>·toh *adj* lower (berth)

καύσωνας <u>kahf</u>·soh·nahs heat
wave

καφετέρια kah·feh·<u>teh</u>·ree·ah cafe

κέντρο της πόλης <u>kehn</u>·droh tees
<u>poh</u>·lees downtown area

κεφάλι keh·<u>fah</u>·lee *n* head

κήπος <u>kee</u>·pohs *n* garden

κιθάρα kee·<u>thah</u>·rah guitar

κινηματογράφος
kee·nee·mah·tohgh·<u>rah</u>·fohs
movie theater

κίνηση <u>kee</u>·nee·see traffic

κινητό kee·nee·<u>toh</u> cell phone
[mobile phone BE]

κίτρινος <u>keet</u>·ree·nohs yellow

κλειδαριά klee·THahr·<u>yah</u> *n* lock
(door)

κλειδί klee·<u>THee</u> n key
κλειδώνω klee·<u>THoh</u>·noh v lock (door)
κλειστός klees·<u>tohs</u> adj shut
κλεμένος kleh·<u>meh</u>·nos stolen
κλέφτης <u>klehf</u>·tees thief
κλήση <u>klee</u>·see n call
κλιματισμός klee·mah·teez·<u>mohs</u> air conditioning
κλοπή kloh·<u>pee</u> theft
κομμωτήριο koh·moh·<u>tee</u>·ree·oh hair dresser
κόμβος <u>kohm</u>·vohs junction (intersection)
κοιμάμαι kee·<u>mah</u>·meh v sleep
κοιλάδα kee·<u>lah</u>·THah valley
κοιτάω kee·<u>tah</u>·oh v look
κολύμβηση koh·<u>leem</u>·vee·see swimming
κοντά kohn·<u>dah</u> adv near
κοντός kohn·<u>dohs</u> adj short
κορίτσι koh·<u>ree</u>·tsee girl
κορυφή koh·ree·<u>fee</u> n peak
κοσμηματοπωλείο kohz·mee·mah·toh·poh·<u>lee</u>·oh jeweler
κουβέρτα koo·<u>veh</u>·rtah blanket
κουζίνα koo·<u>zee</u>·nah stove
κουνούπι koo·<u>noo</u>·pee mosquito
κουρασμένος koo·rahz·<u>meh</u>·nohs tired
κουστούμι koos·<u>too</u>·mee men's suit
κουταλάκι koo·tah·<u>lah</u>·kee teaspoon
κουτάλι koo·<u>tah</u>·lee n spoon
κουτί koo·<u>tee</u> carton

κουτί πρώτων βοηθειών koo·<u>tee</u> proh·tohn voh·ee·thee·<u>ohn</u> first-aid kit
κράμπα <u>krahm</u>·bah n cramp
κραγιόν krah·<u>yohn</u> lipstick
κρατώ krah·<u>toh</u> v keep
κρέμα ξυρίσματος <u>kreh</u>·mah ksee·<u>reez</u>·mah·tohs shaving cream
κρεμάστρα kreh·<u>mahs</u>·trah hanger
κρεβάτι kreh·<u>vah</u>·tee bed
κρυολόγημα kree·oh·<u>loh</u>·yee·mah n cold (flu)
κρύος <u>kree</u>·ohs adj cold (temperature)
κρύσταλλο <u>kree</u>·stah·loh n crystal
κύμα <u>kee</u>·mah n wave
κυλικείο kee·lee·<u>kee</u>·oh snack bar
κυλιόμενες σκάλες kee·lee·<u>oh</u>·meh·nehs <u>skah</u>·lehs escalator
Κύπρος <u>kee</u>·prohs Cyprus
κύριος <u>kee</u>·ree·ohs main
κωδικός περιοχής koh·<u>THee</u>·kohs peh·ree·oh·<u>khees</u> area code
κωπηλασία koh·pee·lah·<u>see</u>·ah rowing

Λ

λάμπα <u>lahm</u>·bah lamp, light bulb
λάθος <u>lah</u>·thohs error, wrong
λαιμόκοψη leh·<u>moh</u>·koh·psee neck (shirt)

λαιμός leh·mohs throat

λάστιχο lahs·tee·khoh tire [tyre BE]

λειτουργία lee·toor·yee·ah n mass (church)

λεκές leh·kehs n stain

λεξικό leh·ksee·koh dictionary

λεπτό lehp·toh n minute (time)

λεπτός lehp·tohs adj thin

λέω leh·oh tell

λεωφορείο leh·oh·foh·ree·oh bus

ληστεία lees·tee·ah robbery

λιμάνι lee·mah·nee n harbor

λίμνη leem·nee lake

λιμνούλα leem·noo·lah n pond

λιγότερο lee·ghoh·teh·roh less

λιπαντικό lee·pahn·dee·koh lubricant

λιπαρός lee·pah·rohs greasy (hair, skin)

λιποθυμώ lee·poh·thee·moh faint

λίρα lee·rah pound (sterling)

λίτρο lee·troh liter

λογαριασμός loh·ghahr·yahz·mohs n check (bill), account

λοσιόν loh·siohn lotion

λοσιόν μαυρίσματος loh·siohn mahv·rees·mah·tohs sun tan lotion

λουκέτο loo·keh·toh padlock

λουλούδι loo·loo·THee n flower

λουρί ρολογιού loo·ree roh·loh·yioo watch strap

λόφος loh·fohs hill

μαγιό mah·yoh swimming trunks, swimsuit

μαθαίνω mah·theh·noh learn

μάθημα ξένης γλώσσας mah·thee mah kseh·nees ghloh·sahs language course

μακιγιάζ mah·kee·yahz make-up

μακριά mahk·ree·ah adv far

μακρύς mak·rees adj long

μαλλιά mah·liah hair

μανικιούρ mah·nee·kioor manicure

μαξιλαροθήκη mah·ksee·lah·roh·thee·kee pillow case

μαργαριτάρι mahr·ghah·ree·tah·ree pearl

μάρτυρας mahr·tee·rahs witness

μας mahs our

μασάζ mah·sahz n massage

μάσκα mahs·kah n mask (diving)

μάτι mah·tee n eye

μαχαίρι mah·kheh·ree knife

με meh with

με άμμο meh ah·moh sandy (beach)

με υπότιτλους meh ee·poh·teet·loos subtitled

με χαλίκια meh khah·lee·kiah pebbly (beach)

μεγαλοπρεπής meh·ghah·lohp·reh·pees magnificent

μεγάλος meh·ghah·lohs adj big, large

μέγεθος meh·yeh·thohs *n* size

μέδουσα meh·THoo·sah jellyfish

μένω meh·noh *v* stay

μεριά mehr·yah side (of road)

μερίδα meh·ree·THah *n* portion

μερικές φορές meh·ree·kehs foh·rehs sometimes

μέσα meh·sah inside

μεσημεριανό meh·see·mehr·yah·noh *n* lunch

μετά meh·tah after

μετακομίζω meh·tah·koh·mee·zoh *v* move (room)

μέταλλο meh·tah·loh *n* metal

μετάξι meh·tah·ksee silk

μεταφέρω meh·tah·feh·roh transfer

μεταφορά meh·tah·foh·rah *n* transit

μεταφράζω meh·tah·frah·zoh translate

μετάφραση meh·tah·frah·see translation

μεταφραστής meh·tah·frah·stees translator

μέτρηση meh·tree·see measurement

μετρητά meht·ree·tah *n* cash

μετρό meh·troh subway

μετρώ meht·roh *v* measure

μη καπνίζοντες mee kap·nee·zon·des non-smoking

μήκος mee·kohs length

μήνας του μέλιτος mee·nahs too meh·lee·tohs honeymoon

μήνυμα mee·nee·mah *n* message

μηχανή mee·khah·nee engine

μια φορά miah foh·rah once

μικρός meek·rohs little, small

μιλώ mee·loh speak

μίνι-μπαρ mee·nee bahr mini-bar

μισός mee·sohs half

μνημείο mnee·mee·oh memorial, monument

μολυσμένος moh·leez·meh·nohs infected

μονάδα moh·nah·THah unit

μοναδικός moh·nah·THee·kohs unique

μονόκλινο δωμάτιο moh·noh·klee·noh THoh·mah·tee·oh single room

μονοπάτι moh·noh·pah·tee path, trail

μοντέρνος moh·deh·rnohs modern

μοτοποδήλατο moh·toh·poh·THee·lah·toh moped

μουσείο moo·see·oh museum

μουσική moo·see·kee music

μουσικός moo·see·kohs musician

μουστάκι moos·tah·kee moustache

μπαγιάτικος bah·yah·tee·kohs stale

μπάνιο bah·nioh bathroom, lavatory

μπαρ bahr bar

μπάσκετ bah·skeht basketball

μπαστούνια του σκι bahs·too·niah too skee ski poles

μπαταρία bah·tah·ree·ah battery

μπέιμπι σίτερ beh·ee·bee see·tehr babysitter

μπικίνι bee·kee·nee bikini

μπλούζα bloo·zah blouse

μπλουζάκι bloo·zah·kee T-shirt

μπλου-τζην bloo·jeen jeans

μποξ bohks n boxing

μπότα boh·tah boot

μπότες πεζοπορίας boh·tehs peh·zoh·poh·ree·ahs walking boots

μπότες του σκι boh·tehs too skee ski boots

μπουκάλι boo·kah·lee bottle

μπρελόκ breh·lohk key ring

μύγα mee·ghah n fly (insect)

μυρίζω mee·ree·zoh v smell

μυς mees n muscle

μύτη mee·tee n nose

μύωπας mee·oh·pahs short-sighted [BE]

μωρό moh·roh baby

N

ναός nah·ohs temple

ναυαγοσώστης nah·vah·ghoh·sohs·tees lifeguard

ναυαγοσωστική λέμβος nah·vah·ghoh·sohs·tee·kee lehm·vohs lifeboat

ναυτία nahf·tee·ah nausea, travel sickness

νέος neh·ohs young

νερό neh·roh n water

νεύρο nehv·roh nerve

νεφρό nehf·roh kidney

νιπτήρας nee·ptee·rahs sink (bathroom)

νόμιμος noh·mee·mohs legal

νομίζω noh·mee·zoh think

νόμισμα noh·meez·mah currency

νοικιάζω nee·kiah·zoh v hire, rent

νοσοκόμα noh·soh·koh·mah n nurse

νοσοκομείο noh·soh·koh·mee·oh hospital

νόστιμος nohs·tee·mohs delicious

Νοτιοαφρικανός noh·tee·oh·ahf·ree·kah·nohs South African (nationality)

νότιος noh·tee·ohs adj south

ντεμοντέ deh·mohn·deh old-fashioned

ντήζελ dee·zehl diesel

ντουζ dooz n shower

ντουζίνα doo·zee·nah dozen

νύχι nee·khee n nail

νύχτα neekh·tah night

νυχτερινό κέντρο neekh·teh·ree·noh kehn·droh night club

νωρίς noh·rees early

Ξ

ξαπλώνω ksah·ploh·noh lie down

ξενάγηση kseh·nah·yee·see guided tour

ξενάγηση στα αξιοθέατα kseh·nah·yee·see stah ah·ksee·oh·theh·ah·tah sightseeing tour

ξεναγός kseh·nah·<u>ghohs</u> tour guide
ξένο συνάλλαγμα <u>kseh</u>·noh
see·<u>nah</u>·lahgh·mah foreign
currency
ξενοδοχείο
kseh·noh·THoh·<u>khee</u>·oh hotel
ξένος <u>kseh</u>·nohs foreign
ξενώνας νεότητας kseh·<u>noh</u>·nahs
neh·<u>oh</u>·tee·tahs youth hostel
ξεχνώ ksehkh·<u>noh</u> forget
ξεχωριστά kseh·khoh·ree·<u>stah</u>
separately
ξινός ksee·<u>nohs</u> sour
ξοδεύω ksoh·<u>THeh</u>·voh spend
ξύλο <u>ksee</u>·loh wood (material)
ξυπνώ kseep·<u>noh</u> v wake
ξυραφάκι ksee·rah·<u>fah</u>·kee razor,
razor blade

Ο

ομάδα oh·<u>mah</u>·THah n team
όμορφος <u>oh</u>·mohr·fohs adj
beautiful, pretty
ομπρέλλα ohm·<u>breh</u>·lah sun
shade
οβάλ oh·<u>vahl</u> oval
οδηγία oh·THee·<u>yee</u>·ah instruction
οδηγός καταστήματος
oh·THee·<u>ghohs</u>
kah·tahs·<u>tee</u>·mah·tohs store
guide
οδηγός ψυχαγωγίας
oh·THee·<u>ghohs</u>
psee·khah·ghoh·<u>yee</u>·ahs
entertainment guide

οδηγώ oh·THee·<u>ghoh</u> v drive
οδική βοήθεια oh·THee·<u>kee</u>
voh·<u>ee</u>·thee·ah road assistance
οδοντίατρος
oh·THohn·<u>dee</u>·ah·trohs dentist
οδοντόβουρτσα
oh·THohn·<u>doh</u>·voor·tsah tooth
brush
οδοντόπαστα
oh·THohn·<u>doh</u>·pahs·tah tooth
paste
οικογένεια ee·koh·<u>yeh</u>·nee·ah
family
οινοποιείο ee·noh·pee·<u>ee</u>·oh
winery
όνομα <u>oh</u>·noh·mah n name
όπερα <u>oh</u>·peh·rah opera
οπωροπωλείο
oh·poh·roh·poh·<u>lee</u>·oh
greengrocer [BE]
οργανωμένος
ohr·ghah·noh·<u>meh</u>·nohs
organized
ορχήστρα ohr·<u>khees</u>·trah orchestra
οτιδήποτε oh·tee·<u>THee</u>·poh·teh
anything
οτοστόπ oh·toh·<u>stohp</u> hitchhiking
οφείλω oh·<u>fee</u>·loh have to
(obligation)
οφθαλμίατρος
ohf·thahl·<u>mee</u>·aht·rohs optician

Π

παγοπέδιλα
pah·ghoh·<u>peh</u>·THee·lah skates

πάγος pah·ghohs *n* ice

παιδική χαρά peh·THee·kee khah·rah playground

παιδικό κρεβάτι peh·THee·koh kreh·vah·tee crib [cot BE]

παίζω peh·zoh *v* play (games, music)

παιχνίδι pehkh·nee·THee *n* game (toy), round

παιχνίδι βίντεο pehkh·nee·THee vee·deh·oh video game

πακέτο pah·keh·toh parcel

πακέτο για το σπίτι pah·keh·toh yah toh spee·tee take away

παλιά πόλη pah·liah poh·lee old town

παλιός pah·liohs old (thing)

πάνα μωρού pah·nah moh·roo diaper

Πανεπιστήμιο pah·neh·pees·tee·mee·oh university

πάνες μωρού pah·nehs moh·roo nappies

πανόραμα pah·noh·rah·mah panorama

παντελόνι pahn·deh·loh·nee pants [trousers BE]

παντοπωλείο pahn·doh·poh·lee·oh minimart

παντόφλες pahn·dohf·lehs slippers

παντρεμένος pahn·dreh·meh·nohs married

πάνω pah·noh *adj* top, upper (berth)

παπούτσι pah·poo·tsee shoe

πάρα πολύ pah·rah poh·lee too (extreme)

παραγγέλνω pah·rah·gehl·noh *v* order

παράδειγμα pah·rah·THeegh·mah example

παραδοσιακός pah·rah·THoh·see·ah·kohs traditional

παράθυρο pah·rah·thee·roh window

παραλαβή αποσκευών pah·rah·lah·vee ah·poh·skeh·vohn baggage [BE] claim

παραλία pah·rah·lee·ah beach

παραλία γυμνιστών pah·rah·lee·ah yeem·nees·tohn nudist beach

παραλυσία pah·rah·lee·see·ah paralysis

παράνομος pah·rah·noh·mohs illegal

παράξενος pah·rah·kseh·nohs strange

παραπάνω pah·rah·pah·noh more

παρεξήγηση pah·reh·ksee·yee·see misunderstanding

πάρκο pahr·koh *n* park

παρκόμετρο pahr·koh·meht·roh parking meter

πάρτυ pahr·tee *n* party (social gathering)

παυσίπονο pahf·see·poh·noh painkiller

παχύς pah·khees *adj* fat (person)

πέδιλα peh·THee·lah sandals

πεζόδρομος peh·zohTH·roh·mohs pedestrian zone

περιμένω peh·ree·meh·noh v hold on, wait

περιμένω στην ουρά peh·ree·meh·noh steen oo·rah v queue [BE]

περιέχω peh·ree·eh·khoh contain

περιοδικό peh·ree·oh·THee·koh magazine

περίοδος peh·ree·oh·THohs period (menstrual)

περιοχή peh·ree·oh·khee region

περιοχή για καπνίζοντες peh·ree·oh·khee yah kahp·nee·zohn·dehs smoking area

περιοχή για πικνίκ peh·ree·oh·khee yah peek neek picnic area

περίπτερο peh·ree·pteh·roh newsstand, kiosk

περνώ pehr·noh v pass

περπατώ pehr·pah·toh v walk

περσίδες peh·rsee·THehs blinds

πετάω peh·tah·oh v fly

πετσέτα peh·tseh·tah napkin

πέφτω pehf·toh v fall

πηγαίνω pee·yeh·noh go

πιάτσα ταξί piah·tsah tah·ksee taxi rank [BE]

πίεση pee·eh·see blood pressure

πιθανός pee·thah·nohs possible

πινακίδα pee·nah·kee·THah road sign

πίνω pee·noh v drink

πίπα pee·pah pipe (smoking)

πιπίλα pee·pee·lah pacifier [soother BE]

πισίνα pee·see·nah swimming pool

πιστοποιητικό ασφάλειας pees·toh·pee·ee·tee·koh ahs·fah·lee·ahs insurance certificate

πιστωτική κάρτα pees·toh·tee·kee kahr·tah credit card

πιτσαρία pee·tsah·ree·ah pizzeria

πλαγιά plah·yah slope (ski)

πλαστική σακούλα plahs·tee·kee sah·koo·lah plastic bag

πλατίνα plah·tee·nah platinum

πλευρό plehv·roh rib

πλημμύρα plee·mee·rah n flood

πληγή plee·yee wound (cut)

πληροφορίες plee·roh·foh·ree·ehs information

πληρωμή plee·roh·mee payment

πληρώνω plee·roh·noh v pay

πλοίο plee·oh n ship

πλυντήριο pleen·deer·ee·oh washing machine

πνεύμονας pnehv·moh·nahs lung

πόμολο poh·moh·loh n handle

ποδήλατο poh·THee·lah·toh bicycle

πόδι poh·THee foot, leg

ποδόσφαιρο poh·THohs·feh·roh soccer [football BE]

ποιότητα pee·<u>oh</u>·tee·tah quality

πόλη poh·lee town

πολυκατάστημα
poh·lee·kah·<u>tahs</u>·tee·mah
department store

πολυτέλεια poh·lee·<u>teh</u>·lee·ah
luxury

πολύτιμος poh·<u>lee</u>·tee·mohs
valuable

πονόδοντος poh·<u>noh</u>·THohn·dohs
toothache

πονοκέφαλος
poh·noh·<u>keh</u>·fah·lohs headache

πονόλαιμος poh·noh·<u>noh</u>·leh·mohs
sore throat

πόνος <u>poh</u>·nohs n pain

πόνος στο αυτί <u>poh</u>·nohs stoh
ahf·<u>tee</u> earache

πόρτα <u>pohr</u>·tah door

πορτοφόλι pohr·toh·<u>foh</u>·lee wallet

ποσό poh·<u>soh</u> n amount

ποσότητα poh·<u>soh</u>·tee·tah
quantity

ποταμός poh·tah·<u>mohs</u> river

ποτέ poh·<u>teh</u> never

ποτήρι poh·<u>tee</u>·ree glass
(container)

ποτό poh·<u>toh</u> n drink

πουκάμισο poo·<u>kah</u>·mee·soh
shirt

πράσινος <u>prah</u>·see·nohs green

πρέπει <u>preh</u>·pee v must

πρεσβεία prehz·<u>vee</u>·ah embassy

πρεσβύωπας prehz·<u>vee</u>·oh·pahs
long-sighted [BE]

πρήξιμο <u>pree</u>·ksee·moh swelling

πρησμένος preez·<u>meh</u>·nohs
swollen

πρίζα <u>pree</u>·zah n plug, socket

πριν preen before

πρόβλεψη <u>prohv</u>·leh·psee
n forecast

πρόβλεψη καιρού <u>prohv</u>·leh·psee
keh·<u>roo</u> weather forecast

πρόβλημα <u>prohv</u>·lee·mah
problem

πρόγραμμα <u>prohgh</u>·rah·mah
n program

πρόγραμμα θεαμάτων
<u>proh</u>·ghrah·mah
theh·ah·<u>mah</u>·tohn program of
events

προς prohs towards

προσαρμοστής
proh·sahr·moh·<u>stees</u> adaptor

πρόσβαση <u>prohz</u>·vah·see
n access

προσγειώνομαι
prohz·yee·<u>oh</u>·noh·meh v land

προσκαλώ prohs·kah·<u>loh</u> v invite

πρόσκληση <u>prohs</u>·klee·see
invitation

πρόστιμο <u>prohs</u>·tee·moh n fine
(penalty)

πρόσωπο <u>proh</u>·soh·poh n face

προσωρινός proh·soh·ree·<u>nohs</u>
temporary

προτείνω proh·<u>tee</u>·noh suggest

προφέρω proh·<u>feh</u>·roh
pronounce

προφυλακτικό
proh·fee·lah·ktee·<u>koh</u> condom

προωθώ proh·oh·<u>thoh</u> forward
πρωί proh·<u>ee</u> morning
πρωινό proh·ee·<u>noh</u> breakfast
πρώτη θέση <u>proh</u>·tee <u>theh</u>·see
   first class
πτήση <u>ptee</u>·see flight
πυρετός pee·reh·<u>tohs</u> fever
πυροσβεστήρας
   pee·rohz·vehs·<u>tee</u>·rahs fire
   extinguisher
πυροσβεστική
   pee·rohz·vehs·tee·<u>kee</u> fire
   brigade [BE]
πυτζάμες pee·<u>jah</u>·mehs pajamas

Ρ

ραδιόφωνο rah·THee·<u>oh</u>·foh·noh
   n radio
ρακέτα rah·<u>keh</u>·tah racket (tennis,
   squash)
ραντεβού rahn·deh·<u>voo</u>
   appointment
ράφι <u>rah</u>·fee n shelf
ρεματιά reh·mah·<u>tiah</u> ravine
ρεσεψιόν reh·seh·<u>psiohn</u>
   reception (hotel)
ρεύμα ποταμού <u>rehv</u>·mah
   poh·tah·<u>moo</u> rapids
ρηχή πισίνα ree·<u>khee</u> pee·<u>see</u>·nah
   paddling pool
ρομαντικός roh·mahn·dee·<u>kohs</u>
   romantic
ρολόι roh·<u>loh</u>·ee n watch
ρυάκι ree·<u>ah</u>·kee n stream

Σ

σμαράγδι zmah·<u>rahgh</u>·THee
   emerald
σαμπουάν sahm·poo·<u>ahn</u>
   n shampoo
σαγιονάρες sah·yoh·<u>nah</u>·rehs
   flip-flops
σαγόνι sah·<u>ghoh</u>·nee jaw
σάκκος <u>sah</u>·kohs knapsack
σαλόνι sah·<u>loh</u>·nee living room
σάουνα <u>sah</u>·oo·nah sauna
σαπούνι sah·<u>poo</u>·nee n soap
σατέν sah·<u>tehn</u> satin
σβήνω <u>svee</u>·noh v turn off
σβώλος <u>svoh</u>·lohs n lump
σεζ-λονγκ sehz <u>lohng</u> deck chair
σενιάν seh·<u>niahn</u> rare (steak)
σερβιέτες sehr·vee·<u>eh</u>·tehs
   sanitary towels
σεσουάρ seh·soo·<u>ahr</u> hair dryer
σήμα <u>see</u>·mah sign (road)
σημαία see·<u>meh</u>·ah n flag
σημαίνω see·<u>meh</u>·noh v mean
σημείο see·<u>mee</u>·oh n point
σίδερο <u>see</u>·THeh·roh n iron
σιδερώνω see·THeh·<u>roh</u>·noh
   v iron, press
σιδηροδρομικός σταθμός
   see·THee·rohrTH·roh·mee·<u>kohs</u>
   stahth·<u>mohs</u> rail station
σκάλα <u>skah</u>·lah ladder
σκάλες <u>skah</u>·lehs stairs
σκηνή skee·<u>nee</u> tent
σκι skee skiing
σκιά skee·<u>ah</u> shade (darkness)

σκοπός skoh·<u>pohs</u> purpose

σκούπα skoo·pah n broom

σκουπίδια skoo·<u>peeTH</u>·yah trash [rubbish BE]

σκούρος <u>skoo</u>·rohs adj dark (color)

σλιπ sleep briefs

σόλα <u>soh</u>·lah sole (shoes)

σορτς sohrts n shorts

σουβενίρ soo·veh·<u>neer</u> souvenir

σουπερμάρκετ soo·pehr·<u>mahr</u>·keht supermarket

σουτιέν soo·<u>tiehn</u> bra

σπα spah spa

σπάγγος <u>spah</u>·gohs n string (cord)

σπάνιος <u>spah</u>·nee·ohs rare (unusual)

σπασμένος spahz·<u>meh</u>·nohs broken

σπάω <u>spah</u>·oh v break

σπήλαιο <u>spee</u>·leh·oh n cave

σπίρτο <u>speer</u>·toh n match (to start fire)

σπονδυλική στήλη spohn·THee·lee·<u>kee stee</u>·lee spine

σπουδάζω spoo·<u>THah</u>·zoh v study

σταματώ stah·mah·<u>toh</u> v stop

στάδιο <u>stah</u>·THee·oh stadium

σταθμός μετρό stahth·<u>mohs</u> meh·<u>troh</u> subway [underground BE] station

σταθμός λεωφορείων stahTH·<u>mohs</u> leh·oh·foh·<u>ree</u>·ohn bus station

στάση <u>stah</u>·see exposure (photos), stop (bus)

στάση λεωφορείου <u>stah</u>·see leh·oh·foh·<u>ree</u>·oo bus stop

στέγη <u>steh</u>·yee n roof

στέλνω <u>stehl</u>·noh send

στενός steh·<u>nohs</u> adj narrow, tight

στήθος <u>stee</u>·THohs breast

στόμα <u>stoh</u>·mah n mouth

στομάχι stoh·<u>mah</u>·khee n stomach

στομαχόπονος stoh·mah·<u>khoh</u>·poh·nohs stomach ache

στολή stoh·<u>lee</u> n uniform

στολή δύτη stoh·<u>lee</u> THee·tee wetsuit

στρογγυλός strohn·gkee·<u>lohs</u> adj round

στυλ steel n style

στυλό stee·<u>loh</u> n pen

συμπεριλαμβάνεται seem·beh·ree·lahm·<u>vah</u>·neh·teh included

σύζυγος <u>see</u>·zee·ghohs husband, wife

συκώτι see·<u>koh</u>·tee liver

σύμπτωμα <u>seem</u>·ptoh·mah symptom

συναγερμός πυρκαγιάς see·nah·yehr·<u>mohs</u> peer·kah·<u>yahs</u> fire alarm

συναντώ see·nahn·<u>doh</u> meet

συνέδριο see·<u>neh</u>·THree·oh conference

συνταγή γιατρού seen·dah·yee yaht·<u>roo</u> prescription

συνταγογραφώ seen·dah·ghoh·ghrah·<u>foh</u> prescribe

συνταξιούχος seen·dah·ksee·<u>oo</u>·khohs retired

σύντομα <u>seen</u>·doh·mah soon

συντριβάνι seen·dree·<u>vah</u>·nee fountain

συστάσεις see·<u>stah</u>·sees introductions

συστήνω see·<u>stee</u>·noh introduce, recommend

συχνός seekh·<u>nohs</u> *adj* frequent

σφηνωμένος sfee·noh·<u>meh</u>·nohs jammed

σφράγισμα <u>sfrah</u>·yeez·mah filling (dental)

σφυρί sfee·<u>ree</u> hammer

σχέδιο <u>skheh</u>·THee·oh *n* plan

σχήμα <u>skhee</u>·mah *n* shape

σχισμένος skheez·<u>meh</u>·nohs torn

σχοινί skhee·<u>nee</u> *n* rope

σχολή σκι skhoh·<u>lee</u> skee ski school

σωσίβιο soh·<u>see</u>·vee·oh lifejacket

σωστός sohs·<u>stohs</u> *adj* right (correct)

T

ταμπόν tahm·<u>bohn</u> tampon

τάβλι <u>tah</u>·vlee backgammon

ταγιέρ tah·<u>yehr</u> women's suit

ταΐζω tah·<u>ee</u>·zoh *v* feed

ταινία teh·<u>nee</u>·ah movie

ταξί tah·<u>ksee</u> taxi

ταξίδι tah·<u>ksee</u>·THee journey

ταξίδι με πλοίο tah·<u>ksee</u>·THee meh <u>plee</u>·oh boat trip

ταξιδιωτική επιταγή tah·ksee·THee·oh·tee·<u>kee</u> eh·pee·tah·<u>yee</u> traveler's check [traveller's cheque BE]

ταξιδιωτικό γραφείο tah·ksee·THyoh·tee·<u>koh</u> ghrah·<u>fee</u>·oh travel agency

ταξιτζής tah·ksee·<u>jees</u> taxi driver

ταυτότητα tahf·<u>toh</u>·tee·tah identification

ταχυδρομείο tah·kheeTH·roh·<u>mee</u>·oh post office

ταχυδρομική επιταγή tah·kheeTH·roh·mee·<u>kee</u> eh·pee·tah·<u>yee</u> money order

ταχυδρομικό κουτί tah·kheeTH·roh·mee·<u>koh</u> koo·tee mailbox [postbox BE]

τεμάχιο teh·<u>mah</u>·khee·oh piece

τελειώνω teh·lee·<u>oh</u>·noh *v* end

τελευταί ος teh·lehf·<u>teh</u>·ohs last

τελεφερίκ teh·leh·feh·<u>reek</u> cablecar

τέλος <u>teh</u>·lohs *n* end

τελωνειακή δήλωση teh·loh·nee·ah·<u>kee</u> <u>THee</u>·loh·see customs declaration (tolls)

τελωνείο teh·loh·<u>nee</u>·oh customs (tolls)

τέννις <u>teh</u>·nees tennis

τετράγωνος teht·_rah_·ghoh·nohs square

τζετ-σκι jeht skee jet-ski

τζόγκιγκ joh·geeng jogging

τζόγος _joh_·ghohs gambling

τηλεκάρτα tee·leh·_kahr_·tah phone card

τηλεόραση tee·leh·_oh_·rah·see TV

τηλεφώνημα tee·leh·_foh_·nee·mah phone call

τηλεφωνικός θάλαμος tee·leh·foh·nee·_kohs_ _thah_·lah·mohs telephone booth

τηλεφωνικός κατάλογος tee·leh·foh·nee·_kohs_ kah·_tah_·loh·ghohs telephone directory

τηλέφωνο tee·_leh_·foh·noh _n_ phone

την teen per

τιμή συναλλάγματος tee·_mee_ see·nah·_lahgh_·mah·tohs exchange rate

τιμή εισόδου tee·_mee_ ee·_soh_·THoo entrance fee

τιρμπουσόν teer·boo·_sohn_ corkscrew

τοίχος _tee_·khohs wall

τοπικός toh·pee·_kohs_ local

τοστιέρα toh·_stieh_·rah toaster

τουαλέτα too·ah·_leh_·tah restroom [toilet BE]

τούνελ _too_·nehl tunnel

τουρίστας too·_rees_·tahs tourist

τουριστική θέση too·ree·stee·_kee_ _theh_·see economy class

τουριστικός οδηγός too·ree·stee·_kohs_ oh·THee·_ghohs_ guide book

τραβώ το καζανάκι trah·_voh_ toh kah·zah·_nah_·kee flush

τραμ trahm tram

τράπεζα _trah_·peh·zah bank

τραπέζι trah·_peh_·zee table

τραπεζομάντηλο trah·peh·zoh·_mahn_·dee·loh tablecloth

τραυματισμένος trahv·mah·teez·_meh_·nohs injured

τρένο _treh_·noh train

τρέχω _treh_·khoh v run, speed

τρόμπα _troh_·mbah n pump

τρόλλεϋ _troh_·leh·ee trolley-bus

τρύπα _tree_·pah hole (in clothes)

τρώω _troh_·oh eat

τσάντα _tsahn_·dah handbag

τσίμπημα _tsee_·bee·mah n bite, sting (insect)

τσίμπημα κουνουπιού _tseem_·bee·mah koo·noo·_piooh_ mosquito bite

τυπικός tee·pee·_kohs_ typical

τύχη _tee_·khee luck

υγρό πιάτων eegh·_roh_ piah·tohn dishwashing detergent

υπεραστικό λεωφορείο ee·peh·rahs·tee·_koh_ leh·oh·foh·_ree_·oh long-distance bus

υπεραστικό τηλεφώνημα
ee·pehr·ahs·tee·<u>koh</u>
tee·leh·<u>foh</u>·nee·mah
long-distance call

υπέρβαρο ee·<u>pehr</u>·vah·roh **excess baggage** [BE]

υπηκοότητα ee·pee·koh·<u>oh</u>·tee·tah
nationality

υπηρεσία ee·pee·reh·<u>see</u>·ah
n **service** (administration, business)

υπηρεσία δωματίου
ee·pee·reh·<u>see</u>·ah
THoh·mah·<u>tee</u>·oo **room service**

υπηρεσία πλυντηρίου
ee·pee·reh·<u>see</u>·ah
pleen·dee·<u>ree</u>·oo **laundry service**

υπνόσακκος ee·<u>pnoh</u>·sah·kohs
sleeping bag

υπνωτικό χάπι eep·noh·tee·<u>koh</u>
khah·pee **sleeping pill**

υπόγειος ee·<u>poh</u>·ghee·ohs
underground [BE]

υπολογιστής ee·poh·loh·yee·<u>stees</u>
computer

υπόνομος ee·<u>poh</u>·noh·mohs
sewer

ύφασμα <u>ee</u>·fahs·mah **fabric**
(cloth)

ύψος <u>ee</u>·psohs **height**

Φ

φακός fah·<u>kohs</u> **flashlight, lens**

φακός επαφής fah·<u>kohs</u>
eh·pah·<u>fees</u> **contact lens**

υπηρεσία φαξ ee·pee·reh·<u>see</u>·ah
fahks **fax facility**

φάρμα <u>fahr</u>·mah *n* **farm**

φάρμακα <u>fahr</u>·mah·kah
medication

φαρδύς fahr·<u>THees</u> **loose** (fitting), **wide**

φάρος <u>fah</u>·rohs **lighthouse**

φέρνω <u>fehr</u>·noh **bring**

φέρυ-μπωτ <u>feh</u>·ree boht **ferry**

φεστιβάλ fehs·tee·<u>vahl</u> **festival**

φεύγω <u>fehv</u>·ghoh *v* **leave** (depart)

φιλμ feelm *n* **film** (camera)

φίλη <u>fee</u>·lee **girlfriend**

φιλί fee·<u>lee</u> *n* **kiss**

φιλοδώρημα
fee·loh·<u>THoh</u>·ree·mah **gratuity**

φίλος <u>fee</u>·lohs **friend, boyfriend**

φίλτρο <u>feel</u>·troh *n* **filter**

φιλώ fee·<u>loh</u> *v* **kiss**

φλέβα <u>fleh</u>·vah **vein**

φλεγμονή flegh·moh·<u>nee</u>
inflammation

φλυτζάνι flee·<u>jah</u>·nee **cup**

φοβερός foh·veh·<u>rohs</u> **terrible**

φοβισμένος foh·veez·<u>meh</u>·nohs
frightened

φοιτητής fee·tee·<u>tees</u> **student**

φόρεμα <u>foh</u>·reh·mah *n* **dress**

φόρος <u>foh</u>·rohs **duty** (customs), **tax**

φορώ foh·<u>roh</u> *v* **wear**

φούρνος <u>foor</u>·nohs **oven**

φούρνος μικροκυμάτων <u>foor</u>·nohs
mee·kroh·kee·<u>mah</u>·tohn
microwave (oven)

φούστα foo·stah skirt
φούτερ foo·tehr sweatshirt
ΦΠΑ fee·pee·ah sales tax
φράγμα frahgh·mah n lock (river, canal)
φράση frah·see n phrase
φράχτης frahkh·tees n fence
φρέσκος frehs·kohs adj fresh
φτάνω ftah·noh arrive
φτηνός ftee·nohs cheap, inexpensive
φτιάχνω τις βαλίτσες ftee·ahkh·noh tees vah·lee·tsehs v pack (baggage)
φυλακή fee·lah·kee n prison
φύση fee·see nature
φυτό fee·toh n plant
φως fohs n light (electric)
φώτα foh·tah lights (car)
φωτογραφία foh·tohgh·rah·fee·ah v photo
φωτογραφική μηχανή foh·tohgh·rah·fee·kee mee·khah·nee camera
φωτοτυπικό foh·toh·tee·pee·koh photocopier

χαμηλώνω khah·mee·loh·noh v turn down (volume, heat)
χαλί khah·lee rug
χαλκός khahl·kohs copper
χάπι khah·pee tablet
χάρτης khahr·tees n map
χαρτί khar·tee paper

χαρτί κουζίνας khah·rtee koo·zee·nahs kitchen
χαρτί υγείας khahr·tee ee·yee·ahs toilet paper
χαρτομάντηλο khahr·toh·mahn·dee·loh tissue
χαρτομάντηλο khah·rtoh·mahn·dee·loh handkerchief
χείλη khee·lee lips
χειροκίνητος khee·roh·kee·nee·tohs manual (car)
χειρότερος khee·roh·teh·rohs worse
χιλιόμετρα khee·lioh·meh·trah mileage
χιονίζει khioh·nee·zee v snow
χλιαρός khlee·ah·rohs lukewarm
χόμπυ khoh·bee hobby (pastime)
χοντρός khohn·drohs thick
χορεύω khoh·reh·voh v dance
χορτοφάγος khohr·toh·fah·ghohs vegetarian
χρειάζομαι khree·ah·zoh·meh v need
χρέωση υπηρεσίας khreh·oh·see ee·pee·reh·see·ahs service charge
χρήματα khree·mah·tah money
χρησιμοποιώ khree·see·moh·pee·oh v use
χρήσιμος khree·see·mohs useful
χρονική περίοδος khroh·nee·kee peh·ree·oh·THohs period (time)
χρυσός khree·sohs n gold

χρώμα <u>khroh</u>·mah *n* color
χρωστώ khroh·<u>stoh</u> owe
χτένα <u>khteh</u>·nah *n* comb
χτενίζω khteh·<u>nee</u>·zoh *v* comb
χτες khtehs yesterday
χώρα <u>khoh</u>·rah country (nation)
χωριό khohr·<u>yoh</u> village
χωρίς khoh·<u>rees</u> without
χώρος <u>khoh</u>·rohs *n* space (area)
χώρος κάμπινγκ <u>khoh</u>·rohs
   <u>kah</u>·mpeeng campsite
χώρος στάθμευσης <u>khoh</u>·rohs
   <u>stahth</u>·mehf·sees car park [BE]
χώρος στάθμευσης <u>khoh</u>·rohs
   <u>stahth</u>·mehf·sees parking lot

Ψ

ψαλίδι psah·<u>lee</u>·THee scissors
ψάρεμα <u>psah</u>·reh·mah fishing
ψάχνω <u>psahkh</u>·noh look for
ψηλός psee·<u>lohs</u> tall
ψύλλος <u>psee</u>·lohs flea

'Ω

ώμος <u>oh</u>·mohs *n* shoulder
   (anatomy)
ώρα αιχμής <u>oh</u>·rah ehkh·<u>mees</u>
   rush hour
ώρες λειτουργίας <u>oh</u>·rehs
   lee·toor·<u>yee</u>·ahs opening hours